TROUBLEMAKER

ONE MAN'S CRUSADE
AGAINST CHINA'S CRUELTY

HARRY WU
WITH GEORGE VECSEY

TIMES BOOKS

RANDOM HOUSE

To the Chinese people,
who have suffered, who have left, who have stayed;
someday soon, no more laogai

Library of Congress Cataloging-in-Publication Data

Wu, Hongda Harry.
Troublemaker : one man's crusade against China's cruelty / Harry
Wu with George Vecsey.
p.   cm.
Includes index.
ISBN 0-8129-6374-1
1. Concentration camps—China.   2. Political prisoners—China.
3. Forced labor—China.   4. Human rights—China.   5. Wu, Hongda
Harry.   I. Vecsey, George.   II. Title.
HV8964.C5W85   1996
365'.45'0951—dc20   96-20956

Manufactured in the United States of America on acid-free paper.

2 4 6 8 9 7 5 3

First Edition

TROUBLEMAKER

Also by Harry Wu

Laogai—The Chinese Gulag

Bitter Winds:
A Memoir of My Years in China's Gulag
(with Carolyn Wakeman)

Also by George Vecsey

A Year in the Sun

Get to the Heart
(with Barbara Mandrell)

Coal Miner's Daughter
(with Loretta Lynn)

Martina
(with Martina Navratilova)

Sweet Dreams
(with Leonore Fleischer)

Five O'Clock Comes Early:
A Young Man's Battle With Alcoholism
(with Bob Welch)

PREFACE

"Chen Ming! Chen Ming, I'm back!"

I saw Chen Ming die. He gobbled down the rich corn bun on his deathbed, but it was too late. I dug him an unmarked grave at Qinghe Farm, in the burying field they call 586.

"Big Mouth Xing, where are you?"

I cannot utter these words out loud. I should not be standing outside this labor camp, a video camera hidden in my knapsack. I should not be here at all.

I saw Big Mouth Xing die. He taught me how to bite and claw for my existence, but then he gave up. He died raving, "Son of a bitch! Son of a bitch!" at the world.

I think of Lu Haoqin, who went mad in a world without women. I think of Ao Naisong, who could not live without his lute.

"Where are you guys? Come on, I will take you to your mothers. It has been too long. You should all go home now."

The reeds are as tall as men, waving and rustling in the wind. Everything is buried in time and space.

"I have corn buns!" I tell them in my heart. "I have food for you. I eat rice and meat every day. We don't have to starve anymore."

Crying, calling, but no response.

CONTENTS

TROUBLEMAKER

1

THE BORDER

The American passport was tucked into the pouch on my belt. Occasionally I would reach for it the way a cowboy in a Western movie might feel for his six-shooter, just to know it's there. Everybody wants an equalizer. It was June of 1995, and I was riding in a taxi through a remote corner of Kazakhstan, trying to slip into China. I felt a shiver—half-love, half-terror. My U.S. passport would not protect me if they caught me inside my homeland. China has a most-wanted list, and I was on it.

The real equalizer was the woman sitting next to me, the redheaded woman from North Carolina. She was my assistant, my eyes and ears, my insurance policy. With a native-born American alongside me, the Chinese authorities were less likely to shoot me in the back, leave me lying out in the desert somewhere. At least, that was my theory.

I had a video camera hidden in the black bag hanging from my shoulder, to document thousands of prisoners slaving in the fields, thousands of prisoners toiling in the factories, prisoners just like me years ago. Just a few more rolls of videotape—then maybe I would stop risking my life.

The Chinese authorities do not like me, because I slip back into China and expose their labor camps. I put them on *60 Minutes* for the prison-made goods they sell to rich countries. I put them on the BBC for the kidneys they scoop out of executed prisoners. The government does not appreciate the publicity.

I thought about my nineteen years in the camps, my entire twenties and thirties, when I could have been married and having children and working as a geologist, living my life. They broke my body, but they did not break my spirit. I told myself, "These sons of bitches stole my youth. They steal millions of lives. Now I will expose them to the world."

I was gambling with my life and with somebody else's life, too: Ching-Lee's—the beautiful wife I had had the fortune to meet five years before, when I was almost fifty-three. She was supposed to join me on the last leg of this trip. But first I needed a traveling companion who could back me up for ten days and then get out with the video-tape.

Although I may seem like a lone wolf who roams the world thumbing his nose at China, I am in fact the head of a research foundation, with colleagues in California, Washington, Sydney, Paris, London, and Toronto. I have contacts in China who will go straight to the labor camps if they are caught. I have helpers who travel with me to China, on the same planes, in the same hotels, but never talk to me or make eye contact. Also, I have traveling companions. Ching-Lee had made two trips to China with me, and a woman from the BBC traveled with me once, but now I needed a new helper, somebody who would watch my back, create diversions, split the work, pick up clues and signals, share hotel rooms and cars and meals with me.

My new accomplice had found me one night three months earlier, when I was speaking at Duke University in North Carolina. Afterward, this tall, slender woman said hello to me. She was middle-aged, intense, earnest. "I saw you on *The Charlie Rose Show*," she said, meaning the popular American interview show, "so I went out and bought your book." She had read *Bitter Winds*, the book I had written in 1994 with Carolyn Wakeman about my life in the labor camps. "I've got two midterm exams at law school tomorrow," she said, "but I thought it was better to hear you talk."

The woman, Sue Howell, told me she had studied the previous summer in Shanghai, the steamy city of my childhood. She told me she had even been taken on a tour of a model prison in Shanghai, which caught my attention because I had heard a Westerner was being held there.

"What was it like?"

"They showed us paintings of happy prisoners and essays by happy prisoners," she said. "They even had prisoners singing and dancing. We were pretty disturbed about that."

We did not sing and dance during my long years in the camps. I can tell you that. We didn't paint. Nor did we write essays. That must have been their dog-and-pony prison, the one they save for people from the World Bank, people from Congress, people who want to think the best of the Chinese system. Sue Howell is smarter than that.

There was a long line of people waiting to talk to me, so I thanked Sue Howell and gave her the phone number of our foundation, should she ever want more information. A month later she called me in California. "I'm planning my summer vacation from law school, and I admire what you do, and I'd like to help you," she said. "I use a computer, and I have access to information. Can you use me for something?"

"How about going to China with me?"

"Aren't you afraid they are going to get you?" she asked, sounding stunned.

"I can't worry," I said. "I've got to do it."

She agreed to meet me and Ching-Lee in Washington a few weeks later. If a man is going to travel with a woman through China for ten days, it is always a good idea for his wife to meet her first. Sue came up from Chapel Hill on May 1, and we met at a hotel near Thomas Circle. She told us she was a child of the 1960s who had learned to question all systems, who had studied to be a teacher, had worked for the disabled, had worked for IBM, but now she was going to North Carolina Central University School of Law to prepare for the next challenge.

I questioned her closely. I could not afford a scatterbrain, an agitator, a victim. I needed somebody who would fit in. Sue Howell had no history of opposition to the Chinese government, had written no scholarly articles, and had taken part in no protests. She just wanted to improve the miserable lives of millions of Chinese prisoners. While we talked, I found myself glancing at Ching-Lee. I am a Chinese man, used to making the decisions, married to a woman who had always worked for male bosses in Taiwan. In five short years, I found myself relying on her, checking her reactions more often than I ever could have expected. What did Ching-Lee think of this independent American woman who would share my hotel room, my fate?

"Why are you rushing into this?" Sue asked me. "The Chinese are ticked off at America right now for letting the president of Taiwan into the country to attend his college reunion. Maybe you should wait until the fall. I'd take a semester off."

I told Sue I had to go while my visa was good. Then I noticed Ching-Lee smiling at Sue Howell. This is America. The women speak their minds. Ching-Lee nodded at me ever so slightly.

"Okay," I said, "let's go."

That was a lot of faith to put in somebody I hardly knew, but Sue Howell was putting the same amount of faith in me. I tried to frighten her. I said there was the possibility of getting caught in the forlorn wastelands of Xinjiang, far from the occasional diplomatic niceties of Beijing. I was sending myself into battle, and Sue Howell would be risking her life for a cause. In a war, if a soldier is killed, you cannot blame the general. It happens. She had to take the responsibility along with the risk.

I told her the rules I had followed on three successful trips to China:

First rule: We undertake this adventure together, staying together in hotel rooms. That way somebody cannot vanish—or be vanished—in the middle of the night without the other person knowing.

Second rule: I am the general. Her job is to be my lieutenant. It's just like soldiers or police or firefighters. If the boss says, "Jump!" you jump. I have to know she will follow my orders.

Third rule: I will not give her much information, will not explain all the details or the reasons. This is hard for Americans to accept, but it has to be that way in case the authorities get their hands on us.

"This is your protection," I told Sue. "If you have to confess, you have to tell the truth. I don't want you to know too much. These guys will know whether you are lying. You are simply my assistant. I ask for the film, you hand me the film. I ask you to talk to the driver, you talk to the driver. You ask me where we are going tomorrow, I don't tell you. You don't need to know. This is not to mistreat you. This is to protect you."

I could see her nodding.

We agreed to meet in Europe in mid-June; we would try to slip into China from the southern tier of the old Soviet Union. I never entered China through Beijing, where security is extremely tight. My theory was that the provincial crossings were still in the rudimentary stages—with typewriters, out-of-date lists of troublemakers, bad phone systems. I was hoping the guards at an antiquated border station would not know I had legally changed my American name from the notorious Wu Hongda/Harry Wu to the anonymous Peter H. Wu. You cannot change your date of birth, however. So that was my gamble.

My first stage on this trip was Xinjiang Uighur Autonomous Region (usually referred to as Xinjiang or Xinjiang Province), in the far northwest of China, where they send our misfits, our outlaws, our dissidents, our class enemies, our thinkers, our questioners, our doubters, our dreamers, our scholars, our optimists, and our pessimists—anybody who thinks or feels—millions of us. I had been to sprawling Xinjiang in 1994—land of the thick, muddy rain, land of nuclear tests, land of prisoners working up to their waists in chemical vats—the badlands.

Now I wanted to go back because I had only slowly realized how China is using gigantic loans from the World Bank in this same region where millions of prisoners work. Most countries in the world agree that you should not use prisoners, political or other, for free labor. I wanted to make sure the World Bank knew how much the regime depended on forced labor; I wanted to make sure the World Bank did not violate its own principles.

The Chinese authorities are trying to dominate a region where Mandarin is not even the major language. The majority of people in Xinjiang are Muslims, people called Uighurs, who speak their own language. I knew only one name in the Uighur language: The huge desert, rich in minerals, now being settled by prisoners—our Siberia, our Wild West, our Australia—is named Taklimakan. It means "the bird can fly in but can never fly out."

I hoped that name would not be prophetic.

In early June, I headed for Europe, a big market for Chinese prison-camp goods. I explained to the Germans, "You don't want to buy tools with blood on them." I explained to the French, "You don't want to buy clothes with prisoners' tears on them." I met with Mme. Mitterrand in Paris. Press conferences, publicity, television shows—I had been making contacts in Europe for years, but I had no way of knowing just how much they would pay off.

On June 15, I met Sue Howell in Frankfurt, and we traveled to Cologne, where I was to give a television interview. On the train ride, I tried to scare her. "Suppose we're caught," I told her. "What if I tell them I did nothing wrong?"

"I'd expect you to do that," she said. "They know I'm American born. I'm a woman. They won't know what to do with me. I'll be safe."

She seemed as committed as ever. In Cologne, we checked into the same hotel room so she could get used to my company. The next morning we went back to Frankfurt and took the overnight flight to Almaty, the capital of Kazakhstan. We arrived around dawn and headed south toward Kyrgyzstan, the new, largely Muslim country that broke away from the old Soviet Union in 1991. When we got there, the border was closed because of a landslide, so we had to backtrack and try a second route, through the Horgas Pass, part of the old Silk Road between East and West that Marco Polo had used some seven hundred years earlier. This road had been sealed to the outside world between 1971 and 1983, while Moscow and Beijing threatened each other with fraternal Communist warfare, but now the border was open again. We arrived at Almaty at nine o'clock at night. By now, we had been up for nearly two days—grimy and exhausted from the dust of the road, in cars with no air-conditioning. My contact suggested we take a night bus from Almaty to Panfilov. We had to keep going to avoid attention.

I never considered sneaking across the border illegally. I stick to a principle on all my trips: Always do it legally. I don't ever want to get caught with stolen papers or a false identity. I was confident that if I could just get in, I'd be like a fish in the ocean: supple, elusive, quick. They would never find me. I know how to travel, how to talk to people, how to find a place to stay, how to find transportation. After all, this is my country; these are my people.

But traveling through Kazakhstan can make a Chinese-American guy nervous. At one checkpoint, the Kazakhs were practicing the new nationalism, the new capitalism. They did not bother the Chinese because they did not have money, and they did not bother the Russians because the Russians didn't either. Sue Howell and I were the only two on the bus with American passports. A Kazakh soldier with a Mohawk haircut, one tuft of hair right down the middle of his head, squawked at me in Russian. I didn't need a translator to know what he wanted. I held out twenty American dollars, and he held out my passport, which he had taken to scrutinize. He grabbed the money, and I grabbed my passport, and then I shoved him out of the way and got onto the bus. He didn't arrest me. He had my money.

At dawn, we arrived in Panfilov. Maybe it was the lack of sleep—I was feeling edgy. I could imagine these people slashing my throat and leaving me in the outback. Still, I wanted to get inside China. We got into a taxi and headed toward the border. Sue Howell noticed how wide and smooth the roads were. "The Russians upgraded all the roads in Kazakhstan so they could roll trucks and tanks into China," I said. "Look how far back the electricity poles are set. This road is wide enough for troop planes to land on." The taxi rolled up to the border station. It was Sunday, eight o'clock in the morning, and the border was closed. The driver told us the only thing to do was to stay in a guest-house overnight. I could only assume the Chinese had lookouts on this side, and with a whole day to kill, I felt exposed.

We looked around Horgas, fast becoming a boomtown, with a bazaar called Market for Both Sides of the Border. Six days a week, people sold cigarettes, watches, alcohol, sugar, money—whatever you wanted—but today was Sunday, the day of rest, even at the Horgas Pass, between

Muslim Kazakhstan and Muslim Xinjiang. Somebody pointed out a handsome old building and said it was a guesthouse. We went and banged on the door, but nobody answered. We banged again, and this time the door opened, and dozens of swallows flew out. Apparently they nested in the eaves inside the house and were used to being let out at dawn. The swallows did not know it was Sunday and the humans were sleeping late.

The guesthouse was a shambles, without electricity, toilets, or much food. What could we do? We ate a few of the chocolate bars we had brought. We found someplace to buy a tin of condensed milk and a few cans of sardines. I took a walk around. Sue took a bath. There was nothing to do but wait. I tried not to think about the other side of the border, my old life in the labor camps: the beatings, the cold, the hard work, clawing for one shriveled carrot in the frozen earth. All those years when I had thought, "If only I could leave this prison, this land of prisons." Now I was a thousand yards away from my homeland, trying not to worry what the authorities would do if they caught me.

On Monday morning, the Kazakhs loaded everybody onto special buses for the short drive to the border. We all swarmed past the passport checkpoint on the Kazakhstan side. Then we got to the Chinese side. It was eleven-forty. We handed our passports to a female border officer with two stars on each shoulder. I could see faces peering at us through a glass partition. Then I noticed. The officer was typing our names into a computer. Son of a bitch. When did these people get computers?

I tried to remain casual. I could not see the screen, so I watched the officer's eyes as she typed. Tap-tap-tap. She entered my name into the computer. Tap-tap-tap. She typed my birth date. Then I saw her eyes open wide. "You are a very important guy," her eyes said. "You are the guy we want."

I turned to Sue and I whispered, "They got us."

2

GOING BACK

"Harry Wu—isn't he the lunatic who was caught in China in the summer of 1995? The one who was released so Hillary Rodham Clinton could attend a United Nations women's conference in Beijing?"

Me for Mrs. Clinton? The world made the judgment that I had plotted this exchange: the wife of the president of the United States for an agitator who visits Chinese labor camps. I'd like to take that credit, but I'm not that smart. Maybe I'm ruining a good story by telling the truth right up front, but here it goes: From the moment I planned my mission to the moment I came home, I never knew about any women's conference in Beijing, never heard about Mrs. Clinton's hopes to attend it, never knew a thing.

People ask why I risked my life to go back to China. People who do not know me judge me as perhaps a madman, at least a crank and a nuisance. They know I touched off an international incident in 1995 when I was arrested at the border and held for two months, my name on television and radio and the front pages of the newspapers. For two months, the world wondered what China's leaders would do with me. Would they send me back to the labor camps? Would they find some way to harm me? Would they let my health deteriorate? I wondered the same thing myself.

I'm nowhere near as noble as a Buddhist monk who sets himself on fire in the public square to protest an injustice. I'm a secular man, with a wife back home, trying to make up for lost time, with no streak of the martyr in him. I've had enough of prison walls. I do not have the courage of Wei Jingsheng, speaking his mind, writing stinging criticisms of Deng Xiaoping, getting sent back to the camps. As far as being the roving zealot who put the president's wife in a tough situation—well, I wish I had known about that conference. I might have slept better during my long nights of captivity. As far as I knew, I was one lonely troublemaker a long way from home.

If that's all it was—me for Mrs. Clinton—then it was a bad deal. I was over there representing the millions of Chinese people who have lived and died in the labor camps. I went back for all my friends who died while I lived. I went back to see the labor camps where I was a prisoner for nearly two decades. Other men were trudging through the fields, looking just like me and Big Mouth Xing and Chen Ming and all my friends. Back in those days, nobody knew about us. Nobody spoke for us. I am lucky. I have come back from the land of the living dead.

In my books, in my speeches, in my poor, inadequate English, I am trying to be a witness for millions of others just like me. Living in the West now, I find it frustrating not to be able to express in English the most subtle thoughts that are in my head in the Mandarin language, but I have made the conscious decision to speak out in English as best I know how. I do not want my books to sound like yet another person but, rather, like the immigrant trying to make himself understood on television or in front of Congress or before the California legislature or while visiting European countries. This is who I am. I just arrived. I want to tell you about the camps in China.

For nineteen years, I was one of those prisoners, held for vague offenses against my homeland. My captors said they wanted to reform me, but really what they wanted was to work me until I dropped. I was lost in the camps that are strategically scattered all over China, where millions of prisoners produce goods for Chinese industry. The authorities have different names for the different stages of their camps. I am an alumnus of three stages: reform through labor (*laogai*), reeducation through labor (*laojiao*), forced-labor placement (*jiuye*). For my purposes, I call the entire system *laogai*.

Laogai—the phrase burns my soul, makes me crazy, makes me want to grab Americans and Europeans and Australians and Japanese by the shirt and scream, "Don't you know what's going on over there?" I want the word *laogai* to be known all over the world in the same way that *gulag* has become synonymous with the horrors of Stalin's prison system.

I went back to China to show the world what is happening in the land of the modern economic miracle. China is booming, making double-digit progress every year. The yuppies have cellular phones now, and they hawk their goods by e-mail. From my house in California, I correspond with their companies by fax. Western businesspeople start salivating when they contemplate the profits they hope to harvest in China. I went back to China to accumulate information so I could caution everybody in the developed nations: Capitalism must never be equated with democracy. This is a very American belief—making money produces freedom and justice and equality. Don't believe it about China. My homeland is mired in thousands of years of rule by one bully at a time, whether you call him emperor or chairman. Don't be fooled by electronics or air-conditioning.

In my homeland, China's rulers change the names of their prisons to make them sound like factories. The prison factories and prison farms have double addresses, double names, but Westerners still visit them and never ask about the abject men and women in the blue shirts hunched over the assembly lines. Many of them are not ordinary workers but prisoners who have been reduced virtually to slaves. The labor of Chinese prisoners is more valuable now than it has ever been. China is selling tea to England, grapes to Japan, tools to France, diesel engines to the United States.

How much of China's economy is produced by prisoners? The only estimate we have ever received from Beijing was in a special white paper on labor camps in 1992, in which the government said 0.08 percent of China's overall output came from prisons. That sounds low, but we really don't know. It is more instructive to look at the numbers of people in labor camps.

The Chinese government has admitted that ten million people have been sent to the camps since the Communists took over in 1949. In 1995, officials said there were 1.2 million workers in 685 camps. This is a ridiculously low figure. I estimate that more than fifty million people have been sent to the *laogai* since 1949. We currently have records of 1,155 camps, with between six million and eight million prisoners in them. I believe that perhaps 10 percent are political prisoners, people who said the wrong words at the wrong time.

The world knows only the tip of the iceberg. The world knows that perhaps a few people were killed at Tiananmen Square or directly afterward. Who knows? I say the incident at Tiananmen Square was peanuts. Millions of people have been lost in the *laogai*. Every one of those lives was precious. The Chinese people have a saying, "We're not looking for the tree but also for the forest." The Chinese preoccupation with the majority has led to abuses by dictators like Mao Zedong. Individuals cannot stand up. The forest is too important.

I speak up for the trees. Each one has a name, a face, a soul, a family. Some of them were my friends. How can I neglect them now that I have freedom? This is my cry. This is my mission. For many people, the bad old days are still here. In some ways, they are even worse. Nowadays, with modern science, some prisoners are too valuable to be kept alive. China is selling kidneys and corneas to wealthy countries. The authorities now kill prisoners in a most sophisticated way while doctors, trained to save lives, are waiting at the edge of the killing field, waiting for the prisoners to be executed—justice on the run blending with supply and demand, ancient justice collaborating with modern science.

Our bodies are also valuable while we are alive. Business is so good that China must keep its troublemakers busy.

Let me tell you about one brave man whom I call Sun, a former prisoner in the Chinese forced-labor system. When we first heard from him, Sun was breaking rocks during the day and making artificial flowers for discount stores in America. He is a teacher who became involved in the pro-democracy movement in 1989 that culminated in the massacre in Tiananmen Square. I wish I could have warned the young people there that soldiers would obey orders from their elderly leaders and fire upon civilians, for the young people had not done their homework, did not understand the minds of the soldiers. The odds were always against the people in the square. The demonstration was too soon, too open, too public, but they did not know this.

Sun was far from Beijing when the killings happened, but he was later detained for "counterrevolutionary instigation" and formally charged with placing posters around the campus where he taught. Among the statements on these posters was this one: "Due to mishandling of the student movement, the party has lost all its credibility and prestige as a ruling party. . . . Upon repeated consideration, we have decided to declare earnestly that we are withdrawing from the Communist Party and the Communist Youth League. . . . Such a ruling party is hated by people the world over and is a shame for the Chinese people."

Like the thousands sentenced for their part in that democracy movement, Sun served three years and was released. He chose to flee to Hong Kong, but the people there could see their expensive digital calendars moving inevitably toward 1997, when Hong Kong will be absorbed by China, and they turned Sun back to the Chinese. He was sent to a reeducation-through-labor camp at a stone quarry in a remote county, where he took the huge risk of smuggling a letter to the outside world, protesting his arrest. I have a soft spot in my heart for anybody who tries to smuggle out a letter because I and a few of my buddies did that once. We took a great risk in writing to Beijing, asking why we were being detained long after the end of our original three-year sentences, but our letter was returned to the camp by the time we had finished our long day out in the fields. The guards threw me into solitary confinement and beat me until I grew so weak, so dispirited that I stopped eating, and they poured liquid down through my nose, using a rubber hose. On the eleventh day, I confessed my sins, and they let me out of solitary. My fellow prisoners captured a frog and made a stew to nurse me back to some semblance of health.

So I appreciated the nerve it took for Sun to smuggle out a letter addressed to the West; it was eventually passed on to the Laogai Research Foundation, which I run from my home in California, with a bureau in Washington, D.C. "I am thrown into this hell because the authorities want to crush me spiritually and physically," Sun wrote. "This is political retaliation and persecution. Being in this critical situation, I have no choice but to appeal to you. I strongly urge progressive forces the world over to pay close attention to human-rights conditions in China and to extend their assistance to the Chinese people who are in an abyss of misery. I strongly appeal to international progressive organizations to urge the authorities to cease persecuting me politically."

Sun wrote that the inmates of the camp work "over fourteen hours a day" moving stones from a quarry to a wharf and then onto a boat. "Many inmates, including me, their hands and feet squashed by big stones, stained with blood and pus, have to labor as usual. As a consequence, many inmates were crippled for life." Any sign of rebellion leads to being beaten "until they are bloodstained all over, collapse, or lose consciousness." Under the best of conditions, he wrote, "living conditions here are harsh. Every meal consists of coarse rice and rotten vegetable leaves." As if that were not bad enough, at night the prisoners at Sun's reeducation-through-labor camp were forced to make artificial flowers.

Sun became even more valuable to the cause in the mid-1990s by exposing how the *laogai* system works and how it is tied to Western markets: "The artificial flowers we make are for export. The trademarks are in English, the prices in [U.S. dollars]. Even the company commander and the quarry director said the flowers are made in cooperation with a Hong Kong company that exports them."

Using forced labor violates international law—even Chinese law—but Beijing insists it does not sell the free labor of prisoners on the international market. It is not so surprising that the government says this, but I find it depressing that all too many American and other leaders believe it. Sun also noted that his camp "has been forcing detainees to make artificial flowers, necklaces, jewelry (trademarks in English, prices in [U.S. dollars]). This can be testified to by anybody who was there, including Hong Kongers."

He actually sent us two labels addressed to Universal Sun Ray of Springfield, Missouri, which, my foundation discovered, imports flowers for Ben Franklin Retail Stores, the name on the third label Sun sent. On July 8 and August 24, 1994, at Ben Franklin Retail Stores in Pleasanton, California, and Reno, Nevada, members of my staff purchased products bearing one or the other of these names.

We sent somebody to the Universal Sun Ray showroom in Springfield who saw dozens of artificial flowers, many of them marked MADE IN CHINA. We could not prove that Universal Sun Ray was aware that these flowers were made at a forced-labor camp, but we did discover that one company executive regularly travels to Asia on business.

Sun noted that he was part of a reeducation-through-labor (*laojiao*) system rather than a reform-through-labor (*laogai*) system. Technically he was not a convicted criminal, just some poor misguided Chinese youth getting a little attitude adjustment. Theoretically, he wrote, "inmates get their pay, have their benefits and holidays, enjoy the right of correspondence, take part in cultural, sports, and other recreational activities, do not labor more than eight hours daily, can visit their families on holiday, can be bailed out for medical treatment, and so on. In reality," he went on, "the *laogai* is hell. I understand that once my letter is published, I might be persecuted even more harshly," he added. "I might even be killed. But I have no choice!"

Sun was the first Chinese prisoner to document goods going from labor camps to America. After his letter was received in the West, he was moved to another camp, but recently we heard he was released. He is one of the lucky ones.

I went back to publicize prisoners like Sun. After I left China in 1985, the prudent thing for me to do would have been to burrow into California and become another new Asian American on the safe side of the Pacific Rim, but word kept arriving of continued abuses in the *laogai*. Even though I knew I might be caught and sent back to prison for the rest of my life, I had to go back.

Even with the angry politicians and their supporters who raise their voices about banning immigration, even with many Americans saying it is time to turn our backs on the rest of the world, I know that deep down America is a generous and decent country. I see its kindness in the way it has always welcomed immigrants, in the way it has cared for others. America is the light unto the world. Do Americans really want to eat fruit and display artificial flowers and use tools that were produced by prisoners? By virtual slaves?

I firmly believe this should not be America's problem, that it should not be something just for the liberal first-world conscience. In the long run, this is a Chinese problem. As an American citizen living in the Silicon Valley of California, I struggle with my identity. I believe there is something intrinsic about the Chinese personality, something that allowed the Chinese to shift from emperor to chairman, something that allows us to treat our own people as slaves.

If the Chinese want to sell their goods in the world, then they must respect the rest of the world, they must respect their own people. Somebody must remind them. This is my job. I appointed myself. I live in another country now, but I cannot forget.

3

STANDOFF

I could tell by the way the guards looked at me that they had me, but I did not want to panic. I motioned to Sue to keep calm, but still our passports did not materialize.

"Would you please wait a few minutes?" one of the guards asked.

"What's the problem?"

"Oh, we've got to check a few things," he said.

This was the moment I had always sought to avoid, the moment when I did not have any control over my fate. I knew it could go in one of several ways: They could hustle me to a back room and arrange for me to disappear—for a decade, forever; or they could escort us across the border and tell us to go back to America. Either I would get my life back, or I would lose my life. I had accepted that risk, but now despite the bravado I felt sick. These people had taken enough of my life, but it was too late to do anything now. I knew my wife and friends in Washington would start making noise as soon as I was reported missing, but that would not help me if I was under the ground, helping to nourish the ancient soil of my homeland.

We waited. They asked us a few questions. What is your name? What is your job? Routine stuff. They were just killing time, and we all knew it. I decided to bluster.

"I'm a free man," I told the guards. "I'm an American. I want to go. Give me my passport back."

Sorry, they said. They had to check things out. Sorry.

After we had been made to wait for an hour or so, a young man in plain clothes came through a door and made a pretense of filming the entire room with a video camera, but he kept zooming back to us.

I was bored and needed some fun, so I walked up to him. "Hey, I'm worried about you," I told him. "You shouldn't be taking pictures here. You'll get in trouble with the law."

He looked at me as if I were nuts. "It's all right," he said.

I gave him the two-finger peace sign, as the hippies used to do in the 1960s, and I walked right past him, so he had to turn and keep pointing the camera at me. I was just messing with him, to see what we could get away with. I walked outside and bought some refreshments, and I noticed the gates were locked. We were in a cage. I went back inside.

At one-thirty in the afternoon, a border policewoman with two stars on each shoulder joined us. You know how it is when two women hate each other on sight? That's the way it was with Sue and this woman. Archenemies. Immediately.

"I just want to practice my English," Two Stars said with almost no accent, asking us questions that were blunt even by Chinese standards. Where were we going? What business were we on? She wanted details. This was not a conversation. This was a grilling. We told her we were scholars going to study the Silk Road. Sue glared at her.

There were questions about why the style of Sue's passport was different from the style of most other U.S. passports. She tried to explain that it had been issued in Italy, on an earlier trip, after she had been robbed, but they did not seem to believe that, or that she was forty-five years old. Under other circumstances, Sue might have been flattered, but we had more pressing problems.

At two o'clock, our minders brought us crackers and bottled water. They changed tactics, changed shifts, but as the time passed, we realized there were no more tourists, no more civilians.

At three forty-five, I asked, "Can I use the telephone?"

They told me no telephone was available.

"Can I send a fax to my embassy?"

No.

"I've changed my mind," I told them. "I don't want to go to China after all. Could you please arrange for transportation back to Almaty?"

No.

Half an hour later I asked again if we could contact our embassy. I demanded to know why we were being detained. This was the first time I used that word, and they did not try to deny it.

At six-ten, an Inspector Ho, with three stars on his shirt, told us he would take care of our problem within the hour.

At six-twenty, a nice young woman from Health Customs spotted us and said she wanted to practice her English. She seemed genuine, but she did not understand the situation. All of a sudden, a police officer motioned her into the back room and screamed at her until she started crying. After that she wouldn't even look at us.

At six forty-five, Inspector Ho returned and said he hadn't forgotten us.

At seven o'clock, he asked me how many times I had returned to China since leaving, and I told him the truth, that I had made three visits. He went away to talk on the phone.

At seven-ten, we noticed all the customs agents going home for the day. Doors were shutting, gates were clanging tight, locks were being clicked.

At seven-fifty, Inspector Ho came back. I could tell by his posture that this was not going to be easy. "I'm sorry, we are closed for the night," he said. "I'm sorry we couldn't verify your passport today. You'll have to wait until tomorrow. We have to ask you to stay overnight in our hotel."

"We're not going to the hotel until we speak to our embassy," I said.

Tomorrow, Inspector Ho said.

Once outside, Sue and I sat down on cardboard boxes on the filthy sidewalk and began our own little sit-down strike. I had the feeling Sue might have done this once or twice back in the 1960s.

At seven fifty-five, Inspector Ho promised to contact one of the U.S. consulates the next day. He pleaded with us to go to the hotel. I knew we'd stalled as much as we could, so I motioned for Sue to head for the car.

What really bothered me was seeing them use Motorola cellular phones. The United States apparently sells modern phones to help the Chinese detain U.S. citizens at the border.

They did not twist our arms to get us into the car. Inspector Ho made sure nobody was going to get hurt on his shift.

At the Karamai Guesthouse, a few hundred yards from the border, we were ushered past the registration desk and taken to an elevator and told there were two rooms for us on the sixth floor.

"We must have one room," I insisted, sticking to my policy. "If they want to separate us, they will," I whispered to Sue. "Let's stay together as long as possible."

We were escorted to Room 611, and the police occupied two rooms directly across the hall. Our room looked down at the border station, and beyond that was the border itself. I noticed a locked gate across the road, but to my amazement I saw that the long chain fence stretched for only several hundred yards in either direction. After that, wide open spaces. Maybe we could make an end run in the middle of the night. I also noticed that two hundred yards from the hotel, there was a post office with a telephone booth. I'd have to check them both out as soon as possible.

Room 611 was small, functional, with twin beds against opposite walls, two chairs, a small table, dresser, bathroom, no hot water. Sue tried to take a bath, but the handle on the faucet came off in her hand, and I could hear her muttering. Sometimes there was no water at all. The hotel looked to be only a few years old, but it was already decrepit.

Our guards invited us downstairs to the second floor, for dinner. Inspector Ho and a younger officer told us dinner was on them. Sue and I kept insisting that we had to call our embassy, and Ho kept apologizing. Sit down, please, he gestured. Don't make trouble. It's not my fault. Here's the waitress. Let's eat.

Ho was a good guy. He knew exactly who I was—Harry Wu, one of the forty-nine most-wanted people in China—but he talked to me like an adult. I told him about the death of my parents, the way I had suffered in the *laogai*, and I could see from his face that he was touched. Everybody in China has suffered or knows somebody who has suffered. That's the crazy thing. When the Red Guards were running around like madmen in the mid-'60s, it wasn't really a case of us against them. It was us against us. You could call it a class war, but it was worse: It was Chinese savaging Chinese. Everybody suffered. The men around the table could have told stories, too, but they did not dare.

They did tell me one story that illustrates just how touchy things were with the Kazakhs across the border. During the spring festival a few months earlier, the Chinese had been setting off strings of firecrackers, the way the Chinese do all over the world. The Kazakh soldiers initially thought it was the sound of machine-gun fire, so they came rushing up to the border, weapons ready. "Why are you shooting machine guns?" the Kazakhs asked on the phone.

"Why are you massing on the border?" the Chinese asked.

The Kazakhs did not believe the Chinese until the Chinese escorted them across the border to see little kids tossing firecrackers to celebrate springtime. Guaranteed that is how the next world war will start.

At eleven that evening, Ho came to our room and said we had to travel to Yining, many hours away, for questioning. Right away.

"Under no circumstances," I told him. "We are American citizens. If they want to talk to us, let them come to the border."

While Ho was negotiating with me, Sue tried to slip past the guards to investigate the hallway. We had not planned it that way, but just like on the television shows I was the good cop and she was the bad cop. She knew they were unsettled by a redheaded Caucasian American yelling at them, so she exploited it to the fullest. "I want to call the American embassy," she shouted. "I'm writing a letter. You must deliver it right away." Then she turned to me and winked. "I'm a bitch."

It was time for the good cop to take over. I was trying to learn things from these guys, and I wanted them on my side. They asked me who

Sue Howell was, and I said, "My assistant." I made sure they understood it was nothing more than that.

They said to me in Chinese, "Hey, what is it with this woman?"

I shrugged my shoulders. "You cannot control American women," I said with a sigh.

When Sue and I were back in the room, I looked around for hidden cameras and decided the room was safe enough for me to clean out my bag. I destroyed some papers that had important phone numbers in code. I cut off the plastic flap on my travel bag so nobody could accuse me of taking pictures surreptitiously. I took a few photographs of the border and also some photographs of Sue, and then she took a photograph of me sitting on the bed, looking almost dapper for a man being held incommunicado, in my boots and slacks and white shirt and my broad-brimmed Indiana Jones hat. Even if I did not get out, maybe my photograph would.

Now that we were alone, reality set in. All day long I had been busy bluffing these people, but now I had to face the big picture. They had me. I was nervous because I had not called home since Almaty, more than a week earlier. Every two or three days, I was supposed to call, and if I didn't, Jeffrey Fiedler, who works with me in Washington, would take emergency action.

I was worried about Ching-Lee, the sweet and capable woman I had met on a blind date in Taipei only five years earlier. How her life had changed. She had gone from an office in Taiwan to a house in California; she had taken her own chances in China. I knew she was strong, but I felt guilty about getting her into this. Most important, I missed her terribly, missed the intimacy of living with a woman I loved. After two failed marriages back in China, I never thought I could love somebody the way I love Ching-Lee. I could not bear the pain of being separated from her. I found my heart doing the same thing it had done back in the camps: It shut down. I knew that if I thought about Ching-Lee, I would become weak and distracted, I would want to live, I would apologize, confess, grovel in front of my tormentors. I did not want to exchange my principles for my life. I forced myself not to see Ching-Lee's face, not to think about her at all. Otherwise, I knew, I would not survive.

The next morning we asked to take a little walk outside the hotel, just for exercise. On the corner, we spotted a shop and were allowed to go inside and buy scarves and other presents. I wanted to keep moving, to try things out, look around, chat with everybody. One never knows what one might find out.

A sign in the shop said INTERNATIONAL TELEPHONE SERVICE, so I took it at its word and asked to call my embassy.

"Please," the officer said. "You have to understand my situation. This is my job. I have orders. I am not allowed to do anything."

We went upstairs for lunch, and Sue reminded them of the promised call to our embassy. When they gave her a vague response, she whispered to me, "I'm going to make a break for it."

She bolted away from the guards and ran down a flight of stairs. The guards outside were not expecting to see a redhead come sprinting through the door, so she managed to race through the gates and get halfway down the block—halfway to the telephone booth—before a young plainclothes officer grabbed her.

"Help! Help me! I'm being attacked!" she screamed as Chinese pedestrians turned and watched.

The officer looked embarrassed as he tried to turn her back toward the hotel, but Sue reached into her pocketbook and came up with a pint bottle of mineral water. She gripped the bottle by the neck and started whacking the poor man.

I decided to exploit the situation, running over to the police and shouting, "What is he doing? This guy is a hooligan!" They tried to explain to me that he was a police officer, but I said, "He is not in uniform! He didn't show his identification."

I was just testing them to see how far we could go. I knew that if I was some ordinary Chinese guy wanted by the police, they would have had me in the back room by then, prodding me with electrical devices, twisting me and bending me. I've been there. I know what these guys can do. Our U.S. passports were keeping us from a beating—at least for now.

Finally Sue stopped whacking the young officer and allowed them to walk her—and me—back to the hotel.

"I made a mistake," she told me. "I looked into his eyes. He's just a kid. He was bewildered by the whole thing."

⌁

At three o'clock, we were summoned to meet with General Luo Yue, the top security officer for the region, who had just arrived from Ürümqi. Luo was pretty suave, but Sue was not impressed.

"I want to talk to my consulate," she told him. "You don't have the right to detain me. I'm an American citizen. I went to make a phone call, and they stopped me. They grabbed my hands. According to international law, you have to let me go."

Luo said he would try to work something out, and Sue just glowered at him, crossing her legs and pointing the tip of her black boot directly at him.

"Where are your manners?" hissed Sue's archenemy, the female translator, who told her that in China it is highly insulting to point your shoe at anybody, particularly somebody of high rank.

"I'm not Chinese, but I might be more polite if you people were not liars," said Sue, keeping her boot directed at Luo, who did not fail to get the message.

Luo tried to get on with his business, saying, "I received an order from Beijing, accusing you of using false names several times to sneak into China."

"I never used a false name or false documents," I said. "I am a naturalized American citizen named Peter Wu. This is my legal name. If I had wanted to use false documents, I could have done that easily. Also, my entrance visa from last year is on my passport. I could have changed my passport easily, but I didn't do it. Your consulate in Houston gave me a visa, so I thought I was welcome."

"Haven't you heard you're on the list of forty-nine?" Luo asked.

"Yes, I have heard about it," I said, "but your blacklist document has never been admitted by your own government."

"Well, you're on it," he assured me. "Why did you come back?"

"I keep hearing that China has changed," I said. "Maybe two or three years ago you put me on a blacklist, but now I received a visa, so I figured I was welcome to return. Why did you give me a visa if you're going to act like this? I just learned from my own experience. In 1957, I was punished as a counterrevolutionary rightist. Twenty-two years later your government apologized and rehabilitated me, so I assumed things had changed."

I was giving him a headache.

"Okay, okay," he said. "I don't want to argue. Please, understand my position. I'm just following orders from Beijing. I cannot let you go. I'll be honest with you. You've come over here at the wrong time."

"What are you talking about?"

"Haven't you heard our ambassador was sent home from Washington?"

"I'm sorry. I was in Kazakhstan. I didn't hear about it."

I knew that China was angry with the United States for letting Lee Teng-hui, the Taiwanese president, attend his class reunion at Cornell University, but I did not know the degree to which the bad feelings had escalated. Now the Chinese were lucky enough to catch one of their top forty-nine troublemakers. They had something to work with.

Suddenly Luo looked nervous.

"Hey," he said. "Later, when you go home and write a book, don't mention my name. This is off the record."

"I don't know when I'll get home, but I won't mention you," I promised. I promised a lot of things to those people. That's how the game works.

~

When Sue and I got back to the room, we argued about her tactics. I understood the idea of playing good cop, bad cop, but I also told her to leave some room for negotiating, to give them some face. This sounds like a stereotype to Westerners, but Chinese people do operate on the premise of face.

Sue decided that was fine for me, but she was going on a hunger strike. "It's the only way I can get their attention," she said. "You need your strength to get around, but I can occupy them with a hunger strike." She skipped lunch while I played the innocent, requesting to speak to my embassy. They said they were working on it.

That night Sue and I stayed up late. We had no choice. It always stays light very late in western China because Chairman Mao had insisted the whole country be on the same time as Beijing, the center of the universe. The great arbitrator, the only Chinese person allowed to have a mind, had wanted the whole country on his time, yet he had lived according to no schedule, rising when he wanted, sleeping when he wanted, eating, fornicating, lecturing, traveling, and giving execution orders whenever he felt like it. Our chairman had been gone nineteen years, but his single time zone lingered on. On one of the longest days of the year, we watched the sun set near midnight, and we discussed our predicament.

We agreed our captors were going to get nasty at some point. I had faced death before, had been through times in the camps when I had thought they were going to blow my brains out, and most of my friends had died young. I could face dying at fifty-eight. "Death isn't the worst thing that can happen to you," I said.

"Hey, a bullet in the brain is an exquisite way to go," Sue said. "I've watched relatives of mine die excruciatingly painful deaths from cancer. I'll take a bullet anytime."

On that morbid note, we ended our second day in captivity.

⌐⌐

Sue's hunger strike was in its second day. She is very slender anyway and normally does not eat much, and I knew she could survive a long time with just water. She was lying still on the bed, looking much worse than she really was.

Meanwhile I was trying to chat up my captors, going for walks with them in the hallways, outside. I wanted to keep in touch with the mind of contemporary China, to see what my options were. I got into a conversation with Ho, the three-star officer, about what would happen to us, and he turned it around and asked what I thought. I said they would keep me and let Sue go, and I asked Ho how much it would cost for a taxi ride from Horgas to Almaty, and he said about a hundred dollars. That night I would slip Sue an extra hundred dollars and tell her to hide it in her document belt.

They came up to the room to issue Sue a personal invitation to dinner, but she declined.

After dinner, I asked to get some fresh air, and they agreed to my request. At first, I walked away from the border, but then I casually worked my way toward the fence, with officers on both sides of me. My eyes had been correct. The fence was only about a quarter of a mile long, and beyond it was nothing but rubble, wide-open spaces, no-man's-land. A person could easily walk around it in a few minutes and head for Kazakhstan—if they didn't shoot him in the back, that is.

When I got back up to the room, I told Sue I was going to escape overnight.

"Are you sure you want to do this?" she asked.

"They don't want you; they just want me," I said. "They'll just let you go. Take care of my luggage. There's nothing worth saving. I'll take some money with me. Bring the camera back, or throw it away. Just get back to Almaty, and call Ching-Lee."

I couldn't stand being cooped up by these people. They already had too much of my life. I waited until Sue was asleep, and then I picked up our carafe and opened the door, as if I were going down the hall to the twenty-four-hour teapot.

The hall was quiet. The room with the two female police officers was closed. Three male officers were supposed to take turns watching the hall from a chair just outside our door, but the guard was sound asleep. I waved my carafe in his face just to be sure. Nothing, no response.

I walked toward the elevator, where the female hall guard sat during the day. Nobody there. I didn't dare use the elevator, so I walked down six flights of stairs, not hearing a soul. I slipped into the parking lot out back. Nobody was stirring. There was a gate, low enough for me to get over. Was it going to be this easy?

For ten or fifteen minutes, I stood in the shadows and thought about it. All I had to do was walk a few hundred yards around that fence, taking a chance with no trees, no shelter—one aging troublemaker running for his life. Were they just setting me up to shoot me in the back? It would be the best possible solution for them, and I did not want to give them the satisfaction. I thought about Sue Howell upstairs, and I remembered my responsibility to her, all my preaching about my being the general and her being the lieutenant. Should I leave her to the mercies of the People's Liberation Army?

I could not do it. One thing I remembered from Catholic school: The captain is always the last to leave a sinking ship. I picked up my carafe and climbed the stairs to my room. The guard was still asleep in his chair.

~

Sue woke up shivering from lack of food, and I told our minders I was growing concerned about her health, so they sent in a Chinese doctor, who very politely tried to examine her.

"Don't touch me!" Sue said. "He's trying to kill me!"

The poor man looked confused, but at least she had enough energy to yell. He was told to stay across the hall until the problem was solved.

In the afternoon, I felt so tense that I began pacing around the room, talking and gesturing and practically bouncing off the walls. Sue attributed it to the caffeine, and she told me, "Harry, let them take you outside for a walk so you can walk off some of that energy."

The guards obliged by taking me outside, where I paced around for a while until I noticed a brand-new black Cherokee-style jeep parked out front. Something was happening for them to bring in hardware like that. I wandered over and saw several police officers sitting in the car, thumbing through the service manuals, all written in English, which did the guards absolutely no good. They could not figure out some of the gadgets in the car, so I volunteered my services, and somewhat to my amazement, they let me slide into the driver's seat. By referring to the manual, I showed them how to work all the extras one does not normally find in a Chinese car, like the four-wheel drive and the automatic brake system. Given the late-June heat, I was relieved to notice a powerful air-conditioning system. I did not have to be a genius to figure out that I was teaching them how to use the car for my own benefit. I was going for a ride in the country.

When I came back, I felt calmer. Sue looked at me and said, "That's better."

I told her, "They're getting ready for something. This is it. They are going to separate us."

"I want to stay with you," she said. "I am responsible for your security. If they don't release you, I'll stay over here and protest. We're partners. American principles won't allow me to do that."

"Sue, you have to understand. The most important thing is to leave here, call the State Department, call my family, tell them I'm caught." I did not want to remind her this was the reason she was here—as a safety valve. They were not about to kill a native-born American; they were going to expel her, and if she got out, so would news of my captivity.

I sat down and wrote a letter to Ching-Lee, telling her how much I loved her. I said if I died in China, it was all right because it is my homeland, and my father and both my mother and my stepmother were buried here. I would be proud to die in China, but I did not want to die.

I also included some instructions for Ching-Lee and Jeff and the names and numbers of some people to contact, which was risky. At first, Sue was dubious about carrying the letter, but I persisted.

"Promise me you'll deliver my letter," I asked her, and then I went over the final details: "They're going to send you to Kazakhstan tomorrow. Maybe they'll make you walk a few miles at the border. They are going to search you, but legally they have no right to do it. Assert your rights. Also, you have a long day ahead of you. You must eat. Here are the sardines and the crackers. They don't know you're eating this. Fool them, and get strong."

While Sue was eating the whole can's worth, I grabbed all the shampoo packets and ashtrays and tea bags and plastic combs that had the hotel's name and phone number printed on them. I also gave her the roll of film, including photographs of General Luo, border facilities, and myself that we had managed to take. I told Sue to mix the hotel souvenirs and the film in with her underwear in her suitcase, and maybe they would be too modest to search there.

I fell asleep. This is a great skill I have, being able to sleep anytime, anywhere. It's from all those years of working long hours in the labor camp, knowing that if you doze off, somebody might hit you with a rifle butt. I used to daydream about having the luxury of taking a nap, so now I can fall asleep in fifteen seconds—making up for lost time.

And yet I am always awake. I always hear what is going on. That night I could hear horns blaring in the parking lot down below and gates crashing open and shut.

I leaped out of bed and went to the window and saw vehicles moving around. I paced around the room for a while, and then I tiptoed to Sue's bed. "They're getting ready," I whispered.

Just before breakfast, they told me that Luo wanted to see me.

"I'll be back in a few minutes," I told Sue.

⌒

As soon as I was out the door, Sue heard a knock, and four guards entered the room, shouting and pointing, meaner than anybody else had been. She attributed this to her archenemy, the interpreter, who was supervising. They forced her to separate everything in the room into two piles, mine and hers.

They even made her go through every item in her pocketbook and her suitcase. Sue made a big show of waving each item of underwear, hoping to embarrass the guards, but they diligently found almost every souvenir from the hotel. Sue refused to leave the room without her goods, and she also refused to let them touch the pouch of valuables that hung around her neck or the documents she carried in her belt. By bluffing, she managed to keep them from finding the hundred dollars she had stuck in the back of the belt. She was very good at standing up to these people, but she could not persuade them to let her say good-bye to me. She wanted to leave her remaining Chinese money with Inspector Ho, to buy a present for his child, but he was not around. Sue reasoned that they had probably taken him off the case because he was too nice.

After an hour, they escorted her to the border, where she had to arrange a taxi ride to Almaty. They really were not doing an American woman any favors by dropping her there at the mercy of the desperado Kazakh taxi drivers, but she managed to find a gentleman who delivered her safely.

Sue was anxious to deliver the message that I was being detained, but she discovered that the State Department had already been notified that I was being taken to the interior. Her frustration turned to rage when the wonderful people from Lufthansa would not let her use her excursion ticket for an early return flight to Frankfurt. She tried to explain that she had been expelled from China, a situation beyond her control. All airlines make exceptions in cases of emergency or personal hardship, but Lufthansa charged her an additional twenty-two hundred dollars to get out of Almaty.

"This had been one of the most painful experiences in my life," she would say months later. "I wanted to get some information, to help the Chinese people. When I got to the border, I felt superfluous. I didn't want to be known for a failure."

I'm not very good at compassionate and subtle words, particularly in English, but I hope Sue Howell knows how much she means to me and Ching-Lee. In those days at the border, Sue did everything she could. I know she would have made a great contribution on a long trip through China, but instead I was on my own.

For four days, I had hoped they would pick me up by the seat of my pants like some character in the cartoons, toss me over the border, fling my suitcase after me, dust off their hands, and say, "Don't ever come back." But that was not going to happen. They had something else in mind for me.

4

THE MAKING OF A DISSIDENT

Maybe I was always a bit of a troublemaker. When I was in grade school back in Shanghai, I liked to test my teachers, just to keep them on the ball. One day my teacher told us to go outdoors, find a plant, and bring it to class, and he would tell us something unique about it. He was a very knowledgeable teacher, but I felt the need to trouble him. Everybody else did what he was told, but I carefully stuck a small stem from one plant into the middle of another.

The teacher described each plant, and then he got to mine.

"Hmmm," he said, "I will have to look at this more carefully." Later he asked the class, "Who turned in this branch?"

I raised my hand. He called me to the front of the room, and he told the class that it is always bad to tamper with science. And just to make the point, he delivered a dozen whacks across the palm of my left hand with a ruler.

Things got worse at home. My father was a businessman, strict, typically Chinese. When he was not around for dinner, all the kids and my stepmother would joke and move around, but when he was home, we sat at our places and ate silently, our hands always on the table. Good manners to the Chinese mean never eating with one hand below the table. That day, however, I could not eat with my left hand because of the spanking in school, so I rested it on my lap.

"Why are you hiding your hand?" Father asked. "Let me see."

I held out my left hand with the red welts across the palm, and when I told him why I had been spanked, he evened things out, whacking me across the right palm a dozen times. I therefore received both a science lesson and a manners lesson in the same day.

There is no such thing as an equal relationship in China. In America, a son can call his father Dad or maybe even by his nickname or his real name, but in China everything is formal. Master is Master, servant is Servant, husband is Husband, wife is Wife, child is Child. This mentality goes back a thousand years and has shaped our political culture as well.

My father, Wu Pao-Yi, did not talk about himself to his children, and he did not expect them to talk about themselves. We knew he was an official in a bank and ran his own knitting-yarn factory, but we had no idea how many properties Father had, what he did at work, how much money we had. I knew he had been born into a modest landlord family in Wuxi and had been sent to Shanghai to study with the Christians, with the Westerners. He was firm about the boys' role: "Your job is to be good students. Become intellectuals. Above all, stay out of politics."

My father's main lesson to us was to stand on our own feet. One time I got into a fight with two other boys, and I came home crying. My father looked at me and said, "Never cry. And never give up."

Like all kids, I wanted attention from my father. If this was his attention, I accepted it. I vowed never to cry. And never to give up.

There is an old Chinese curse that goes "May you live in interesting times." I was born at the onset of interesting times, on February 8, 1937, just before a clash in Beijing that set off a full-scale war with the Japanese, who had earlier invaded northern China and installed a puppet government in Manchuria. In the early months of my life, thousands of wealthy people left Shanghai just ahead of the Japanese.

My real mother, Kuo Zhong Ying, died in 1942. I do not remember her very well, and the circumstances of her death remain murky to me. We did not have much family, no grandparents by the time I came along and few other relatives, but one of my cousins once told me that my mother and father had quarreled, and implied that perhaps my mother had committed suicide. I could never ask my father about this because he was too stern, too remote.

The Chinese tradition is that a person must be buried in his or her native province, but with a three-way war going on—among the Japanese, the Communists, and the Kuomintang, the ruling government—it was not safe to take my mother's remains home. Father buried Mother in an elaborate wooden coffin, and he paid a lot of money to keep it safe until she could be taken to Wuxi.

Within a year, my father told us bluntly that he was getting married again. He arranged for us to appear at the ceremony, and we expected the worst from our stepmother, but Chen Ren Tai smiled and hugged us and broke down all the terrible images we had conjured up of stepmothers: cold, distant, self-centered.

We learned more about our new mother on April 5, when all Chinese remember their ancestors. Although my father had adopted Western ways, he did not neglect the Buddhist and Confucian rites, which on this holiday meant bowls of food set out on a long table, candles glittering, incense burning, his pouring the wine. Three times he poured the wine, and three times everybody kowtowed, a formal and elaborate bow. We did it in order: first my father, then my older brother, then me, then my oldest sister, then the little ones. All were very quiet, very serious.

Nobody would have blamed my stepmother if she had bustled about doing the odd jobs, keeping busy, staying out of the way of this ceremony for a departed first wife, but my stepmother bowed deeply in front of the statue. My stepmother even honored my mother's coffin. Every year the men in the family are supposed to paint the coffins of the departed, but my father was always very busy at work, and we dared not ask him to come with us. Instead, my stepmother hired a ricksha and took my older brother and me to the cemetery. I can still visualize us—my stepmother carrying the paint bucket and brushes in one hand and grasping my hand with her other hand, and my older brother, Hong Yi, walking alongside, clutching her dress.

At the coffin, my stepmother opened the paint can and put a brush in my brother's small hand, then wrapped her own hand around his hand and guided him while he neatly spread the paint. Then she took my hand and repeated the ritual until the job was completed—the elegant hands of an upper-class woman, a stepmother, painting the coffin of her predecessor.

With the help of the Westerners, the Japanese were stopped in 1945, and although the civil war continued, there was a semblance of the old order. We took my mother's coffin home to Wuxi and buried her there.

My stepmother taught me how to love and respect other people. She made our house happy again, and soon there were four boys and four girls. I only wish I could have spared her the pain, the terror, that my life would bring to the family.

In 1948, when I was eleven, my father sent me to the St. Francis School, where most of the teachers were Italian priests. My favorite was Father Capolito, who taught science and took me on outings on weekends, bringing along picnic lunches, teaching, always teaching. The Italian priest became another father for me. I will always remember him putting his thick, warm hand on the top of my head as we walked together in the garden. He was very Western-looking, with thick lips, a bald head with a silver fringe around the sides, big, round eyes, a big nose.

In the ancient Chinese fright masks, the eyes are always large and round, like Western eyes, but Father Capolito and his fellow priests were different from the images these masks conveyed; they personified how humans should be: strong, kind, proud, individual, faithful. This strong Christian, Western strain in my family made me different at a time when it was not healthy to be different. I learned to stand up for my beliefs; I also learned to ask questions, to be smart, stubborn, logical.

Soon I was baptized as a Roman Catholic, sang the hymns and attended the masses, and said grace before meals at school, but we never said Christian prayers around the house because my father remained Buddhist. Many years later I dared to ask why he had never become a Christian although he graduated from a Christian college. He told me, "I had to find a way to commemorate your mother, and Buddhism is the way."

I learned from my father. I looked to the West, but I never renounced the style, the ceremony, the tradition, the respect of Buddhism. Buddhism does not demand total allegiance. Buddhism is a philosophy. Buddhism can coexist. And yet I became a Christian in some part of my heart. Christianity has its history of martyrs: men and women nailed to the cross, their sides pierced with arrows, their tongues cut off because they would not renounce their beliefs. Jesus Christ, with his crown of thorns, was a martyr.

While I was detained in China in 1995, James R. Lilley, the former U.S. ambassador to China, said on *ABC News Nightline*, "The United States has got to get the Harry Wu case solved," as if I were a manila folder, not a human being. And then he said, "He has a martyr complex in the true Chinese tradition."

That was easy for him to say. Do I respect Christian martyrs for not giving up their principles? Of course. Did I want to be a martyr myself? Never. My whole instinct has been to survive. My teachers, those proud Italian fathers, were an example to me, showing me that integral to basic human nature is the will to survive, to stay alive. It is human nature to love and be loved. This goes beyond religion. Human beings are not animals. They need to be treated with respect. I learned this when I was young.

Of course when I enrolled in college, I became a scientist and studied Darwin, evolution, the formation of the earth, the fossils, the bones, the dinosaurs, the evolution of animals, the place the human race came from. I believe the world was not created by God in a flash of light, in six days, the way the Bible says but, rather, through evolution. My scientific instincts work against religious beliefs, but still I feel there is something there.

So perhaps for me, Christianity is not faith in dogma, but morally and philosophically I believe Christianity is my faith. The sense that human beings are connected to a God, that we should treat one another as God's children, helped sustain me in the dreadful years to come.

~

We lived in an apartment complex with a lot of foreigners, Italian, French, Spanish, and it became fashionable for privileged Chinese like us to take a Western name. I was named Wu Hongda at birth, but

I was also called Harry, and my brother was called Henry. Chinese people have trouble pronouncing the Western *r*, so a friend might call for Harry to come out and play and get Henry instead. My oldest sister, Han Lian, made a decision: "One of you has to change your name." She put a piece of paper in one hand behind her back and told me to guess which hand held the paper. I guessed right, and so she said, "okay, Peter." I really didn't use that name much, but it was an extra identity: the rock of the church of Jesus Christ.

Because my father had had a strong liberal arts education at St. John's University in Shanghai, I was surrounded by the Western classics. One of my earliest favorites was Victor Hugo's *Les Misérables*, which I read first in Chinese, later in English. Even as a child of comfort, I felt a total bond with Jean Valjean, hunted for stealing a loaf of bread. No matter how he prospered, no matter what good works he performed, Valjean knew that the rigid law of France still considered him a criminal and that an inspector would hunt him down. Little did I know as a child that my love for this book would cause my arm to be broken during the Cultural Revolution.

When I was seventeen, I read Melville's *Moby-Dick* in English, and later I read it in Chinese. Most people think Ahab is crazy, but I loved him. I can hear Captain Ahab shouting, "Ship, ahoy! Hast seen the white whale?" People say, "Yes, but Ahab dies," and I say, "Yes, but the whale dies, too." I am no Ahab, but I admire what he did. Ahab chased his white whale, and now I chase the white whale of communism.

A third book I remember is Hemingway's *The Old Man and the Sea*. I never tire of reading how the old fisherman holds on to the giant fish even though it nearly costs him his life. I have two favorite sentences in that book: "Man is not made for defeat," and "A man can be destroyed but not defeated."

My experiences could have happened only in Shanghai, the most Westernized city in China, worldly, affluent, dangerous, corrupt, beautiful, mysterious. The Shanghai of the 1930s was where people went for commerce or culture or pleasure, for the famous cooks, jewelers, and tailors; for gambling, opium, women. The British had built opulent neighborhoods next to squalid slums and brought traffic cops from India, Sikhs, with their beards and their turbans, fierce-looking guys who stood out in the middle of the traffic. You had Westerners driving cabs, teaching school, dancing in the cabarets. It was an open city.

Shanghai was also a center for an exotic new sport called baseball. The American servicemen had taught the game in Shanghai and Guangzhou while the Japanese had introduced it in Manchuria and Beijing. I started playing baseball in school when I was eleven, and the older boys stuck this little guy with glasses in right field, always the last position to be filled. But gradually I showed I was a good athlete, and I moved to the infield, to the middle of the action. I loved baseball because the player has to be smart, has to think ahead, has to be flexible. I loved all the English terms: *double play, home run, base on balls*.

When the Communists took over, they left baseball alone for a long time. Instead of playing for a private school, one played for the state, but that was all right. The more control over our lives they took, the more I loved baseball. They couldn't bother us out on the field. The rules were always the same: three strikes, four balls. By 1954, I was captain of my high school team. The idea of baseball is to sacrifice yourself. I learned the lesson of sports: Never give up, never think you failed, always try again. A team can be five runs down and still win the game. I hated internal bickering on our teams. I was a team player in those days.

When I went to college, I even had my picture in the *People's Monthly*, the *Life* magazine of its time. I was proud of my body, and I was mentally strong and would fight to win.

In 1949, when I was twelve, the Kuomintang fled to Taiwan, and the Communists took over China, supported by the majority of the Chinese people. This was just another step in the history of Chinese killing Chinese in the name of the motherland. The Kuomintang killed Communists, landlords killed peasants, revolutionaries killed landlords, Communists killed Catholics, Tibetans—anybody who disagreed. Chinese killed Chinese.

To this day, I still think America could have done more to help China after the Second World War, the way it helped Europe under the Marshall Plan. The Americans basically abandoned China to the Communists, but Mao did not show America any respect. Ever since then, there has been this great debate in America: Who lost China? Famous academics like John K. Fairbank and diplomats like Henry Kissinger have the patronizing attitude that communism is bad in most places but maybe not so bad in China.

We were the ones who had to live with it. Father Capolito and the other priests went home to Europe, and many of our affluent neighbors took their money and their families to Hong Kong, Asia, Europe, the Americas, but my father would not leave. He was Chinese, he said, and he would fit into whatever system came next.

In 1952, Father did not come home for a month, but we did not ask questions. One night he returned and told my stepmother the Communists had interrogated him in his office, and he had refused to give false information about his associates. He was assigned to a small bank and given a worker's income, but two years later he retired from banking and quietly taught English at a neighborhood school.

He tried to remain a loyal Chinese citizen, the ideal Communist, but it was almost chemically impossible. What the Communists wanted from us we could not do. We could not pretend. My father was proud of my going to Beijing to study geology, and he warned me to watch my stubborn ways and to stay out of politics, as if there were a choice.

5

THE BIG COUNTRY

"We're leaving," General Luo said. "We've got orders to take you."

"Where?"

He would not say.

"The woman?"

"We'll deliver her to Kazakhstan."

I was concerned about Sue's safety, but there was nothing I could do about it now. They took me to the jeep out in the parking lot, and we left the border and headed east. The Chinese could play this game very well. They had experience hiding their dissidents.

Three times I had slipped back into China with cameras and notepad; three times I had lurked at the edge of labor camps and cataloged the ongoing horrors. There are more than a thousand such camps scattered all over China. The authorities could send me anywhere: back to my coal mine, back to the farms. They probably had my old blue uniform waiting for me.

"You are fascinated with our labor camps?" they could ask. "Well, we're giving you a guided tour. One camp a month. That should satisfy your curiosity for the next eighty years or so."

I thought about the way they would just herd us into a railroad car in the middle of the night and steam off, for hundreds of miles, because the potatoes needed picking in the next province. Poets and peasants, teachers and truck drivers—all became Chinese slaves in Chinese camps. I had never meant to be among them again.

This time we drove inward, inward through this big country, so dry and barren up in the northwest, with hardly any sign of vegetation. Surrounded by officers and guards, I had a grandiose sensation that I was not some abject captive prisoner being shuttled to his fate but, rather, I was being transported across my homeland in modern-day style, in an air-conditioned jeep.

I was not a prisoner. I was Chairman Mao himself, departing from Horgas on a whim, on five minutes' notice. Let's take a road trip. Mao would wake up one morning in Beijing and decide he needed to visit Qingdao or Guangzhou, and he wanted to roll that day. No matter what had been planned for that day, if Mao had a desire to inspect a dam or swim in the Yangtze or purge a rival politician, his staff had better be prepared to travel. Advisers, cooks, medical staffers—they had no time to pack a suitcase or say good-bye to their families. This also meant that extra staff always had to be on duty—including the pretty young "attendants" whom Mao liked; they all had to be ready to accompany the chairman on his impulsive jaunts. There were no pretty attendants on this expedition, just a bunch of quiet officers escorting one lost troublemaker across a giant country.

I was driven to Yining, about six hours from Horgas, to a government guesthouse that serves only high-ranking officials. General Luo and a younger officer named Chu stayed in the same suite with me, and I made it my business to badger them.

"Where are my detention orders?" I squawked at Chu. "Where is my arrest warrant?"

"Don't ask me, okay?" Chu said. "I'm just a low-level officer, and you are a very special case."

"I don't want to be special!" I said. "Don't do me any favors. Remember in the Cultural Revolution when the Red Guard arrested Liu Shaoqi? Liu took out a copy of the constitution, and he said, 'I am not only a Chinese citizen, but I am chairman of the country. I am protected by the constitution.' Remember? But the Red Guard pushed him around anyway, saying, 'Forget it. You are special. You are the enemy of the party, the enemy of Chairman Mao, the enemy of the country. We can do anything.' Liu was beaten and deposed, and finally they let him die of tuberculosis. Everybody knows about that. In 1980, Deng rehabilitated him, but it was too late. I don't want to be special. That just means the constitution becomes nothing. This country is lawless."

Chu just looked at me and said, "I don't have the right to discuss this. I just know that you're special, and I'm doing my best to treat you well."

I looked at his face. He was a human being caught in a tough position. "I thank you very much," I said. "I appreciate what you're saying. Here's a gift." Knowing they had not confiscated any of my belongings, I reached into my traveling bag and gave him a Swiss Army knife. He was very appreciative, and he gave me a key ring. We exchanged gifts. Decent guy.

~~

Without explanation, on the morning of June 24, we boarded a small, Russian-made propeller plane with about twenty-five civilians on it. We arrived in Ürümqi, the capital of Xinjiang, an old desert town now swollen from the oil business and the labor-camp business. I had been there a year earlier with Sue Lloyd-Roberts, a correspondent who often works for the BBC, watching the uneasy dance between the Uighur natives and the outsiders: the settlers, the authorities, the Han (ethnic Chinese). Xinjiang is a colony of China, almost like Tibet. The Chinese are making it over in their image.

This time I never saw the center of the city. We drove from the airport to the outskirts of town, where we stayed in the Friendship Hotel, a nice place but empty, totally empty, just for me. They never put handcuffs on me, never searched my bag. They treated me like a captured dignitary. I decided to see whether any privileges went with this, so I wrote another letter to Ching-Lee and told General Luo I expected him to mail it to California. "You did not arrest me," I told him. "I want to send it to my wife." The letter was never delivered.

Just outside my bedroom, the guards were smoking and drinking and laughing and playing cards. They tried to teach me how to play Chinese poker, but I was slowing down the game, so I told them I would read a book instead. None of these guys asked me any political questions or harassed me. They seemed to have no idea where I was going and were merely baby-sitting for me. On Monday morning, Chu said good-bye, and I never saw him again.

Next I was taken to the train station in Ürümqi, which I recognized from my trip with the BBC reporter in 1994. Then I was merely anonymous, now I was incommunicado. General Luo ushered me into a private compartment with three new guards while he and two other guards shared another compartment. Later I would stand up and look out the window but also keep my eye on the two compartments. I saw one of the guards open one suitcase that contained handcuffs and shotguns—in case their honored guest got out of hand—and another suitcase that held my money and my documents. They were all in plain clothes, and nobody on the train seemed to notice they were escorting a special guest.

Why a train? And where were they taking me? At first, I thought they were taking me to Beijing, but I could not get an answer, and maybe they did not know. I wondered whether they would toss me off a bridge out in the middle of nowhere, but if they were going to kill me, they could have done that at the border.

The train was in terrible condition: run-down, dirty from constant use. At first, I looked out the window and tried to watch northern China going past, but after a few hours I started to get bored with the mountains in the background and the repetitive dry, dusty land, just rocks and rubble and, in the lowlands, few people, few animals. I kept telling myself, "Keep your brain in neutral; make them think you're not worried."

On my three successful trips, I had penetrated the empty spaces of China, where the lost souls are hidden, but now I was an honored guest, riding the rails in my own private car. I had achieved the highest station in Chinese life. I was being treated like Chairman Mao.

Our wise and caring chairman almost never flew on his spur-of-the-moment journeys, so his staff kept entire railroad trains ready for him. In his raging paranoia, Mao felt that one special railroad train would be too easy to sabotage, so his staff had to maintain three identical trains, and he would personally choose one at the last moment. I've always wondered why, if Chairman Mao was so universally beloved, anybody would conspire to blow up his train.

Naturally, when Mao traveled, his staff would close off stations, cancel trains, disrupt the lives of thousands of people. Because the chairman never slept or made love at predictable hours, whenever he wanted a little peace and quiet, without the clattering of the wheels underneath him, the train would be shunted to a siding, an entire province thrown into chaos with no explanation.

I should have been honored, but I felt guilty about the expense of my private journey. But the government was used to such excesses.

After a while, I stopped staring out the window, and I read a few magazines and started some books and defeated all the guards at chess. I had gotten out of practice, but when I was in prison camp, I could play two games at once without a board.

The guards—all in their late thirties, all colonels, they told me—would not discuss my situation, but a few of them loosened up, and we talked about American cars. They were fascinated to learn that I owned two. One of men had been in the border war with Vietnam in 1979, and we talked about that.

Finally the topography changed. Somewhere after Jiuquan, the yellow soil yielded to the lush green fields of early spring wheat. This was a land on which people could at least survive. The train clattered along through Xian, the site of more than eight thousand life-sized ceramic statues from the time of the first Qin emperor, which were unearthed only in 1974. I thought to myself, "Maybe they will turn me into a statue and bury me standing up." Instead, we just kept rushing east, through crowded towns, where people jammed onto platforms of railroad stations, waiting.

⌒

Seventy-two hours after we started, we approached Zhengzhou, the scene of one of the ugliest days of my life. It was after I was released from camp and had traveled to Zhengzhou as a geologist. There I witnessed a mass execution of forty-five prisoners. I thought of the bodies sprawled in an open field and began to fear for my life, but I had long ago learned that such imagining saps your will. "Relax," I told myself. "Don't think about it."

We were four hours late arriving in Zhengzhou, and the police had closed down the station. Through the window, I saw two black fancy cars, an Audi 100 and a shiny Honda, and about twenty policemen on the platform. I looked at the license plates and saw that the first two numbers were 41 and 42—which signified Henan Province and Hubei Province. This meant they were transferring me from Zhengzhou to Wuhan, where I had worked just before leaving China in 1985.

Wuhan is inland, far from the international cities of Beijing and Shanghai. An American could be hidden in Wuhan for a long time. There would not be enough foreigners, enough journalists, enough diplomats to pick up on rumors. I was apparently going to be treated as a former resident of Wuhan, a native rather than a foreigner. According to law, the prisoner is usually sent back to the city where he is registered, his case handled by local police and local courts.

I was escorted out of the train and walked ten yards to a car. Then I noticed that a great many police officers had stopped all the people, blocked them from using the station. Chinese railway stations are always crowded, but the police had cleaned this one out, just as they would have done for Chairman Mao.

The crowds, held back by lines of police, watched as the motorcade—motorcycle escorts, two unmarked cars in front, black with lights flashing, two vans, three more cars in the back—squealed away from the station. And the people of Zhengzhou would probably never know who the guest was. As the two escort cars pulled ahead, I was transferred to a van, eleven officers accompanying me.

We roared onto a new highway, two lanes, under construction, almost finished. Only Beijing, Shanghai, and Guangzhou had had major highways, like U.S. interstates, but now there was a Zhengzhou–Wuhan highway, too. We slowed down to a crawl as traffic backed up because of construction. The guards had thoughtfully brought a bottled drink and biscuits for me, but the relaxed mood of the train had vanished. I tried to pick up a Chinese newspaper from the floor of the van, only to be rebuffed by a snarling local police officer.

"I just want to read the newspaper," I said, prodding him a little, but he looked at me with the surly face of authority that says, "I could stick a hot poker between your ribs right now, and nobody could stop me." Every Chinese person knows that look.

General Luo calmed him down. Luo was smooth. I suddenly realized I wanted to stay with the big guys. Now I wanted to be treated like a special case.

They forced all the other drivers off the road to make room for us, and we rolled toward the border of Hubei Province. According to Chinese regulation, every distinguished visitor who is traveling to another province must be accompanied by the senior officer of the first province right to the border of the next one.

At a town named Guangshan, on the border between Henan and Hubei, everybody got out and shook hands, the Henan police saying good-bye, very politely, while the van carrying me and Luo and the Hubei police rolled south toward Wuhan.

Early on June 29, I recognized the river and the downtown, and then I realized we were heading to the outskirts of Wuhan. The memories came flooding in: a marriage breaking down, the romance with a young college student, the hope of a new life in America. I never imagined I would be back in Wuhan, a prisoner again.

The vehicle stopped by a large compound surrounded by a high wall and guarded by white-gloved police sporting Uzi-style guns. These guys were serious. They made the plainclothes security officers present identification cards.

"I don't have an identification card," I said. "I guess that means I can't go in."

They laughed and said they would make an exception in my case.

6

HOW CHAIRMAN MAO
REFORMED ME

I never consciously made the decision to be a troublemaker, a man at war with his own country. In my youth, I thought I was part of the new generation, Chairman Mao's children, who would run their homeland no matter what the political system. Everything we did was for our father, our Chairman Mao, with his benign smile. Sweet Mao. Smart Mao. Protective Mao.

I saw him once. On October 1, 1956, our National Day, I was selected to be one of the thousands of honor guards at the celebration in Tiananmen Square. From a distance of perhaps five hundred yards, I saw him waving, not energetically, not with any emotion, a proud and distant papa greeting all his good little boys and girls.

Just to be in the presence of Mao was a great honor, because the public did not see much of Mao. Many years later we would learn that Chairman Mao had spent much of his time in his pajamas in his villa with his young female assistants, but we did not have gossip magazines and television talk shows telling us things like that. In those days, he was a god, a symbol, the father of our homeland, and we respected him. I saw him on the balcony far in the distance, waving to us, and I was so proud to be there.

My father, forced to sell his books and his furniture to keep his household going, warned me, "Stay out of politics," and I thought I would serve my country as a geologist. I would lead a normal life. I was the captain of my high school baseball team, I had fallen in love with a neighbor, a girl named Meihua, whom I planned to marry, and I was accepted by the Beijing College of Geology. While I was studying to be a scientist, however, the country was being ruled by a smug, arrogant, raving leader who could overrule trained engineers, trained teachers, trained doctors.

Why study any discipline when a man in pajamas in Beijing can strut out of an orgy and decree that people should build steel mills in their backyards? To satisfy this particular whim, to make the fires for these neighborhood steel mills, people began cutting down the trees, and the rivers flooded more extensively than ever. To produce the necessary ore, they melted down their cooking utensils. What was being manufactured at the steel mills? Cooking utensils.

Zhou Enlai, who followed orders from Mao, ordered two million prisoners from Shanghai and the provinces of Jiangsu and Zhejiang to work on the dam across the Hui River. They went out to labor without the proper clothes, equipment, medical care, or training, and a year and a half later, half of them were dead.

In 1955, I began college in Beijing only to discover I had already been judged an outsider, a member of the bourgeois class. I was a better student than most of the party members, but that was seen as incidental. We were supposed to be studying a practical science, but we spent much of our time in political meetings. I was asked to study to join the party, but I would have had to criticize my father as a capitalist, and this I could not do.

Mao's offhand remarks became our dogma, his cunning asides became excuses for us to criticize one another. At first, we were not supposed to question government policy, but in 1956 we heard that Mao was welcoming diverse opinions. Unfortunately I took Mao at his word.

In the fall of 1956, the Soviet Union sent its army to stop a popular movement in Hungary. China's government newspaper, *People's Daily*, ran two long articles entitled "Comments on Proletarian Dictatorship Experience," explaining why the Soviets had to suppress the uprising.

We were called to study groups to discuss the articles, and I spoke my mind, saying the invasion was a violation of international law. The secretary of the party branch said I was criticizing my own country and the party, but I denied it. Little did we know that Mao's henchman, Zhou Enlai, had gone scurrying to Moscow to convince Nikita Khrushchev to send tanks and troops to Budapest to crush the Hungarians.

This was the first time I had ever been singled out as a political troublemaker. Most of my classmates were more pragmatic than I, and they just repeated what the Communists wanted to hear. After the party leaders had collected enough "opinions," they stopped the meeting, and they made a report, featuring me prominently.

Two days after the meeting, the party cadres organized a march in solidarity with the Soviet invasion, and they urged me to make a self-criticism. I was a nineteen-year-old kid who wanted to study and play baseball and write letters to his girlfriend. I apologized to the Soviet Union and figured it was over.

The irony was that at the same time, we began to hear about Mao's most famous expression: "The policy of letting a hundred flowers bloom and a hundred schools of thought contend is designed to promote the flourishing of the arts and the progress of science." By March of 1957, it was part of our curriculum. I can only assume that Mao never meant what he said, that he was setting a trap for millions of people like me, who might utter some "counterrevolutionary" thought. In May of 1957, Comrade Ma, one of the party leaders in my class, began putting pressure on me to skip baseball practice and attend meetings. I told her about my oldest brother, who had been held for months at his school, who was refused permission to return home on holidays, because he had received letters from our oldest sister in Hong Kong. It didn't make sense. Whatever happened to the hundred flowers?

By now, I was a marked man. In late May, Meihua wrote to me telling me to forget our relationship. I was stunned and managed to obtain a five-day leave to see her. She would not tell me why she was so distant, and my school began sending telegrams saying that I had overstayed my leave. My father urged me to get back to Beijing as soon as possible.

Meihua met me at the railroad station and handed back a silver cru-cifix I had given her. There was no explanation from the blank-faced girl, who clearly hoped my train would leave on time, ending the unbearable silence between us. Did the Communists threaten her and her family to get her to avoid me? To this day, I do not know.

I was saved by summer recess in 1957—a two-month field trip out-side Beijing, where we all worked at our chosen field. For two months, we were geologists, not party activists. Even Comrade Ma seemed to enjoy working with rocks and dirt rather than slogans. But at the end of August, I knew I had to go back and face the party. I went back to Shanghai to say good-bye to my family. I went upstairs to see my step-mother, whose lung and heart problems had confined her to bed. Her sensitive face looked sad as she kissed me, a highly demonstrative ges-ture for a stepmother to show a twenty-year-old stepson, and I knew this was her way of saying good-bye to me, probably forever. "Don't worry about me," she said. "Take care of yourself." I took a last look at her and rushed back to Beijing.

On October 20, 1957, my statements about Hungary returned to haunt me. At the front of the cafeteria, a large poster appeared with twelve separate charges, listing my crimes: "Harry Wu is a counter-revolutionary rightist. He opposed our party's foreign policy. He opposed the Soviet Union," and so on.

The Communists charged me with disloyalty to the party, which had paid for my education and my books, which had given me so much. I said to them, "The party has no money. The party does not produce anything. The people feed the party, not the other way around." But they did not accept that. I said that the party treated nonmembers like third-class citizens. They would remember this when they pressed charges against me.

This is the tradition of China. You must love your motherland, which meant both Mao and the party. You must not question. They kept telling us this was a new order, but to me it was just a repetition of the past three thousand years, with Mao as the uncrowned emperor. Chinese leaders have always said, "I am the son of the dragon. When I die, my son will be authorized by the gods. Nobody can replace me. If you oppose me, you oppose the gods."

My family was falling apart, which was exactly Mao's intention. He saw the family as the enemy of Chinese society because it hindered loyalty to the great secular emperor. To this day, I can sing the famous ditty Mao forced us to learn in school:

> The earth is so wide, the sky is so large, the love of the party is larger than them.
> The love of the father and mother is good, but the love of Mao is better.
> Everything is good, but the best is socialism.
> Maoism is the treasure of the revolutionary. Anybody who opposes it is our enemy.

This is why I am so pessimistic about the future: The Chinese people cannot distinguish between the government and the motherland. You hear Americans saying of their country, "Love it or leave it," but those are just words, or at least they have been so far. Traditionally in China, the top crime is political crime. For a long time, if the leaders did not like what someone said or wrote or did, they would kill the person's whole family: his brother, wife, children, father, and his wife's father, mother, brothers, children. It's a little more benign now, but they still find ways to punish a person if he or she criticizes the motherland.

In the West, even the kings had to acknowledge the Christian religion, had to deal with it as a separate force. In the West, there was a little balance. In China, the emperor is the lawmaker, the scientist, the husband, the parent, human nature itself. Even our one Christian revolution, the Taiping Rebellion of the mid-nineteenth century, was done in the Chinese way. One man, Hong Xiuquan, thought he was God and urged the peasants to follow him. The Qing dynasty fought against Hong and his followers, and millions of people were killed. In the mid-twentieth century, there was another uprising against religion, this one Communist, and again the urge was to suppress, to kill.

Everywhere we went, there was always a huge poster of Chairman Mao: Mao the swimmer, Mao the poet, Mao the thinker, Mao the family man. I am convinced that if it had not been Mao, it would have been somebody else. The mentality was already there, and Mao exploited it perfectly. The Communists do not have any concept of love, except the love of Mao. Society consists of human beings, but if human beings have no value, then society has no value.

Sometimes it was easy to make a confession. In the summer of 1958, we made another field trip, this time to Shandong Province. For the first time in my life, I saw the true life of the peasant majority: no running water, no electricity, little food, little connection to the life in Beijing or Shanghai. I realized what a privileged life I had led, as a member of an upper-middle-class family with a piano and carpets and a refrigerator. These people had nothing. Now I understood a little bit about the stated goal of communism: to equalize things, to make life better for the masses. When I returned, I was able to write an honest self-criticism.

The Communists would hold competitions among counterrevolutionaries who were just begging to criticize themselves. Whoever did the best might be praised, but confessing was just a way to survive, just a game to keep everybody in line. I made confessions, but I was not forgiven. In Christianity, when you confess your sins to yourself or your pastor, you feel you are forgiven, you feel the spirit within you, but when I made my confessions in the party meetings, nobody said, "Go ahead, Mao loves you." Their stated policy was forgiveness, but they acted in ways that only made me feel guilty. I knew then that I had to leave this country.

I and three other students, branded as rightists, hatched a plan to escape. Wang got his hands on three hundred yuan as an advance from the school for a field trip, but he was forced to change his plans. Soon I discovered that he had forged my name on a withdrawal of fifty yuan. I could not accuse him for fear of getting all of us in further trouble, so I took the blame.

On April 27, 1960, a Public Security officer unexpectedly walked into my classroom and announced that I was charged with several crimes, including taking fifty yuan. I was sentenced to "reeducation through labor." I insisted on seeing the accusation, but he told me I had only a few minutes to gather some clothing. I rushed to my dormitory room and managed to destroy some papers that would have incriminated my three friends in our abortive escape, and then, with the other students watching, I was hustled into a jeep and driven away from the campus.

~

Thus began nineteen years in the *laogai*, nineteen years of so-called reform, nineteen years of menial work without pay, nineteen years without explanation, without hope. I have told much about my life in the camps in my earlier book, *Bitter Winds: A Memoir of My Years in China's Gulag*, written with Carolyn Wakeman. All you have to do is multiply my experience by a million, by fifty million, to know that it still goes on, subsidized by corporations, subsidized by the World Bank, subsidized by all the governments that encourage trade with China.

This is why I keep on fighting. This is why I insinuate myself into China, visit the camps, photograph the lost people as they trudge behind the barbed wire and the walls. This is why I was trapped and sent to the interrogation in Wuhan in the summer of 1995. The system has never stopped. When I saw prisoners in China, I said, "That was me. That is still me."

After being taken away from college, I was kept in the north, where it is cold half the year. The guards tried to frighten me right away, showing me a few dead bodies hanging from hooks in a back room, like meat on a rack. Cooperate—that was the message—or else this will happen to you.

At first I could not eat the watery soup, the corn buns that tasted like sawdust, but a rough peasant named Big Mouth Xing stole one of my corn buns and warned me, "Nobody here will take care of you. You have to take care of yourself." In fact, Big Mouth Xing taught me to fight for my life.

In the cold of winter, when I was starving, I learned to admire the rat, who stores his food neatly, beans with beans, seeds with seeds, in subterranean tunnels engineered so cleverly that water cannot reach them. We would spend our working hours trying to notice a rat scurrying into its hole, because if we did, we could dig down and find clean food.

Xing also taught me to get over my prejudices about food. He showed me how to get protein by catching rats and snakes, how to skin them and cook them and eat them. The rats and snakes sustained us when our masters would not.

We had classes in which we were expected to confess our sins. The authorities immediately spotted me as an intellectual, a city boy, and they gave me extra attention.

Once, early on, my oldest brother came to visit me, bringing a pair of shoes. I had not seen him in five years and knew he had suffered, and now he was a different person, angry, suspicious, righteous. He denounced me in front of the guards, which I understood was the new way to behave, but I did not like it. I wanted to know about our parents, but he would not discuss them, and we hurled angry words at each other.

Not for almost nineteen years would I discover the terrible truth: that my brother had just come from the funeral of my stepmother, who had committed suicide on May 19, after receiving my letter from camp. I will forever feel guilty about the death of this kind woman.

In late October of 1960, I talked my way into a steel factory near Beijing, where there would be more food, more order. There, for the first time in my life, I hit a man, clubbed a gang leader in the head with a stone to stop him from bullying me. On January 27, 1961, I was transferred to an iron mine, where I started to smoke for the first time in my life, and soon I developed lung problems.

We began to hear about people starving in the countryside because of Chairman Mao's mad projects in the Great Leap Forward. John K. Fairbank, the noted Asia scholar, has estimated that between twenty million and thirty million people died of famine between 1958 and 1960. Mao's Red Terror also produced twenty million prisoners at the time of the famine, more than twice the number today. Millions of corpses of prisoners were buried in hastily dug mass graves, around which wild dogs roamed at night. The dogs looked healthier than the survivors.

In April of 1961, I was sent by train to Qinghe Farm and reunited with Big Mouth Xing. I had often warned him not to eat unwashed grass and weeds, but he knew nothing about germs. He ignored my warnings and developed diarrhea and grew weak. He fought to obtain more food and was sent to solitary confinement, where he died cursing the world.

I knew things were bad when they first transferred me to Camp 585, a section of Qinghe reserved for the most unhealthy inmates. The unmarked burying field of 586 was adjacent, so they would not have to carry us far when we died. When prisoners at 585 grew too weak to go out to the fields to work, they would lie on the floor, a pail on one side for food, a pail on the other side for human waste. The cook would come by with a large pail of something resembling soup and would dole it out with a ladle, being careful not to spill a drop, lest the prisoners curse him for his clumsiness. They zealously counted how many soupspoons' worth he had given them. Twenty-six—okay. Twenty-five and a half—you no good son of a bitch.

My friend Chen Ming grew thinner and thinner, too weak to move, and eventually slipped into a coma. The medical staff, such as it was, pronounced him dead and hauled his body off to the side with five other bodies, for delivery to Field 586. Sometime around midnight, the staffers noticed that Chen Ming's hand was moving, and then his eyes were open, so they hauled him back next to me. When I awoke, I thought he was a ghost, but then I realized I must fight to save my friend. I shouted for Old Wang, the cook, even though it was the middle of the night. "My friend missed a meal," I said. "You must feed him now."

The cook said Chen Ming would have to wait until morning.

"This is unusual," I shouted. "He has come back from hell. Do something special for him."

The guards nodded at Old Wang, who went off to the kitchen and forty minutes later returned with a vision from heaven—two hot, fresh, authentically yellow real four-ounce corn buns, the kind our mothers had given us when we were children.

I can never forget the stunned look in Chen Ming's eyes as he smelled paradise right here on earth. With the zeal of a healthy man, he swallowed the two corn buns—and promptly went into shock from the surprise of real food and expired right in front of us.

I had no illusions about what I had done. I had killed Chen Ming, killed him with kindness perhaps, but killed him nonetheless. For the first time since I had been thrown into this frigid hell, I found myself addressing my Maker. The words were not the prayers I had learned back in Catholic school. First I prayed for Chen Ming, but then I railed at God and demanded that he show his face in this desolate corner of Qinghe Farm. "Where are you?" I shouted. "If you are universal, where are you now? Do you want me to die?"

God did not appear, but somebody was looking over me. I do not know whether this was the voice of my father or the voice of God, but somebody whispered to me, "Survive. Get through this. Someday you will tell the world."

The next morning, sick with remorse for killing Chen Ming, I fought the guards for the right to accompany him to 586. I thought I would be buried there soon, but I surprised myself. I came back from the land of the skeletons. I was not a hero; I would have to turn myself into a beast many times, fighting and bullying and lying and confessing, but I would survive.

The diplomat James Lilley, who said that I have "a martyr complex," knew nothing. His were the pompous words of a privileged Westerner. If I wanted to be a martyr, I had my chance back at Qinghe Farm. I wanted to live.

In April of 1962, I was transferred to Tuanhe Farm, south of Beijing. I would sit and listen to Lu Haoqin describe the first and only time he had sex with a girl, a subject even more tantalizing than our food fantasies. Lu went mad with longing, and he began to ask me and other male friends to have sex with him, and eventually he was used by some of the men in prison, and he died.

Another friend, named Ao Naisong, used to talk of the beautiful music he had played on his lute. Ao was the bravest man I met in the camps. He had the courage to stop a Maoist mob from tearing apart a prisoner who had resisted reeducation, and later Ao had the courage to walk off into the fields and kill himself.

For whatever reason, I made the choice to live. I kept waiting for May 24, 1964, the day my three-year period of "reform" was supposed to be over, but my release date came and went. This was not a time for leniency. Outside, China was tense, as if waiting for the Cultural Revolution, when young people would call themselves the Red Guards and take the law into their own hands, destroying the past with their bare hands.

As the Cultural Revolution developed in 1966, the police made sure we saw copies of *People's Daily* describing the changes in China, for if they hadn't, the Red Guards would have said, "Hey, don't you want these guys to know about us?"

On September 17, 1966, some Red Guards came storming through our compound, chanting slogans like "It is right to rebel!" and "Wipe out revisionism!" They asked for a malcontent and were given a guy named Xiu, and they beat him badly, right in front of us.

The Red Guards went rampaging through the storage rooms, where the prisoners' meager belongings were kept, but I had buried my last few books, my Shakespeare and Tolstoy, my Hugo and Twain, out in a field. A year later somebody discovered them and traced them to me, and the guards and servile prisoners threw me on the ground and pranced around me like savages. This was the heart of Mao's revolution—crazy people with clubs in their hands. One of them smashed his shovel on my left arm, breaking it just below the elbow, so that the bottom part hung limply. They made me kneel and watch as they set my books on fire—a bonfire of literature to serve Chairman Mao.

Other countries had rockets going into outer space, but China had street gangs burning books and torturing people. Teachers were sent into the countryside to "learn" from the peasants while Mao closed down the schools, which in the long run may have been his greatest crime of all—the murder of Chinese education.

The prison doctor put a splint on my arm, but there is a permanent scar and a bump on the bone, and the arm aches from time to time, and so does the memory of my books going up in flames.

In December of 1969, 150 of us were told we had been reformed and reeducated, but there was one catch. The country was mobilized for impending war with the Soviet Union, so we were transferred to the Wangzhuang Coal Mine in Shanxi Province.

Digging coal under the ground is a dangerous business under the best of conditions. Skilled miners and engineers supervised the construction of the mines and the removal of the coal while the rest of us were there for our expendable bodies.

One day they staged an execution in the yard of the mine. A street criminal named Yang Baoying, who had been held back for further reeducation, had subsequently overstayed a short leave given him so he could visit his family. As punishment, he was put in solitary confinement, where he had written "Down with Chairman Mao" on a cigarette pack—or so they said. They bound and gagged him, and the loudspeaker squawked that he was an enemy of the people.

I had seen enough people tortured and killed, so I stayed in the back of the pack, but my friends up front said the executioner blew off the top of Yang's head as he lay inert. My friends insisted that his brains had been scooped out and given to Captain Li Tonglin, who eagerly took them to his aged father, who would eat them in hope of restoring his own fading mental powers. They were sending the old message that the powerful have always sent to the powerless: This could be you.

There was one difference between reform camp and work camp: the presence of female prisoners, most of them convicted of penal rather than political crimes. Some were used as prostitutes by the guards and the miners, but others settled into marriages. A friend of mine named Wang invited me home one Sunday, where his wife served me real dumplings, introduced me to a woman named Shen Jiarui, and pointed out that if I married her, I could have my own household.

Shen Jiarui was a complicated woman who had gravitated toward "dangerous" people: outsiders, dissidents, foreigners, troublemakers. She was seven years older than I and had three grown sons, already in trouble with the government, and a daughter. We were married on January 22, 1970, and lived in a renovated cave.

~

News traveled slowly to the labor camps. We heard about momentous events months after they happened.

One day late in the fall of 1971, we were summoned into the yard and commanded to take out our copies of *The Quotations of Chairman Mao*. We were under strict orders to keep this book with us twenty-four hours a day, even while we were sweating in the fields or the mines, just in case we wanted an extra dose of enlightenment. Only one person was allowed to interpret or explain the deep wisdom of the chairman, and that was the defense minister, Lin Biao, who had written the preface to Mao's little red book.

That morning we were shocked when the political instructor demanded that we all tear out Lin's preface, in unison. Nobody moved. We had seen people killed for mocking the name of Mao, but now we were told that if we did not tear out Lin's page, we would be committing a crime. One loud ripping sound was heard across the courtyard, and then we held out the page in our left hand and gave it to the guards, and we went back to work. We did not even dare discuss this among ourselves because we did not want to burden our friends with the possibility that we had spoken treason against the chairman.

Finally, in January of 1972, they summoned up enough courage to tell us that Lin and members of his family had apparently commandeered an airplane and tried to flee to Russia but ran out of fuel and crashed and died in Mongolia. This had happened, we were told, on September 13, 1971—several months earlier.

In 1974, the government was going through a dance of showing that we were really not prisoners, so I was given a short leave to visit my family. First, of course, I had to present my *laogai* papers to the local party official, the snoop on the block, which reminded neighbors once again that the Wu family was in disfavor. I found my father much older, now recovering from a stroke, my brothers and sisters scattered and mute, beaten down by the system, and I mourned my stepmother, but nobody would tell me the circumstances of her death.

I also suspended the pain of rejection and went to see Meihua, who was now married with three daughters. It was seventeen years since we had seen each other, and she seemed shocked to hear I had been in the camps since 1960, but she refused to explain why she had rejected me.

Some terrible fear had come between us, the shadow of Mao, the suspicions and the threats, and she could barely look at me. We spent a tense few minutes chatting, and then I left. I was almost tempted to think that the camp was my real home now.

⌐

One day in September of 1975, I heard the terrible shriek and rumble of three coal cars breaking loose, and then I was crushed under the wreckage. I was unconscious for three hours while rescuers dug through the rubble. A police officer named Liu did not want the other prisoners to be frightened by the sight of my dead, broken body, so he sent a coffin directly into the mine. When they pulled the debris off me, however, I nodded to my friends. "Please spare my brain," I muttered to myself. I was not supported by images of God looking over my shoulder, but this prayer was answered. I suffered seven fractures in the back and leg and shoulder, and my wife cared for me at the clinic during the long weeks of healing. The facilities were just good enough that a man could recover from a broken body and go back to work. I still had value to the government.

⌐

In 1976, it could truly be said, the earth shook. On January 8, Zhou Enlai died. In July, Zhu De, the commander in chief of the Red Army in the 1930s and a member of the Politburo since 1956, died. On the night of July 27–28, there was a massive earthquake measuring 7.8 on the Richter scale, in Tangshan, just east of Beijing. We were too far away to feel it, but authorities claimed that nearly a quarter of a million people were killed.

Then, on September 9, 1976, Mao Zedong died. We heard rumors in the mine, but we did not dare ask about them for fear that our curiosity would be construed as happiness. Only later did I hear subtle whispers about the political struggles that had taken place, with Jiang Qing, Mao's widow, at the center along with three others. Somebody used the term Gang of Four, but I had no idea what he was talking about. Only now, with Mao's departure, could China take a breath of air and act with some slight semblance of reason.

My old college friend Wang wrote from Xinjiang. He admitted that he had taken the fifty yuan so many years before and hoped I could use his letter to request exoneration.

I showed the letter to Captain Li Tonglin, who said it would only complicate my case. Li told me he was under orders to get some of the political prisoners back to civilian life and would arrange a teaching job for me. Li and I had started out as wary adversaries, but soon he asked me to tutor his two daughters so they could qualify for better schooling in the cities. Now he and his wife showed me the dossier on my wife, which showed she was considered unstable and dangerous and would be a hindrance to me in civilian life. This sounded like the same old Maoist character assassination, so I thanked Captain Li and his wife for their advice but insisted my wife come with me.

On February 16, 1979, a truck took us to Pingyao, to begin life anew. I was forty-two years old. For the first time in my life, I was a free man.

7

STARTING OVER

The first thing I learned about civilian life was that in the wake of the Cultural Revolution, there were only victims; nobody was a former member of the Red Guard. Nobody ever said, "I tortured somebody. Those were the good old days." People talked only about how much they had suffered.

Living in this society, I felt scared, isolated, alone. In the camps, another prisoner would steal my corn bun if I turned my head for a second, but out here, in the world, life was more complicated. Everybody knew how to mislead someone, how to pretend he or she was innocent. Everybody knew how to get something from society. China was a country of survivors.

The Communists tried to brainwash me all over again. Mao had been gone only three years, and some people still professed to believe this stuff. Since I was on probation, the police would have periodic meetings with me, and they would ask, "Why didn't your thought-reform work very well?" They were always giving examples of counterrevolutionary rightists who had suffered, who had reformed, who had seen the light, who had turned a horrible experience into a new life. Why couldn't I be like these paragons of Communist life?

"I'm sorry," I told the police. "I accepted thought-reform, I worked hard, I went over Mao's thoughts twice, and I reviewed Marx and Stalin. Maybe I'm stubborn, but I'm working on it all the time."

In the new China, after Mao, people put a finger to their lips and said, "Ssssh, better not talk about it. Things are better. Ride it out."

Soon after I was released from the camp, I went to visit my father, who was old and frail, beaten down by a stroke, no longer the proud and distant Shanghai businessman of my childhood. Others in my family feared me because of the taint of the camps, resented me because their lives would never be free of suspicion. My father had suffered more than any of them; he had been forced to kneel at a town meeting and hear himself denounced by his own Number Two Daughter and his daughter-in-law. The flower of Chinese society, the Red Guards, had come rampaging through his home, stealing and destroying and whipping him with belts, leaving him diminished in body and spirit. I was just glad my father was still alive, glad that we could get to know each other a little now that I was an adult.

I asked whether he regretted not leaving China while there was still time. Yes, he admitted, it was a mistake. Our whole family was destroyed, and so were our friends who had stayed. He was back in touch with many of his old friends who had left, and their lives were better than his. He did not want to see me suffer the way he had. "There are very many ways to succeed in this life," he told me. "Steal, lie, cheat—whatever. But one thing that never fails is bootlicking. Any society, any time—it works. Everybody wants to listen to something good about himself. But you are my son. I know you. You do not have this skill. You will never be a bootlicker. This country is not for you. You have to go."

"How can I go?"

"I'll do it for you," he said.

My oldest sister, Han Lian, had left for Hong Kong in 1950, when I was thirteen, and had married someone from a wealthy family. We had not seen each other in thirty years. I remembered her as very pretty, as spoiled by my father, who gave her a bicycle, clothing, a piano—because she was the oldest. In 1969, she had emigrated to San Francisco, where she and her husband quickly found good jobs. My father wrote to her and said he had only one wish left in life: that she help get me to the States.

My sister wrote back, saying she would honor my father's request, and for that moment he seemed strong, still the leader of our family, but I soon realized how far he had fallen. He received a letter from an old friend, Sir John Keswick of Jardine Matheson Holdings, Limited, the huge trading company that has been thinly disguised in James Clavell's novels. Sir John, who spoke several Chinese languages, had been friendly with my father until he had to leave the country after the Communist takeover in 1949, when his firm lost a great deal of its holdings. Now he was coming back for a visit, and my father was very uncomfortable. "My home is ugly, my furniture is damaged, my belongings are gone; I am not respectable," my father told me.

I said, "This man is British; he understands. He was your friend thirty years ago. He respects you, he wants to see you." And I promised to help my father entertain Sir John when he arrived.

My older brother became nervous about the visit, but I told him that as the Number One Son, he had to respect our guest.

In September, my father found a way to avoid meeting his friend from the old days. He died quickly and peacefully, safe from any more humiliation.

My oldest brother and I argued before the funeral because I wanted to say how my father had been accused unjustly. He told me to accept the reality that we lived under Communist rule. I promised to behave myself, but when I saw the faces of my family and friends at the funeral, I remembered my father telling me I could never be a bootlicker, so I impulsively stood up and eulogized him as a man of old-fashioned character. Afterward I felt the distance from the rest of my frightened family.

As I straightened out my father's few remaining belongings, I discovered that the Red Guards, in their stupidity, had overlooked some of my father's treasures: a beautiful book bound in silk string and a lovely stone painted with thick black-ink brushwork. I wrapped these two objects and presented them the next month to Sir John Keswick, who was saddened to have missed his old friend by only a few weeks.

The last thing I could do was reunite my three parents, all of whose lives had been destroyed. The Red Guards had decreed that "ashes are for the bourgeois class," but somebody at the cemetery had discreetly notified my family about getting my stepmother's ashes, and my father had hidden them in an urn during the terrible years. I could not locate my mother's ashes because the barbarians had toppled all the head-stones, but we retrieved a statue with her name on it. I bought a piece of land in Wuxi, near Lake Tai, and buried my father in a cement box, with my mother's memorial on the right and my stepmother's remains on the left.

Soon my youngest brother joined them. He had been in unstable condition ever since he was beaten for protesting the Red Guards in 1968. My brother was one of the sad stories of our time: He had tried to separate from his counterrevolutionary family by going to a poor and remote village to receive reeducation from the party and work with the peasants, and he had even joined the Red Guards. But his efforts at hand-painting a portrait of Chairman Mao were not deemed good enough, and the party accused him of insulting "our great revolution-ary leader," and he had been punished. Recently he had gone to Bei-jing to apply for work but had been caught up in a sweep of the city before our National Day and was apparently beaten by the police. When I went to the morgue, I discovered bruises on his body. I took my brother's ashes and buried them in Wuxi, praying that my brother would find peace in the presence of his parents.

In those first months out of the camps, I still had hopes of living a nor-mal life with Shen, my wife from the coal camp. She had been steril-ized before I met her, as part of China's crackdown on population growth, so I could never have children with her. But a month after we arrived in Pingyao, one of Captain Li Tonglin's daughters came to live with us to continue her studies. Zhen-Zhen was around thirteen at the time, and I enjoyed teaching her about music, food, the English language, Captain Ahab, and Jean Valjean. I took her to the secondhand bookstores to replace the Western books that had been taken from me when my arm was broken. In the few short months she was with us, Zhen-Zhen became, in my heart, my daughter.

In the summer of 1980, my wife and I moved to Wuhan, where the government had arranged for me to lecture at the Geoscience University. After Deng took over early in 1979, he needed all the talent and experience he could find to get the country moving again, and in this interlude of hope, I and thousands like me had gone from virtual untouchables to useful public servants. His regime overturned the guilty verdicts of more than 27,800 counterrevolutionary cases and exonerated the individuals, according to a report issued on December 25, 1982, by the party committees of the Ministry of Public Security, the Supreme People's Procuratorate, and the Supreme People's Court. Often the cases involved more than one person, so the true number of exonerated victims is estimated at more than 50,000 by Human Rights Watch/Asia.

At the university, I ran into some of the party officials who had driven me to the camps twenty years earlier. They never apologized, never discussed it at all. Their attitude was "Sorry, old friend, but times were tough. See? We made it back." The bitter part of me could not forget, but there was a sentimental side of me that I now could acknowledge.

My niece, Xiao Niu, which means Little Ox, a term of endearment, the daughter of Number Three Brother, who had been teaching in exile in Xinjiang, came to live with us to receive better schooling. One day my wife slapped her and called her a liar, but I was sure Xiao Niu was not to blame. I had to send her to other relatives, and I had to face the fact that things were not good in my marriage.

Sometimes I would think about Meihua, my first girlfriend, the innocent kisses of our childhood, her fearful face when we met briefly in 1957 and 1974. I did not want to bring harm to her, and through a sheer act of will I resisted any contact.

My wife was still very much involved with all three of her sons, which I could understand, but when I talked of starting over in America, she told my supervisors that she would not endorse it. Angrily I told her that I had stayed with her in 1979 against the advice of Captain Li, but now she was taking the side of the Communists. The last straw was when her youngest son, whom I had adopted, sold three paintings that had belonged to my father. After that, I divorced her.

From the cultured world of my family, I now had almost nothing. All I had was one beautiful print by a famous artist named Zhang Shan Zi, who had visited our house when I was young and had been invited to the White House by President Roosevelt in the 1930s. Zhang worked with special ink on very delicate paper, often illustrating the old proverb about the downhill tiger, who emerges in the evening very hungry, very fierce, while the uphill tiger has eaten, is satisfied, and has retreated to the hill.

This print was of two downhill tigers, both looking for their evening meal. It was 2.5 feet by 4 feet and was designed to be separated from its silk mat. It even had Zhang's personal red seal, the individual stamp that every educated Chinese person uses to identify his documents, his books, his artwork. Because this print was classified as a national treasure, it was not allowed to be sold or taken out of the country even though it was my personal property.

I had also managed to save a painting of my mother, done after her death. The artist had incorporated a photograph of her with his own painting of a vivid red shawl on her shoulders, and then he had added calligraphy above the portrait. Some of the brutes from the Red Guards had damaged some of the calligraphy, but I managed to paste back the remainder. Because I have only vague, sad memories of my mother, I had to keep this portrait showing her young and hopeful.

Later, when the time came to leave China, I folded the two pieces of art, which meant they would always have crease lines. But I would rather have crease lines than discard the works forever to a society that did not respect its own history.

After my divorce, I started seeing a young woman, a student in a different department at the college where I taught. Even though my marriage was over, our relationship was against the rules. Lu Qing and I would ride our bicycles to the parks, trying to be anonymous, as people do in this crowded country where somebody is always watching. The way I looked at it, I was single, had spent my early manhood as a celibate, and did not expect to spend my middle years the same way. But I was well aware of the age difference, particularly when we began talking about marriage. "I am twenty-six years older than you," I would tell her. "Think how you will feel when somebody says, 'Isn't that nice; the man is walking with his daughter.' " Lu Qing said she did not care, and I knew she meant it. This was the intense love that a man should enjoy when he is in his late teens perhaps, but I had never known anything like it.

We had to assume the party knew about the romance because it had spies everywhere—on the block, on the floor of each apartment building, in every office. Lu Qing's political instructor did bring it up with her, saying, "You have to be careful. Your job is to study. You should not be under the influence of that man." When she said we planned to get married after her graduation, the party official called her parents and scolded them.

Her parents were opposed to the wedding, but Lu Qing reminded them that she had just turned twenty-one, that she was an adult who could make up her own mind. She even stole her birth certificate to remind the party that she was old enough.

The Communists called a meeting at party headquarters to decide whether two adults could get married, and I was afraid her parents would cause trouble because of my age and my status as a former prisoner and my job at the school. The father kept quiet, however, and the mother, who had been strongly against me, seemed even more annoyed with the party officials. "My daughter is an adult," the mother said, "and we respect her decision."

After her mother's surprising turnaround, Lu Qing and I were married at Christmas of 1984. We could not live together because she had now graduated and was working in Shanghai, so we commuted on weekends and holidays.

In the summer of 1985, I persuaded my school to let me do my research in Shanghai, so we spent two months together as man and wife. But by then, I was looking to get out of China.

What had pushed me over the edge was a field trip with two graduate students to Zhengzhou on September 23, 1983. We were in our dormitory that morning when my students heard a "parade" outside the door—horns, loudspeakers, shouts, the rumbling of feet, grownups and children flocking down the street as if to a game or a circus. We were told it was execution day, and half the city's population of over half a million was turning out for the big event. I had seen quite enough death in my life, but my students were young, and they pestered me— "Teacher, Teacher, let's go." So we went.

First we heard the clatter of police on motorcycles, then the rumble of forty-five flatbed trucks, each bearing one miserable human being, standing up, swathed in rope, with a sign plastered on him: THIEF, MURDERER, RAPIST. And maybe the signs were right, but how could I believe the government?

In camp, I would have known the man or the story. What did he do—write some silly thing about Mao on a wall? Was he being killed to frighten the rest of us? In camp, I knew nobody deserved to die like that, but on this noisy, booming, festive street in Zhengzhou, I began to think, "Well, maybe some of these men deserved it." But all forty-five of them?

The prisoners were neither defiant nor repentant, just miserable. They did not raise their fists and proclaim some noble cause or plead their innocence. They knew they were guilty—guilty of living in the wrong time. Or maybe there was never a good time in China. The government was staging this horror show to impress the people. As the old saying goes, "Kill the chicken to frighten the monkey."

The parade led several miles outside the city to an open cornfield, where a ring of police officers held back the crowd. Other officers emerged from several dozen black cars and dragged the prisoners from the flatbeds to the killing grounds. One official fired a flare as a signal, and every prisoner was held by two policemen, one on either side, while a third held a rifle a few inches from the prisoner's head and pulled the trigger. Forty-five shots at once. The bodies fell limp while a team of inspectors walked down the line. If a body twitched, a pistol was fired at it point-blank.

I was close enough to see it all. I was stunned at how organized it was. This government could not feed its people, but it could kill forty-five human beings in unison for the entertainment and education of many thousands.

There is an old saying in Chinese that when you see something special, you have "lucky eyes." Many of the people that day reacted as if they had seen a great goal at a soccer match or a memorable performance in the concert hall. They acted lucky. After most of the police officers had driven off in their black cars, hundreds of people surged forward for a closer look. Hundreds, thousands of people pushed me closer and closer to the sad, limp bodies on the ground. Children and weaker adults were knocked down. I managed to keep on my feet, but I was pushed directly into the midst of the bodies. To my disgust, I saw I had human blood on my shoes. I maneuvered myself out of the area and observed the crowd, milling and shoving as the police moved it back with swagger sticks or gun barrels.

One officer took a long stick and daubed it in the brain cavity of a dead man. He then brandished the bloody stick six inches away from the faces of some onlookers, as if to smear blood all over us. We slunk backward, not wanting to be touched by death. But we were all touched by death. All the time. I noticed that the spectators who had stayed back were a more sober lot, neither cheering nor laughing. Their sober looks indicated that they understood the grim tragedy of their country.

The next day the government displayed grisly photographs of the bodies. Officials described the alleged crimes but never the fine details of trials or sentences or appeals. I was a stranger to this city and did not want to be singled out for having a curious mind, but just from listening to conversations, I could tell that some of these executed prisoners had done little more than criticize the government or refuse to follow mundane orders. They had bucked the system, and the system had blown off their heads.

That day in Zhengzhou was the beginning of my life as an investigator of the way justice is carried out in my homeland. Surreptitiously

I began seeking more information about mass executions. One thing I discovered was that the government does not necessarily notify the doomed prisoner's next of kin, but the family must pay for the bullet and the cremation before his ashes are released.

In Zhengzhou, people said, these executions would happen once a month. In Shanghai around the same time, 69 were killed. In Wuhan, 101; in Beijing, 79. China has 2,000 counties, 300 middle- to large-size cities, so if you multiply 2,300 municipalities by an average of 20 executions a month, and multiply that number by 12, you can just imagine how many people are executed in China in one year. And we all understand that Deng Xiaoping and his assistants keep track. They do not like the international publicity. They actually stopped public executions in 1984 but resumed them in 1989, after Tiananmen Square. The monkeys needed frightening again.

Other countries kill, too. Wars, revolution, famine, racial hatred, border disputes—it happens. But show me another country in the world that allows mass public executions on this scale month after month in province after province. Maybe two hundred years ago, maybe one hundred years ago, but not now, in the age of television and computers. China is still a place where we kill our own.

~

I made up my mind to go to America. My new wife was young and eager to start over. My sister had written a letter saying she would sponsor a temporary visit by me, but my visa application was turned down by the U.S. consulate in Shanghai. I was angry and asked why. The officials said I had to prove I would return after my visit. I got my party leader at school to say that I was a good teacher with a good income, that the school planned to hold my job for me.

After the three-month waiting period, I decided to try in Beijing for my second application, which is all one is allowed. I thought I might change my luck in Beijing, but the clerk at the U.S. consulate did not even look up at me. Rejected. "What are you doing?" I shouted. "You didn't even look at it! What's your reason?"

"I'm sorry, I cannot give you a reason," he said, proving to me that China is not the only country with maddening bureaucrats.

"You're crazy!" I shouted, making such a racket that an American official walked over.

"What's the problem?" he asked.

I said, "I miss my sister. I haven't seen her in thirty years. My father's last wish was that I visit her."

The officer said, "I sympathize with your situation, but too many people apply to see a sister or a brother and then do not come back. We give priority to people who visit their parents or their children or a husband or wife. Your situation with your sister is a low priority."

"I just want to visit America for the first time," I said. "I will come back."

He glanced at my file and said, "You have good credentials. You should get sponsored by a university to teach. Here's what I suggest. I have a quota, and I can't let everybody go, but if you get an invitation from a school in the United States, you would qualify as a visiting scholar."

Then came the great stroke of good luck that would change my life. I had written a paper about a very advanced French design for a drill that would transmit information to a computer without scientists' having to send samples to the laboratory. My paper had been published in a Chinese journal and then reproduced in a scientific journal in Paris. Somebody at the University of California saw my article and wrote to me, inviting me to lecture and continue my research at Berkeley. Totally out of the blue, without my asking, the letter just arrived one day in the mail. The man in Berkeley added that he still had to apply for a grant, that he did not have the finances, but I wrote back, "I can cover my own expenses. Please issue the invitation as soon as possible."

According to the U.S. rules, my sister's affidavit was good for only one year, November of 1983 through November of 1984. The Berkeley invitation arrived in September, and I called my sister to ask her to extend the affidavit.

"That's enough," she wrote back. "I did it once, it didn't work. I don't want to do it." Just like that. Now that our father was gone, she was not cooperating.

I went right away to Beijing to apply again, with little more than a month left on the affidavit. I had to take my chances. At the consulate, purely by luck, I bumped into the same official who had been so polite on my last trip. He recognized me right away. "How are you doing?" he asked.

It felt great to have somebody talk to me with respect. "Okay," I said. "The University of California has invited me to work there."

"Berkeley," he said. "That's a great school. Congratulations." He reached for his pen. Did he notice that my affidavit was about to run out? I have no idea. He just signed his name to a one-year visa and told me to enjoy myself in Berkeley.

I don't remember his name. It was ten years ago. His face, his voice, his manner were the America I believed in. It was the country that had always said, "If you have something to contribute, come over." I often wonder whether he remembers that intense geologist who came to the consulate and fought for a visa. When he watched television in the summer of 1995, when he saw the crazy activist who got caught by the Communists, maybe he said, "Oh my goodness, that's the geologist." I hope he's proud of me.

8

COMING TO AMERICA

I called my sister and said I would be arriving at the San Francisco Airport and asked her to pick me up. She sounded boggled.

When I arrived on November 20, 1985, she asked, "How did you do that? How did you get out?" She knew she hadn't helped me much.

I said, "The University of California at Berkeley helped me get out. I'm going to work over there. I got a temporary visa permitting me to work."

She did not say "Good." She did not say much at all. After thirty years, we were strangers to each other. She took me to her home, which was not very large but did have a spare bedroom, which she never offered. Instead, she gave me a convertible couch in the living room. Every morning she would close it up, and every night she would pull it out. The signal was pretty clear: temporary.

Han Lian and her husband could not hide their annoyance with me. One morning her mother-in-law was at the house and I was folding away my bed when we all smelled something burning. My sister's husband came running out and yelled at me, "What are you doing? What are you doing?" He was blaming me. Then the mother-in-law said she was making toast in the kitchen, that it was her fault, but I got the message. I was a backward country boy from the mainland, not to be trusted with complicated things like toasters.

When I arrived, I had my father's tiger print, now permanently wrinkled, a few clothes, forty dollars left after selling all my books, and that was it. Han Lian did not seem to care whether I needed anything. She had always been pampered as a girl, but now she was even more self-centered.

I went over to the famous university across from San Francisco. Famous university—it is beautiful, situated on the side of a hill facing the bay. While we had the Red Guards in the '60s, Berkeley had the Free Speech Movement, the hippies, and the Black Panthers. I had gone from a claustrophobic society to one that was dizzyingly open. Everything was available. But one had to have money.

There is a modern subway underneath the bay, connecting San Francisco and Berkeley, but it cost five dollars for the round trip. I registered with the school and was given a place to work. After a few days, I asked my sister to lend me some money until I had some coming in. Her husband had a good job at a bank, and she had a good job, too, but she said she wouldn't lend me anything.

One day her mother-in-law invited me to lunch, which was nice of her, and I said, "Thank you, but could I have the money instead? I need the money to get over to Berkeley." She gave me twenty dollars, and she must have mentioned it to my sister, because the next day my sister gave me an envelope filled with coins. That got me across the bay a few more times. I knew I had to get out.

I found a room near Berkeley that I could share with five Chinese students. It would cost ninety-three dollars a month. I asked my sister whether I could borrow the first month's rent; she refused. After eight days at her house, I left.

I tried sleeping in the little office I shared at the university, but at nine o'clock in the evening the janitor would politely tell me he had to lock up for the night. After that, I slept in what had once been People's Park, the famous block that street people and radicals had tried to reclaim from the university in 1969. When it rained, I stayed in a bus station or a subway station.

One of my first jobs was in a doughnut shop, standing up, making dozens of doughnuts at a time. Back in the camps, if you fell asleep on the job, the guards would beat you, but here if you closed your eyes, the sizzling grease would spatter your arms and face. I did this for only a few months, but the pungent, burning grease left a lasting impression on me. To this day, I can never bring myself to touch a doughnut. My research position did not pay a penny, so I could not afford the ninety-three dollars for rent on that tiny apartment with the five students. From nine in the evening till six in the morning, I still needed alternative places to rest. Often I would go to the Berkeley Library, cover my head with a newspaper, and fall asleep.

My wife's visa took six months to come through, so I wrote letters to her in the meantime. I told her she needed to choose an English name, the way many Asian people do when they come to the States, and I suggested she call herself Diana.

When she arrived in June of 1986, I could tell from her face that something was wrong. Lu Qing or Diana, she was not the romantic young girl of a year before. I gave her a month or two to get accustomed to life in America, but there were always letters she had to write, phone calls she seemed to be making when I was not around. In August, she told me she was in love with somebody else, a man a few months older than she, whom she had met in Shanghai. I felt terrible, but I had long since learned to hide my pain. I didn't want to appear vulnerable to anybody.

I said, "Look, it happens — the age difference, being separated for so long. I understand." I told her I would do whatever she wanted, and she asked that we stay legally married until her green card came through, and I said, sure, whatever.

It wasn't that simple. The U.S. immigration authorities were cracking down on green-card marriages, arranged to get somebody into the country. They were expecting couples to be married in every sense of the word, living under the same roof, in the same bedroom. We kept up the façade for a while, but then she moved in with the family of Martin Hussman, a very nice older man who had helped me get settled in California. When I agreed to help Diana's new boyfriend emigrate from China, Martin lost patience, so the guy never came over as far as I know. But Diana eventually got her green card, and we were legally divorced. I think she still lives in the Bay Area.

⌒

I drifted away from my sister, too. We did not correspond for years, but when I married Ching-Lee, in 1991, I sent her an announcement, and she twice invited us to dinner. At Christmas, we sent a card. When *Bitter Winds* was published in 1994, I sent her a copy so she would know what had happened to me and our family during all those years, but I never heard from her. My feeling is that her mentality was conditioned in Hong Kong, where people feel superior to mainland people because of what Mao did to us, because of what we did to one another. Now Hong Kong is going over to China in 1997, and its citizens will get a taste of the mainland. When I was arrested in China in 1995, my sister never called Ching-Lee. I did not expect her to. To her, I only create problems.

⌒

Before that, though, I was closing in on fifty, and my dreams of a family were fading fast. I did not think I would ever get to be a professor at Berkeley, and I thought I was too old to work in the field in geology. I needed money. I worked in a liquor store for $4.50 an hour, better than the $3.25 I had earned in the doughnut shop, but I always had to keep one eye on the front door. I took a part-time job taking care of an old man, helping him shower, clean up. I didn't mind it—two hours a day, $8.00 an hour, the best job I had in America. I worked in people's gardens, painting, cleaning up, fixing doors—for $5.00 an hour. Then I got a job at a photo-processing company, eight to nine hours a day. I believed in the United States. If a person works hard, he'll get by.

In 1986, I was asked to give a talk about China at the University of California at Santa Cruz. I had already discovered that Americans knew little about China because after 1949 the government had pretended mainland China did not exist. It took twenty-three years for a president to visit the People's Republic of China, and the man who always said he hated communism played right into Mao's hands by legitimizing Mao's rule. What stunned me most in California was that

Chinese Americans knew nothing about the labor camps; they did not know the word *laogai*. When I gave my talk at Santa Cruz, I could not help crying when I talked about the dead. The teachers and students listening to me were stunned.

"We sympathize, and we want to help," some people said. "We can tell you have suffered. What can we do?" Others would say, "Maybe you are just an isolated case," and I would say, "No, I am not; there are a million more like me. Nobody in China has ever heard of me," I went on. "I'm just one of hundreds of thousands. If I had died out in the fields, nobody would remember me. I'm ashes. And now look at me. You think I'm a hero? I'm just somebody who survived. I come here as a representative of those nameless, faceless people."

That night in Santa Cruz, I realized somebody had to teach Westerners what was happening in China. I knew I should turn over a new page—get a life, as Americans say—but the *laogai* would not let me go.

In December of 1987, I met Wu Yuan Li, who had been a deputy secretary for Policy Plans and National Security Affairs until 1970, and was now a senior consultant at the Hoover Institution on War, Revolution, and Peace, on the campus of Stanford University. When he heard that I was a survivor of the *laogai*, he encouraged me to teach about it and said there might be something for me at Hoover, which I later discovered is known as a deeply conservative, right-wing institution.

I obtained an interview with Ramon Myers, the curator of Hoover's East Asian Studies Department, and he asked whether I had published any papers or had a degree in the social sciences or political science or had any scholarly recommendations.

"No," I said, "I have a degree in geology. I am currently working at Berkeley in the Civil Engineering Department."

Myers told me that the Hoover Institution worked only with people from Taiwan, not with people from the mainland, and I could see he had already written "denied" across my form. I thanked him for being honest with me and said I did not want to waste any more of his time.

"I have twenty minutes until my next appointment," he said. "Let's talk. What do you really want to do?"

"I want to study the Chinese gulag. The *laogai*."

Myers seemed curious, so I started talking about the camps, and we kept going for two hours, and then he said, "Okay, I've changed my mind." He picked up my application, on which he had already written "denied," and he went to his secretary and got a new form and welcomed me as a visiting scholar. He arranged for me to help him with his paper on Chinese issues, and he got me a grant of eighteen thousand dollars to study the *laogai*, the only grant Hoover has ever given me, but the support from this institution has been invaluable.

Knowing I had an outlet at Hoover, I made a commitment to expose the *laogai*. I quit my job at Berkeley and my outside job, and I went to work for a company called Meftech, which manufactured electronic chips. The owner was a Taiwanese guy named Chen who became a friend of mine. At first, I was in charge of the warehouse, the shipping and receiving, but then I became an assistant manager, making thirty thousand dollars a year. I bought a used car, and I was, at long last, living. The company taught me about importing and exporting, handling shipping documents, negotiating, the nuts and bolts of tax and customs laws, moving goods across borders—knowledge I would soon use in my business dealings with the Chinese prison system, which masquerades as private industry. I was no longer a scientist. In my heart, I was now an activist.

I started compiling a catalog of the biggest concentration-camp system in human history. As Deng Xiaoping and the other old men were trying to guide China into the world marketplace, the Communists were becoming more sophisticated. For the first thirty years, the labor camps were primitive, a form of punishment for alleged crimes, civil or political. But now these camps were part of the gross national product. China was changing. China was going commercial. China was into marketing. And China was doing it, in part, with people who were little better than slaves. The Communists were now using double names for the camps—calling them reform camps internally but factories or farms for the sake of the innocents abroad who did business with them.

Under Deng, the prisoners not only continued the primitive work, like reclaiming wasteland, constructing roads, opening up mines, building dams, and undertaking agricultural projects, like the growing of tea, cotton, and grains, but they also manufactured electronic, mechanical, and chemical products, which could be exported. In the end, I would find 120 different forced-labor products sold on the international market.

China kept telling the world it was changing—and it was. The whole idea was to make money now. These large camps absorbed foreign investment and technology and sent trading and technical delegations abroad. They were the Chinese equivalent of multinational corporations, but they had a huge advantage: Their labor force was partly free. The prison warden was now an entrepreneur. He had to meet his own expenses, and if he produced a profit, he made money for himself and paid bonuses to his employees. For the first time, the guards and the police were now part of the profit system.

It was to everybody's advantage to avoid international regulations against forced labor, but the Chinese authorities still had to pay lip service to the world's standards. In 1988, the Ministry of Justice published a criminal-reform handbook that stated, "The primary task of our *laogai* facilities is punishing and reforming criminals. To define their functions concretely, they fulfill the task in the following three fields: punishing criminals and putting them under surveillance, reforming criminals, and organizing criminals in labor and production, thus creating wealth for the society." What they were really talking about was slave labor. They were not ashamed.

My first book was eventually titled *Laogai: The Chinese Gulag*, and the Hoover Institution graciously allowed Westview Press to publish it in 1992. Now that I had assembled the facts, I realized there was a lifetime of work for me.

In 1989, China became more visible—in a ghastly way. In June, the pro-democracy movement surged into Beijing, into the huge open space called Tiananmen Square, where I had served in the student honor guard for Chairman Mao more than thirty years earlier. This time people were not honoring Chairman Deng or the Communist Party but were protesting the arrests, the censorship, the control, the bullying, the labor camps.

I had nothing to do with Tiananmen Square. It was not my generation. If the kids had asked me, I would have said, "Are you crazy? Make
sure you have the police and the army on your side before you start this
stuff." The kids at Tiananmen Square might have thought they were
replicating the demonstrations in East Berlin and Russia and Hungary
and Czechoslovakia at the end of the Soviet Union. Those European
people went up to the soldiers and said, "Hey, you're not going to shoot
me for this lost cause, are you?" And the soldiers knew in their hearts
that they could not kill their own people.

This was not the case in China, where leaders still know how to
intimidate and control the army and the police. I would have told the
students that Deng and the other old men would not hesitate to kill to
keep power, but I was just a shipping manager in California. Like the
rest of the world, I watched television and read the papers. Horrible —
tanks running over kids on bicycles; police shooting people in the
back; soldiers chasing people down Beijing's back alleys, stabbing them
with bayonets; security agents pulling people out of their homes, out of
their stores, shipping them out to camps. And for what?

Of course I protested. I went to San Francisco and stood outside the
Chinese consulate and held up balloons with the Chinese characters
that say LIVE FOR DEMOCRACY, DIE FOR FREEDOM. That's all I could do:
hold up balloons. I did not have the political or the financial ability to
help people, but maybe I served by raising the issue in the West.

In June of 1990, the Foreign Relations Committee of the U.S. Senate
held the first hearing ever about the Chinese gulag. Neither Senator
Alan Cranston nor Senator Jesse Helms knew the word *laogai*, but both
men knew something was going on. Many members of Congress in
both parties, with their vast knowledge of the Soviet gulag, Hitler's concentration camps, and the killing fields of Cambodia, did not know
anything about the *laogai*.

There is a Senate rule that foreign citizens are not allowed to testify
at committee hearings, but the senators circumvented that by inviting
Steven Mosher, who teaches at Claremont McKenna College in Cali-

fornia, speaks fluent Mandarin and Cantonese, and was one of the first Americans to disclose the forced abortions and other abuses in China. Mosher agreed to make a brief statement and then introduce me as his expert witness to talk about my own experiences.

The day I testified before Congress, three Chinese officials were standing in the hall, staring at me with cold, vicious eyes that said "We should have finished you off back in the camps." They knew who I was, they knew where I lived, and they knew what I did. I could not guarantee that they would not do something to me in California, but I had to keep going. People were starting to pay attention.

In the spring of 1991, Representatives Frank Wolf and Chris Smith visited Beijing Number 1 Prison and returned with proof that socks made in its factory by forced labor were very likely exported to the United States. This was against U.S. laws, against the U.S. tradition of fair play, and there were now public officials willing to make the charge.

China was fighting back, spending money on goodwill campaigns and tourism campaigns, putting out a so-called bill of human rights in order to retain the most-favored-nation status granted by each U.S. president. The Chinese government was trying to adapt Western ways to soft-pedal what it was doing. Somebody had to set the record straight. I began getting the itch to go back to China.

At the same time, I was doing some writing with a friend of mine, John Creger, a teacher who encouraged me to explore the psychological part of my life. "Let it out," he would say. "That's the only way you can survive. Get everything off your chest." Confront the beast. Face the devil. The only way I could deal with my past was by talking about it, writing about it, shoving it in other people's faces. But when John and I began dredging up my memories of my friends and my family, the distance was too great. I needed to refresh my memory. I wanted to go up to the Great Wall of China and symbolically remove a few bricks and look inside.

To prepare for a possible return to mainland China, I decided to visit Taiwan, just across the Formosa Strait. And then something unexpected happened to me. I fell in love.

9

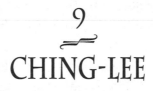

CHING-LEE

While I was planning my trip to Taiwan, my old boss from the dough-nut shop kept telling me that his wife had a friend over there who would be perfect for me. Like the people of every other civilization, we Chinese believe we are experts at matchmaking. "You are not young anymore," my friend told me. "You should have a family. You cannot just be a wild dog wandering around the graveyard all your life."

"What are you talking about?" I said. "I've been divorced twice. I'm not even thinking about getting married again. Forget it." That was my bluff, my bravado. I was half a century old, my life had been disrupted by history, and part of me wanted to risk everything to challenge China, but the other part of me still wanted a wife, still wanted a family. I could not admit this, either to myself or to my friends.

Meanwhile my friend wrote to the woman in Taiwan, insisting she meet me. My old boss's wife, Glenda, said that I was writing a book about China (she did not think it had much chance of success), that I was trained as a geologist, and that I had just left China for the first time. She neglected to mention my time in the camps.

Ching-Lee called California to get more information. "What are his shortcomings?" she asked.

"He is a good man but very stubborn," Glenda said.

In Ching-Lee's mind, I could have been anything from a former Red Guard who had torn down schools and hospitals to an intellectual who had been sent off to the countryside to learn from the peasants. The friend said I would make a perfect husband.

"Marry a person from China? It's impossible," Ching-Lee said, well aware that the forty-year gap between Taiwan and China had made our backgrounds extremely different. "But I was curious about this man from China," Ching-Lee has said. She thought, "Maybe we can be friends."

After she agreed to meet me, her friends told me that she was the assistant to the vice minister of economic affairs, that she was a working woman, unmarried, already in her forties. They said we were a lot alike—determined, strong, individualistic, stubborn.

We arranged to meet on January 4, 1990, on Fu Zhou Street in Taipei, near Ching-Lee's office. The sun had already gone down, and the corner was not well lit, but I knew my friends were right. I always trust my first instincts. As soon as I saw her soft, intelligent face, I knew this was the woman I would marry and live with for the rest of my life. She was nicely dressed, elegant but subdued, not trying to show off. When she spoke, her voice was educated and worldly but also Asian and charming—the best of both worlds. I instantly knew she was the one.

I asked her to recommend a place for dinner, and she could have named the best restaurant in Taipei and I would gladly have taken her there. Instead, she proposed a modest coffee shop in the neighborhood. We sat down and ordered steaks, and I found I could talk easily to her. I did not have to play games. I knew I had to tell her the truth about myself.

"I was a prisoner for nineteen years," I said.

She looked shocked.

I quickly explained that I had been a political prisoner caught up in the craziness of Mao's system and had spent my time working on the farms and in the factories of the *laogai*.

"What is the *laogai*?" she asked. "It sounds like a life on another planet."

I realized she did not have a clue about the labor camps. Here she was living across the straits from mainland China, growing up under threats of invasion, missiles, war, destruction, but Beijing had managed to keep this ugly secret from most Taiwanese.

Ching-Lee's people are educated and active. Her father, Chen Hsien-Cheh, from Hunan Province, had been a navigator on a bomber for the Chinese air force during the Second World War. He left for Taiwan in 1949 and has never been back. Her mother, Chen Yen You-Mei, from Henan Province, has written nearly a hundred children's stories, most of them fairy tales, and has had half of them published.

Ching-Lee was born in Chengdu, in Sichuan Province. She moved with her family to Taiwan, first to Tainan and later to Taipei, studied at National Chung Hsing University, and then worked for the government. When I met her, she still lived with her parents, in a large, comfortable apartment in Taipei, and they had traveled to California once. She admitted right away that she was hoping to do something more interesting with her life.

"My first impression of Harry was not that impressive," Ching-Lee has said, "but after we talked for a few minutes, I said to myself, 'Wow, he's really different.' He had such terrible experiences. He told me, 'I have nothing, but now I am in the United States, writing my story.' I was very impressed that he told me about the *laogai* on our first date. He was honest with me. I knew he wanted to go back to China, but I knew only a little about China," Ching-Lee told a friend. "I worked for the government, but I was not interested in politics."

Before the evening was over, I invited her to take a trip with me to a beach resort, where it is peaceful and quiet in the winter. Everything happened so quickly. Within two weeks, I was in love with Ching-Lee in a way I had never imagined I could be. I could talk to her. I could laugh with her. There was a closeness I had never felt with another human being. I could not lie to her. I had to tell her of my plans to return to China, the dangers of my being caught, perhaps shot in the back of the head, anonymous and lost. I had to tell her about the Chinese government officials at the congressional hearings, the occasional click on the other end of my telephone. The future I was proposing to her was not the normal life of working hard all day and coming home at night. I was describing a life of controversy and strong emotions and perhaps even danger. She was neither Chinese nor American, and I could see she had her doubts about getting caught up in this.

"Look, even if you marry a Taiwanese," I argued, "nobody can guarantee you won't divorce. Human beings are the same all over. We all want a good marriage. No matter where you come from, you want a good wife or a good husband. I'm a human being, the same as you."

My arguments must have swayed her, because she said she would think about marrying me. In those few short days together, I could see her growing curious, trying to understand this driven man who had materialized in her life. I went back to California, and we talked on the phone and made plans to get married in February of 1991. I think she was hoping I would get over my obsession with the camps, but I could not escape it.

Just before I went back to Taiwan to get married, Columbia University in New York held a major conference on human rights in China. People wanted to know about Tiananmen Square, what had caused it, what the backlash had been, and I was invited to give a speech.

Right after that conference, Orville Schell, one of the foremost Westerners writing about China, put me in touch with David Gelber, a producer with CBS who wanted to do a program on the camps. By now, I had a U.S. green card, which meant I could travel to China and return to the United States. Gelber wanted to know whether I would be interested in going over there and gathering photographs, videotapes, interviews, documents — anything to illustrate these camps for Western viewers.

I had to ask myself whether the Chinese would understand the difference between working for CBS and working for the government of the United States of America. These are people who think the Republican and Democratic Parties are just like the Communist Party — for insiders, the chosen elite. Would I risk my life on their grasping that I did not work for the United States government? "Forget it," I thought. "You're getting married. Relax. Lock it up, hide it, put it in cement, and drop it in the Pacific Ocean. You don't have that many years. Give it a rest."

It was five years since I had left my homeland. I wanted to see and hear things for myself. I wanted to go home.

⌒

Ching-Lee and I were married in Taipei, in court, on February 11, 1991. Her family and her best friend—just a few people—were present, and we invited some friends to dinner that evening. I loved her parents right away, and they filled a gap in my life. I had been terribly lonely much of my life, but now I had a wife and parents. Only a fool would jeopardize that.

After our honeymoon, Ching-Lee finished her work in Taipei, and I returned to California. I knew I had to tell my new wife that I was thinking of going back to China to investigate the camps.

"It's too dangerous," Ching-Lee said. "You have suffered enough. Let other people do it. You deserve a good life."

For a short time, I thought about going off secretly, but I knew I could not deceive her. She was too smart, too proud, too good to be treated that way. I did not want her hearing about me on the seven-o'clock news in Taipei: "American jailed in China." What if she turned against me? What if she thought, "This is more than I bargained for"? It was quite possible. Ching-Lee had grown up in a stable environment, but now she had a husband who wanted to take a terrible risk. I wasn't going to deal drugs or smuggle illegal weapons, but the Chinese could accuse me of being a criminal, a spy, if they caught me visiting their camps.

I went back to California—to my own apartment, television, car, bed, kitchen, privacy—and I envisioned the prisoners in their blue uniforms trudging out to the farm. What time was it? Evening in America—morning in China, people going to work. There would be a red flag planted at the edge of the work site. If the prisoners crossed that, the guard with the rifle would shoot them. I would be lying in bed in

California, and my mind would be racing to a coal mine in China. I knew I had to go, and I knew I had to tell Ching-Lee.

"I know you've made up your mind to go," Ching-Lee said on the phone. "If you don't go, you will always resent it." There was a pause. "I am going with you," she said. "I will use my annual leave from work."

"No way," I said. "You can't take chances just to help me."

"It's not just for you," Ching-Lee said. "It's for me, too. I was born in China. I have not been there since I was a baby. It has been so close but so far from me. Now I want to set foot in my homeland. I want to do something for China."

"It is too dangerous," I told her, but I could hear the strength in her voice. This was not a docile Chinese wife shuffling after her husband. After this telephone conversation, I never had a doubt that Ching-Lee was a strong, modern woman who would stand by me.

But could she run or even crawl to escape danger? I had learned to do this in the camps. Strike the bully first. Bite the man who is stealing your corn bun. Speak up to the guard. Lie. Tell the truth. Do whatever is necessary to survive.

I was just beginning to feel like a human being again. Could I expect Ching-Lee to think like a beast, to act like a beast? She did not push or shove or speak in a loud voice, and I was afraid her polite Taipei manners would give her away to the Chinese.

There was also a language problem. The Taiwanese people speak Mandarin, the official language of China, but because Taiwan has been separate for almost half a century, the two languages have evolved in different ways. Taiwan has many words that reflect the subtleties of the West, of freedom of expression. It has technical words, slang words, English words that have not yet been absorbed by mainland Mandarin. Accent is not a problem, but just one phrase can give a speaker away. In Taiwan, when people speak of fast-food noodles, they call them *soaked noodles,* but in mainland China they say *convenient noodles.* If Ching-Lee ordered noodles on the street in Shanghai or Beijing, somebody just might prick up his ears and say, "Hmmm, Taiwan."

There were other questions about Ching-Lee. Could she get used to the primitive conditions in mainland China? This woman of high-tech offices and high-rise apartments and beach resorts would have to travel in a land of rudimentary plumbing. Could I test the dignity of her life? Would she feel threatened by the situations she might face? There were many things I could not teach her, many situations for which she would not be prepared. I did not have the time, I did not have the energy, and I wasn't smart enough to anticipate.

In my mind, my bride was sweet and innocent and virtuous. Maybe every husband needs to feel that way about his new wife. I had never thought of her as "material" for my trips. I had other volunteers—people used to living on the margin, people with a need for danger. I did not want those qualities in my wife.

"It is not dangerous," Ching-Lee insisted. "We are not going for political purposes."

She was glossing over the reality. We both knew I was going to collect information on the camps. We both knew I was going to use tactics that would be considered illegal or, at the very least, unfriendly. I knew I could handle anything these people could do to me, but I did not want her to be caught and to suffer.

"You are my husband," she insisted. "I must go where you go. I can help your morale. I can work with you. I am your partner."

I had lived by my own wits most of my life. I think I had truly been alone since the day I said good-bye to my stepmother, saw the look of pain on her face, sensed that we would never see each other again. In the camps, I trusted a few male friends because we needed one another for survival, but this was different. Ching-Lee's voice on the telephone told me she would back me up wherever we went. I was not alone anymore.

10

BACK INTO THE TIGER'S MOUTH

I wrote my will and carried it to Taiwan and gave it to my in-laws. Just in case. I was going back, back to the land I had left six years earlier. I could not stay away. My intention was to visit the old places, see the old inmates, the guards, to make a documentary and write a book about my life in the *laogai*. Then nobody in the West could say he or she did not know.

But I had to admit there was something darker about my mission. I needed to go back, needed to play with fire, needed to run with the bulls, needed to cross a six-lane expressway, needed to walk the tightrope. My whole life had been about testing the system, taunting the system, surviving the system, and now that I was a free man in the West, I could not stay away.

As soon as I arrived in Taipei, I spent time with Ching-Lee, going over my plans. I had never done anything like this before, but I had talked to some people, and I had come up with three basic rules for the trip:

First rule: Never argue with me; just do what I say.

Second rule: Try to keep a distance between us out in the field. We will sometimes use walkie-talkies to communicate. Try not to walk alone in open country. Try to stay with crowds, or between trees and buildings.

Third rule: If I am arrested, beaten, or killed, don't try to rescue me or my body. Just leave the scene as quickly as possible, get to Hong Kong, Taiwan, or the United States, and inform the people whose phone numbers and addresses I have given you. (All numbers were written in code in case the address book was confiscated.)

"Safety is the most important thing," I told her. "If we have problems, you take off. I will stay behind. I know how to deal with these people. They will go after me and leave you alone. You must escape. No questions. Just do it." She listened and nodded.

We had a cover story in case anybody stopped us. Chen had closed down Meftech in 1991—I was getting by on grants and speaking fees—and there was a huge supply of leftover Meftech business cards, letterheads, envelopes, and shipping ledgers. It would have been a shame to waste them.

CBS had given me two cameras that would fit inside modest-size traveling bags. We had cut small holes in the two bags and fitted Velcro flaps over them. When we wanted to operate the camera, we opened the flap. One of us would operate the camera while the other would be the lookout. I also told Ching-Lee that Chinese people and outsiders would be meeting us at prearranged sites to pick up the film we had already shot. These people, whom I called pigeons, were working not for the money but because they believed in what I was doing.

I had a second system arranged for security, telephone lines in different cities that lay ready twenty-four hours a day, just waiting for the call. I had set up a code to let people know what I needed, but I wouldn't make the call myself. I would have another person behind me, a friend, a companion, maybe just a brave stranger, to make the call, to keep an eye on me.

"You never know," I told Ching-Lee. "The Chinese might be watching me. They could arrange for me to be killed in an accident. I could suddenly disappear, and the Chinese would say they never found me. It's happened. That's why I need people around me, watching—just in case."

How did I know this stuff? Not from any James Bond movie or from a book but from my past life in the camps. Back then we needed secret signals, double languages, just to communicate with one another. We'd trust a few people, and we'd develop key words, key signals.

~

We knew that our biggest problem would come at the border. By now, I had some slight visibility in the States, from my speeches and my testimony in Congress, so it was possible the officials would be looking to keep Wu Hongda or Harry Wu out. Ching-Lee got her visa easily in Taiwan; the borders had been relaxed, and both sides wanted the business.

We flew from Hong Kong to Tianjin, not far from Beijing, and I held out my visa. To my surprise, nobody even glanced up at me. I presented my American travel documents, obtainable by any legal alien with a green card, and I walked through the passport control, an ordinary man on a visit to his homeland. Although six years had gone by since I had left China, I felt nothing. Ching-Lee was not so blasé. When we landed, she was filled with emotion at seeing her motherland. No matter what politics divide Taiwan and the mainland and even though she had heard many of my stories about the *laogai*, her heart was Chinese.

The next morning we discovered that foreigners are discouraged from renting cars, so we had to hire a driver and van, known as a bread vehicle. I knew that some drivers worked with the police, so I chose my driver through the dubious science of physiognomy: I just liked the way his face looked. I told him we were going to visit a friend who was a security officer at Qinghe Farm, and he did not ask any questions.

When I had been sent to this camp twice in 1961 and 1967, I had arrived in a boxcar with snarling dogs (and snarling guards) watching over me. I had never had the liberty of seeing Qinghe Farm from the road, and it was not until 1988, when I bought a satellite photo of the region, that I realized how huge it is. (A Chinese-American supporter named Chang paid eighteen hundred dollars to a legal commercial service for the satellite map.)

As soon as our bread vehicle crossed Yonghe Bridge over the Yongding River, a sign warned LAOGAI CAMPS AHEAD. The driver told the police some story, and they let us through. Suddenly it all came back to me—the terror of being sent to camp, of not knowing whether

I would ever get out. We could see endless fields of reeds, grass, rice, and corn, clusters of dark-red buildings, the twenty-foot brick wall covered with electric wires, now topped by an even taller watchtower, the dark-gray iron gate, tightly closed. Above the gate a sign said BEIJING QINGHE SHRIMP FARM, the sanitized name for foreigners. But to the men trapped inside, day after day, year after year, it was really Beijing Number 1 Laogai Detachment. This was the old 585 section, where they had sent us when we were too weak for heavy labor. This was where my best friend, Chen Ming, had died from the shock of eating a real corn bun that I had obtained for him.

Riding along with Ching-Lee, I felt a manic, obsessive buzz. I could not sit still. I had to get out and shoot a video of me standing outside this hateful place, to prove to the world—to prove to myself—that I had survived. I told the driver, Mr. Tian, to stop right away because my wife needed to urinate. He protested, but I told him it was urgent, so he stopped the van and we walked along the small winding path.

In front of us was the notorious Field 586, the burying ground, where I had left Chen Ming's body to the wild dogs. Chen Ming's bones were inside that field. Big Mouth Xing had fertilized that ground. Thirty years had passed. The Berlin Wall had been knocked down, the Soviet bloc had been dismantled, the American war in Vietnam had come and gone, but men still trudged behind the dark-red Chinese prison wall.

I spotted a Public Security officer rushing over to investigate our van, but I wanted a photograph of me at 586. "Hurry up!" I whispered to Ching-Lee. She took some shots of me. Then my college-educated Taipei wife squatted, peasant-style, to relieve herself.

"What are you doing here!" shouted the officer, who wore a straw hat and an incompletely buttoned shirt.

"I am sorry; my wife is looking for a place to urinate."

"You can't come to this place," he screamed. "Leave as soon as she's finished."

Ching-Lee was not ready to leave. When she was finished, she whispered, "Why don't you go chat with him for a while? I want to videotape him."

I turned back, facing the officer, and pointed toward the pigpens in the camp. "Are these pigs about two hundred pounds?" I asked. "What do you feed them?"

He regarded me with new eyes. "Where are you from?" he asked.

"We are from Shanghai, but we are going to Chadian to visit a friend who works at the finance department in the farm's headquarters."

He seemed disarmed. "In Shanghai, they raise pigs differently," he said.

Ching-Lee was taping the most mundane conversation you can imagine, but it was important to me. It proved that Harry Wu dared to engage a security officer in conversation.

We got back into the van and noticed hundreds of prisoners digging a large ditch, their upper bodies bared. The guards were standing around with rifles, with red flags marking the boundaries: Anyone who stepped beyond the line would be shot to death.

"It's exactly the same," I whispered.

The men stared at us impassively. They seemed reduced to the level of beasts at the side of a road, with their glistening muscles, their hard stares.

"If I had met you at that time, seeing you were one of them, I don't know whether I would have married you," Ching-Lee admitted.

And it was true. There was a taint to those lost souls. I caught myself thinking, "Maybe they deserve it."

I whispered to Ching-Lee, "It's lucky you did not know me then." I turned to the driver and asked, "Who are these people? What are they doing?"

"They are prisoners," he replied. "Some were sentenced because they made trouble at Tiananmen Square. They were forced to labor here."

I pretended to be surprised. "They are prisoners?"

Ching-Lee wanted to take more film of the camp, so she got into the act. "I have never seen prisoners working. What do they eat? Are they beaten? Mr. Tian, could you drive back and let me see it one more time?"

I played the role of the patient husband. "You are curious about everything," I told her. "There's nothing to see but prisoners working!"

Being a polite man, the driver made a detour past the prisoners once again, before we went back to the Chadian train station. I gave him some lunch money and told him we were taking our rented bicycles to visit old friends and would be gone two hours.

We attached our side bags, with the cameras inside, and started pedaling the bicycles into the countryside, past fences made of barbed wire. Ching-Lee told me that I had been so full of bravado as I planned the trip, but now, every time I spotted a police officer, I immediately became alert. We pedaled from one camp to another, noting their clearly labeled functions: paper mill, electronics manufacturing, rice mill, machinery factory, chicken farm, and cow farm. We saw thousands of prisoners working in the vineyards, in the rice fields, and on the roads.

We have a saying in Chinese, "The young cattle are not afraid of the tiger." That was Ching-Lee. She did not have enough experience to be instinctively afraid of these people. We would face each other, pretending to be having a conversation or maybe an argument, and she would keep shooting. I would get nervous and say, "Okay, enough," but Ching-Lee would whisper, "It's all right; I want to keep shooting." Typical photographer. Just one more.

I knew what these places were. I carried the memories. Qinghe Farm had existed for nearly forty years, since Mao started learning from Stalin how to create his own gulag. I wanted to rush into the fields and liberate all these men, some of them peasants, some of them office workers, some of them petty criminals, all of them guilty of being male, being Chinese, being expendable.

Ching-Lee sensed my sadness and drew close to me. I thought to myself, "I do not know why I have survived, but I have. Now I am married to this beautiful, strong woman. I have a cause. I must keep going."

After we pedaled back to Chadian, I told the driver we were not going back to the hotel right away, and I asked him to drop us off at any restaurant of his choosing. We paid him and went into the restaurant, and as soon as he drove away, we rushed to the Tianjin train station. No sense staying around in case the driver was curious. We were in Beijing a few hours later.

~

My next problem was to get several reels of tape out of the country as quickly as possible. One of my contacts hid a duplicate copy somewhere in China, just for safekeeping, while another took the original from Beijing.

Was it time for me to quit? It was a nerve-racking time in the capital. June 4 was the second anniversary of the Tiananmen Square massacre, and there were still extra police units on the streets, just to intimidate people. Nevertheless, we decided to play tourist for a day. Ching-Lee stood on a rampart overlooking Tiananmen Square, and I took a photograph of her giving a sedate little wave, just like our dear departed Chairman Mao.

As we toured the country, I began to notice that most of the taxi drivers were hustling for money, and many of them did not have a high opinion of Communist society. One driver's wife, in Shanxi Province, who was active in the Communist Youth League at her company, told me, "The party members are worse than the ordinary people." I asked why she was a party member, and she said, "Personal benefits. If you don't join the party, you will not be promoted; if you cannot get a promotion, you will not have power. If you are powerless, you will not have a better life."

I compared her attitude with that of people in the 1950s, who actually believed party members devoted themselves to the public good. Revolutionary zeal had died decades ago. No wonder many Tiananmen Square leaders had been able to hide inside China for months. After a few days, I realized I would be able to travel around the country without worrying about the average citizen turning me in for looking suspicious, but China still had millions of police officers and soldiers keeping a clamp on the rest of the population.

~

We had our first serious scrape on June 13, when we pedaled out to Tuanhe Farm, on the outskirts of Beijing. This is where my heart had been broken, because my original sentence of three years for rightist activities had expired, but I was informed that my services were still needed, indefinitely. It was at Tuanhe that I had punched a weaker man in the face over a turnip, that my friend Lu Haoqin had gone mad with desire, that my friend Ao Naisong had realized he would never play his lute again.

These memories came flooding back as Ching-Lee and I hid our bicycles in a cornfield. I found a small building used as a pumping station and from a hole in the wall took photographs of a squad of men working in the cotton fields a hundred yards away. I tried to film them, but I became so emotional that my whole body started trembling. "I cannot hold the camera," I whispered. Ching-Lee took the camera. I tried telling myself, "You are a free man; you are just visiting a place where another Harry Wu once lived." But in that moment, I knew I was still in prison. They still had me, and maybe they always would have me.

The trick was not to let them catch me again. We became more daring as we biked into a vineyard about ten yards from the red-flagged warning zone. I was pretending to fix my bicycle while Ching-Lee was operating the camera, both her hands inside the bag.

"Stop!" a policeman yelled, waving his straw hat to two other policemen. "Go to the front to stop him—hurry!"

I turned to Ching-Lee. "Remember what I told you! We split up. Hurry!" I pointed down the road and said, "Turn right at the next intersection. You will see a big road. It takes fifty minutes to get to the Yongding Gate. Don't worry about me. Leave here quickly!"

I wanted them to get me, not her, so I pedaled calmly, conserving my energy, knowing it was impossible to get away because they had radio communication and patrol cars. No matter what, I could not afford to look nervous. I had to be stronger than the bullies.

"Halt!"

Two bicycles converged at the crossroads ahead of me. One man blocked me while the other swerved into me on purpose, knocked me sideways, then threw me to the ground. They stepped on my back, twisted both arms behind my back. I knew they were trained to cut off my circulation, to knock me out, to kill me if they wanted.

"Where are you running?" one screamed.

Nothing had changed at Tuanhe Farm, but I did not tell them I was a former inmate. "What are you doing to me?" I gasped. "I am a tourist from the United States. How dare you beat me!"

When they heard I was a foreigner, they relaxed their grip, pulling me up. "Are you really from the United States? What in hell are you doing here?"

I dusted the dirt from my clothes, trying to appear poised. "It is against the law for you to beat people," I said. "What kind of place is this?"

"What is this place? This is a *laogai* camp!"

"What is a *laogai* camp?" I shouted back.

"You don't know what a *laogai* camp is?" one of them snapped. "This is where we keep prisoners. Don't tell me you don't know!"

He had a point. Everybody in China knew somebody who had disappeared into the gulag.

"How could I possibly know?" I snarled. "Here you are! These are my travel documents!"

When I opened my bag, I deliberately dropped my American dollars, my Chinese foreign-exchange certificates, and my Chinese yuan. The unspoken message was "Plenty to go around, boys." They could not read English at all, but they could read the numbers on the paper currency.

"Who was that woman?"

"Which one?"

"The one who just spoke to you."

"I don't know her."

"Didn't you two come together?"

"No. I was only fixing my bike and asking her for directions. By the way, how can I get back to Beijing from here?" You've got to be a psychologist with the police. Let them think they are in charge, but try to set the agenda. Now, instead of discussing my trespassing, we were discussing directions. Maybe there was a way out of this.

"Even if you are from the United States, this is a forbidden area," one stubby officer said. "According to the regulations, you must be fined."

I knew there was no such regulation, but I was glad he thought there was. "I don't know anything about *laogai*," I said, "but laws are laws. I'm willing to pay a fine because I'm in a hurry to go back to Beijing."

They suggested we discuss the matter in their office, but I could not take any chances of encountering some higher official who didn't tolerate bribes. Besides, this was my old place, and I just might run into some crusty old guard who remembered me. "Please, do me a favor," I said. "It's getting late. Would you please take the fine and turn it over to the authorities for me?" With my heart pounding, I reached into my bag and grabbed handfuls of yuan, which I pressed into the short man's hands. His partner protested, so I grabbed another bunch of yuan and stuffed them into his hands. "I have to go," I said. "Sorry!"

I walked toward my bike and started pedaling, fearful that somebody might shoot me in the back. I kept pedaling, all the way back to Beijing.

Ching-Lee had packed everything and was ready to leave for the airport. I was proud that she had followed the rule and was ready to get out of town. She had thrown her camera into a brook because she was afraid of having it used as evidence against her. We would have to settle with CBS later, if we survived. (Fortunately, we had another camera.)

The next day we visited my old college, where the party zealots had turned on me in the late 1950s. Because Mao was being downsized in the new China, I was surprised to see his statue staring benevolently at the new generation. I stood in the courtyard and looked up at the window of my old room, Number 332, North Dormitory Number 5. I remembered the day when the Public Security officer, wearing his blood-red badge, had escorted me across this same courtyard, past my classmates, and with the agent lurking behind me, the frantic way in which I had destroyed evidence that could have been used against me.

As we walked the campus, I spotted Yu Ji Gang, one of my old coaches, now nearly eighty years old. I bowed to him very politely because I still believe in the old Chinese saying "A teacher is forever." For a moment, he seemed a little vague about who I was, but then I reminded him that I was famous in my day—captain of the men's base-ball team, coach of the women's team. I was Wu Hongda. Then he brightened and reminded me of several of my classmates and team-mates, and I knew he remembered me. He patted me on the shoulder, the way coaches will do, and I bowed to him, honoring his years. He had never done me any harm. Did he remember the day I was led from this campus in disgrace? There were so many of us—and so many others willing to turn us in.

While I was talking with Yu, two middle-aged men came over, and I recognized them as former colleagues. I was worried that they would cause trouble if they knew I was visiting from the States, but then I remembered I had not done anything against the Communists yet, so I relaxed.

"I have come back," I thought to myself. "They did not defeat me."

There was no indication that anybody was following us as we contin-ued our trip, flying the short hop from Beijing to Taiyuan and then driving four hours to the Wangzhuang Coal Mine, also known as Shanxi Provincial Number 4 Laogai Detachment.

Anyone could tell right away that this was not an ordinary mine, as in other parts of the world, what with watchtowers jutting up from the wall surrounding the mine. My bones began to ache as we approached the old place with the same three questions posted above the door:

Who are you? I am a convicted criminal.
Where are you? This is a *laogai* camp.
What are you doing here? I am here to accept reform through
    labor.

It was so familiar, twelve years gone backward in a short taxi ride. It was here that Yang's brains had been blown out so Captain Li's father could eat them. It was here that I had married Shen Jiarui. It was here that my back had been broken when three coal carts broke loose and crashed near me. And it was from here that Captain Li had arranged for my release. I had left these blackened faces, blackened clothes—and if you asked me, blackened souls—to start my new life. Now I was back, with a new wife on this gorgeous June day, just as if it were yesterday while other men with blackened faces and blackened clothing bent their bodies to push the carts. I was going back as an old boy, as they say in the English prep schools. I just wanted to look over the old place, for old times' sake. Even if we were captured here, there was nothing they could use against us. We were just sightseeing now.

We knocked at the door to the office, and I told the security agents I was a former resident of the mine, now rehabilitated and living in the States. Ching-Lee watched and listened quietly as these gruff old guards, dressed informally in short sleeves and short pants, greeted me. As we joked and gestured at the buildings and the hills, it could have been a vacation lodge in the countryside.

Like a typical tourist, Ching-Lee pulled out our second video camera and asked whether anybody minded if she shot a few frames. They treated the handsome woman from Taiwan and the old miner from the States with respect, smiling for our expensive camera. A few of them displayed red certificates, meaning that they were former prisoners who had gone over to the other side. They laughed and waved at the camera as Ching-Lee charmed them and photographed their smiles and their waves. If she also caught the watchtowers and the walls and the guards—well, that was just an accident.

To my amazement, I discovered a familiar face—Liu, the officer who had rushed a coffin right into the mine back in 1975, when the coal cars crushed my body. "Do you remember me?" I asked.

"Of course," he said. "You are the only miner who ever refused his coffin."

We both laughed uproariously. It was nice to be a survivor. Liu was prospering; he was now the chief of the entire Wangzhuang Coal Mine.

"Didn't you go to the United States? Why did you came back?" Liu asked, welcoming us to his home.

I tried to be cool, but my hands were shaking as I thought to myself, "How can I be the guest of this man?"

"Have you had your meal?" Liu asked.

"Yes, Vice Chief Yang had lunch with us. We also went to one of the pits. I wanted to see my old home. No matter what, I can hardly forget everything that was here!"

"What do you do in the United States?" asked Chief Liu as he served me a cup of hot tea. "How much money do you make?"

In China, people will immediately ask someone his job, his age, his salary, and the number of children he has. It is considered a friendly gesture, not nosy.

"I do research work in an American university," I said. "I make forty to fifty thousand dollars a year."

Chief Liu translated that figure into yuan. As a good Communist, he was not supposed to care about money, but he seemed impressed. "Wow," he said. "Are you able to spend all this money?"

"Sure," I replied. "No matter whether you are a proletarian or a capitalist bourgeois, everybody who works hard does all right in the States. Money, family, good car, entertainment, whatever—it is easy in the States. You can do it."

I thought about the way the Communists must turn everything into a political struggle, must put the people down, trap them, kill them. I tried to hold back my anger as I told Liu, "Twelve years ago when I worked here as a laborer, I would have been regarded as garbage to be cut into pieces. But now I am respected in another society. Maybe in your *laogai* camp, there are more people like me, people who could live their lives with dignity."

He did not flinch when I used the term *laogai*. We were old acquaintances, and he saw me now as a man of value because I was American. I had recognized three or four other officers who had been there when I was. I could still remember the blows and the hunger and, most of all, the insults, the lack of respect. As I walked toward the waiting taxi, Liu asked me whether I could drive a car. Not only that, I said, but I own two cars. He seemed wistful that at the age of sixty, he was too old to ever drive a car.

He invited me to stay overnight at his house, but I refused, with gratitude. "Tonight I'm flying from Taiyuan to Beijing, and tomorrow I will fly directly to San Francisco." That wasn't true, but I didn't want him to know too much.

The next day, June 17, we visited another mine, Guozhuang, also called Shanxi Provincial Number 13 Laogai Detachment, where some of my old camp mates had been moved. The country was booming, the cities smelled of coal fires, a dreary yellow film covering everything, and China's need for energy would keep these old miners locked in the camps forever, with no hope of civilian life.

My friends Chen, Hang, and Sun had been fifteen or sixteen when they were arrested. Now they were old enough to be grandfathers, and still they were virtual slaves. Our nine years together at Wangzhuang enabled us to express our friendships in a short sentence, even a gesture or a facial expression. They understood that I lived in America now and probably could afford to give presents to my friends. Chen did not ask what I was doing at the coal mine. There is an old saying, "He who has come comes with ill intent, certainly not on virtue bent." The less he knew, the better.

"I just got here," I said. "I have a camera in my backpack and I want to take some pictures from high on the mountain. Take me to the place you think is the most stimulating."

He took me to the top of a hill, from which we could see rugged walls wriggling along the mountain ridges. China has a great history of walls. Emperor Qin Shihuang built the Great Wall to block the Mongols from invading, to secure his own rule. Emperor Mao built these walls to isolate seven thousand miners from the rest of China.

My friends had enough respect for me to pose as guards, to escort me around the mines. Ching-Lee videotaped them telling their stories about their experiences. I asked Sun whether he still liked gambling, and he said he had run up a debt. I said, "I will pay off your debt under one condition: You must swear you will never gamble again." (I gave him three hundred dollars in front of his wife, and naturally he promised to reform, but two months after I returned to the States, he wrote, asking me for two thousand dollars because he had run up another debt. This time I refused to respond.)

After we shot the last scene at the mines, I realized that a lifetime of "thought-reform" had diminished my friends from the coal camp.

Their limited literacy had been used for reading ghost stories; their limited wisdom had been used for gambling; their leftover strength had been used for fighting. I believe they all once had dreams, but now there was no future, no happiness, no hope. The system had snuffed them out.

I could not afford this sadness, because I needed my wits. Trouble was in front of me in the person of Li Fang, a sixty-year-old inmate. Theoretically he still labored in the mine, but his main job was running errands for the police. My three "guards" were supposed to deal with any problem, but they could not afford to be spotted in my company, so they turned away.

"Don't you recognize me?" asked Li.

I stifled my inner panic and said, "Oh! My old friend, Li Fang!"

I quickly handed him a pack of Phoenix cigarettes, taking out a match and passing it to him. "It's nice to see you," I said. "Is everything going well? I don't smoke. You keep this pack."

While he was smoking, he said, "I heard you went to the United States."

"Who said so?"

"I just heard it." This guy acted like a police agent, volunteering a small fact, hoping for a bigger fact in return.

"How could that be possible?" I replied. "How can a person like me go abroad? This is my wife. We both work at a university in Wuhan. We were just about to go downtown and eat something. These cigarettes are on me, my old friend." I knew he was not the kind of man who socialized out of friendship alone. Maybe he was chatting for the free cigarettes, or maybe to get information on us. Or both.

"We went to Beijing on a business trip and came here to see some old friends, like Chief Liu at Wangzhuang," I said, letting Li know that I was all right with Chief Liu. Besides, we were dressed in ordinary mainland-style clothes, smoking cigarettes made in China. By the time he finished smoking, Li was filled with information, some of it true, some of it not. By the time he got back to the mine, it would be too late for him to report to the Public Security officers. And early the next morning we would be moving on.

~

Shanghai was booming. My hometown had changed drastically in the six years since I had been there: The dense old neighborhoods were being torn down in favor of skyscrapers; construction cranes were everywhere. Humble people who had hunkered down during the invasion of the Japanese and the rampaging of the Red Guards were now being evicted from their homes to make room for high-rises for the new technological elite.

The *laogai* was booming, too, smack in the middle of Shanghai. On June 18, we visited the Shanghai Laodong Steel-Pipe Factory (*laodong* means "labor"), with me posing as an executive for an American company. I wanted to get one signed contract and documents and photographs from one manufacturing facility that was also a labor camp. The steel-pipe company was a perfect candidate. We already had a brochure listing Wong Shing Ping as the warden of the camp and another document listing the same guy—same name, same photograph—as an engineer and president of the factory. The addresses were the same, the telephone numbers were different, but the telegraph numbers—89896—were the same. My job was to get more proof. I walked around the Shanghai Laodong Factory just to make sure it conformed with the maps and addresses. Sure enough, one gate led to the "factory" and another gate led to the prison, but both gates opened onto the same complex.

We went inside, and I introduced myself and my secretary, Chen Ching-Lee, and we presented our business card—Meftech was going strong. The managers, wearing police uniforms, were quite hospitable, the way you would expect top management to be in the States. After we talked business for a while, I asked to see the manufacturing area, and the security man agreed. I winked at Ching-Lee, who excused herself to visit the bathroom, where she would start the camera that was hidden in her handbag. When she came out, he led us into the factory area, where I saw hundreds of prisoners, heads shaved, wearing identical uniforms, all hunched over their machines. Somehow the atmosphere was even worse than that on the farms.

These prisoners would not even look at me, because they had been stripped of their identity.

I was supposed to be the tough one, the cool one, but I began quivering, not from fear, but from the sadness of seeing these lost souls laboring over heavy machinery. I knew that any one of them could have been me. Ching-Lee was aware of my discomfort and leaned over and squeezed my arm. The security man asked whether I was all right.

"I'm sorry," I said. "I was just thinking about the standards of these prisoners' skills."

I slipped in the word *prisoners* and was never corrected. It was just taken for granted. The guided tour continued, but I had other things on my mind. "It's very noisy out here," I said. "Could we go someplace quiet?"

The man invited us into his office, and I asked him whether he could guarantee the quality of his company's products.

"No problem," he said. "You will understand after I give you this example: A West German manufacturer bought our steel pipes and labeled them as being made in West Germany. Our products are good enough for the West Germans. How about that!"

When the official left the room to speak to somebody else, I spotted a document on the table, with red lettering, names, and phone numbers on it. Ching-Lee looked around and nodded—coast clear—so I took it. I wasn't thinking, "Is this worth fifteen years in prison?" because I could not afford to have thoughts like that, but I knew I was stealing. The way I saw it, I was exposing the system.

When we got outside, we examined the document. It was better than I could have expected. It had the seal of the factory on it, with a map and addresses of all the local labor camps. The document was the record of a meeting at which *laogai* and party officials discussed how to quell possible riots or escape attempts: "On June 12, 1991, Number 7 Reform-Through-Labor Detachment and Xinjing Township, together with the armed police unit and the procuratorial unit stationed in the detachment, convened a joint security meeting in the auditorium. . . . The purposes of the meeting were to . . . carry out defense and security work along the mass line, to strengthen joint security, to prevent incidents within the prison, and to ensure law and order in the prison."

And so on. I was sure the Western business partners would be shocked to learn that this steel-pipe factory was also a prison.

The next day I stole another document, at the Huadong Electric Welder Factory. A man left us alone, and I grabbed it. Good luck again. This document, issued by the Political Department of the Shanghai Labor Bureau of Laogai, suggested that the prison system was controlled by the Communist Party: "There should be a harmonious relationship between party and government organs, which support and complement each other. Tasks in reformation and production should be completed fairly well."

(When I got home, I presented these two documents to a House subcommittee hearing. At my trial in 1995, the Chinese would use them to suggest that I was a spy, but I was not working for the FBI or the CIA or the intelligence services of any nation. I preferred to think of myself as an investigator working for the truth.)

~

Also in Shanghai, I visited the Laodong Machinery Plant, where hand tools were made, bound for the United States. The managers had to explain why they could not let me near the assembly line: "Actually, we need to speak quite openly with you," said Lu Weimen. "In the United States, Congress recently made quite a fuss about the special nature of our kind of enterprises." Despite his caution, he told me exactly how the system works: "We always go through the import-export-company system," meaning they set up companies to handle the shipment of the goods. That way nobody quite knows where the goods come from. These guys were getting wise to the ways of the world.

~

In Shanghai, Ching-Lee asked whether she could visit my childhood home, but I reminded her we had agreed not to visit my family.

"I don't understand," she said. "Your own blood little sister, the place where you grew up—why can't you go see them?"

"Ching-Lee, I want to, but I can't. I don't want to cause them trouble. Eventually the government is going to read and see what we've done here, and they will associate me with my relatives. If my relatives have seen me, they will have endless trouble. It's better if they never see me at all. I know these people."

Ching-Lee changed tack, saying, "All right, tomorrow I will hire a taxi to Wuxi. I want to pay respect to my in-laws' graves. No matter what, I am their daughter-in-law."

I looked to the heavens and sighed, "Ching-Lee, I understand your heart. You should go. We should all go to pay respects. I, too, am thinking deeply about my family. But—we cannot go."

It was so frustrating to be in the heart of my native city and not to be able to visit familiar faces and sights. It made us realize the huge gap between our lives in America and life in China. On our last night in Shanghai, we stood on the top floor of our hotel, the Shanghai Portman Shangri-La, looking at the bustling city below.

"Let's go! Let's not come back anymore. Come on, hold my hands!" Ching-Lee said softly to me.

We had been on the road a long time, and now we had to go through the hardest trial of all: getting out. At ten o'clock that evening, I was supposed to meet an American who had promised to carry our last film and documents out so that Ching-Lee and I could pass through customs the next day. I did not know his real name, and when I got to his hotel room, one dim lamp was lit in the corner, so I could not see his face.

"You are very punctual. May I ask what I can do for you?" he said.

"There are a few videotapes, rolls of film, and documents here," I said.

He was silent for a moment, and then he said, "I can't take the videotapes and the film, but the documents are okay. I need to make a contact. I'll call you at eleven. Is that okay?"

I was surprised and worried because the other drop-offs had been perfect. When the man did not call at eleven, Ching-Lee said, "Call him back."

"He didn't call me," I said. "It means he isn't willing to do this job. What's the point in calling him?" Then I realized the man might have compromised us. "Let's pack," I whispered. "We'll leave at once."

We rushed to visit an old friend in Hangzhou, south of Shanghai. Li (not his real name) was stunned to see me, but I knew our friendship from the *laogai* would ensure that we would protect each other at all times. He was also wise enough not to ask questions.

"I need you to go to the airport," I told my friend. "This is my wife's luggage, and this is her ticket from Hangzhou to Hong Kong. Please check the luggage after the customs checkpoint. There is some money in this envelope. Return the ticket to her two hours before the plane takes off."

"I'm not familiar with the road to the airport," he mumbled. "Maybe we should change plans. This is all so sudden."

"No time to negotiate," I said. "How you get there—that's up to you. I will see you two hours before takeoff." One can talk that way only to a trusted old friend. I knew Li would do it for me.

We had duplicate copies of the videotapes hidden somewhere in China, just in case anything happened to us, but we needed copies of the eight last rolls of film and the documents from the plants. We had to take a chance. We found a tiny express film-processing stand in Hangzhou, and operating on the old expression "money talks," I told the vendor we were in a rush, did not need prints, but did need the negatives developed on the spot. The lady stopped her work and developed the eight rolls while we sat and watched her. For double the price, she had no problem keeping her eyes off the negatives.

My friend came through. He got Ching-Lee's luggage to the airport in plenty of time, and we put the tape in the luggage, none of us showing any sign of recognition.

As for the documents from the plant? Ching-Lee folded them and hid them in her shoes and underwear.

I stayed behind and watched Ching-Lee pass through customs. If they were after me, they wouldn't stop Ching-Lee, because I was still on line. Once she was safe, it was my turn. I walked up to the counter, presented my ticket and my American travel document—and nothing happened. Ching-Lee and I flew on to Hong Kong, just ordinary tourists.

I was eager to see the tapes, eager to see the documentary CBS would make of my trip. I had relived my life in the *laogai*. Maybe I had gotten it out of my system.

11

SECOND TRIP

There was just one little problem with the trip: CBS liked what it saw so much it wanted more. The *60 Minutes* people decided to make a trip of their own. They proposed we try again, this time with a network crew, after getting permission to enter China to work on some other story. CBS was offering to finance another trip to China, to investigate corners of this huge country that I had never seen. I did not want all my efforts to expose China's cruelty negated by my own lack of expertise with a camera, which had marred some of the tapes. I never claimed to be an electronics wizard, but this time I practiced with the camera and learned to hold it more steadily and would go a few places on my own first, before CBS arrived. This time, I agreed, we would do it better.

CBS would send its A team. The correspondent would be Ed Bradley, the famous journalist on *60 Minutes*. I knew that Ed Bradley, as an African American, would have a special passion about slave labor. Instead of merely doing a documentary about me, CBS now planned to do some investigating of its own.

My itinerary would be different this time. I was familiar with the east coast, the cities, but the center of the *laogai* system is out west—the Siberia of China. The Russians had given us the example of their gulags with forced labor, and now China's rulers were imitating them—with a vengeance. A former intelligence analyst in Washington who now works for a U.S. senator told me, "When I was working for the CIA, we saw a lot of photos from satellites and U-2 spy planes. We could see trains loaded with people going out to Qinghai and Xinjiang, but they would come back empty."

For more than forty years, the Chinese government had been sending its prisoners out where there was space to lose a million here, a million there. One of those millions was particularly important to me: Wei Jingsheng, the eloquent symbol of China's democratic resistance, had spent four and a half years in Qinghai before the government moved him closer to Beijing. To this day, I have not met Wei Jingsheng, but I admire him greatly. The irony is that Wei comes from the very class the government is supposed to represent: the workers. Wei's father was a middle-level Communist cadre, and Wei was an electrician at the Beijing Zoo, and although he put out a magazine in his spare time, Chinese intellectuals did not respect him.

Nevertheless, Wei had become a hero to his generation. When Deng Xiaoping said, "Our goal is four modernizations," Wei had the courage to place an essay on a wall in Beijing saying he agreed with Deng, but he added, "We need a fifth modernization: democracy." This was seen by everybody as a direct, personal attack on Deng and his policies, and it caused Wei to be sent to Qinghai. I wanted to stand outside the camp where he had been to show what China does to its best and its brightest.

A man could disappear in Qinghai Province—particularly a Chinese citizen with a camera in his hand in a place he was not supposed to visit. Orville Schell warned me I was crazy to jeopardize my life in this way. I gave him a box of my documents and told him to publish them if I did not return. "I am not gambling. I know the risks," I said. "If I were going out like a blind person riding a donkey, I would pay the price. They know me well, but I know them well, too. As Sun-tzu said in *The Art of War*, 'Know the enemy and know yourself, and you can fight a hundred battles with no danger of defeat.' "

I started out alone, intending to link up later in Shanghai with the team from CBS. When the clerk in the Chinese travel agency in Hong Kong politely stamped my visa after a wait of only twenty minutes, that only raised my suspicions. What if they allowed me in only to arrest me as a Chinese citizen? I somehow felt better when I had trouble entering China on a small boat from Hong Kong to Jianshazui Port, near Guangzhou. A young female customs officer called in two other officers to discuss why a Chinese citizen would be using an American travel document. "Whom are you going to visit? Don't you have relatives?"

"To tell you the truth, I still have some relatives, but we don't see each other anymore. Because in 1957, after I was persecuted as a rightist, I went to a camp, and my relatives and friends all left me. This time I want to go to Shanxi to visit a friend."

All Chinese hate to be reminded of the bad old days, so they changed the subject and asked whom I was visiting. I dropped the name of Li Tonglin, who was now chief of the Yangquan Security Police Bureau of Shanxi Province and had been my disciplinary officer at the Wangzhuang Coal Mine. Although our friendship had begun as a game of cat and mouse, eventually his daughter had come to live with me and my first wife.

The officer returned my travel documents and let me proceed. I had no intention of visiting Li Tonglin, of course, but his was not a bad name to drop. Because the footage shot on my first trip was not usable, I had to return to the second coal camp to show that prisoners were still being used as miners.

Although still under police surveillance, my three old friends lived outside the barracks, so I slipped into their small house undetected.

Upon discovering me, Sun blurted, "You came back!" without asking any more questions.

I knew the day shift ended at two o'clock, but there was always activity an hour before and after the shifts. I wanted to film the prisoners in line, dirty, tired, back from the mine. "I want to go up the hill," I said, knowing I could look over the wall into the camp.

My three friends agreed to help. If asked what we were doing, we would claim to be studying nature. To avoid the scrutiny of the guards in the watchtower, my friends and I lay down behind a large rock, my camera in my bag, a zoom lens attached for long distance. Two o'clock came and went with no activity. "Aren't they going to work?" I asked Hang.

"They're working," he said.

"But I didn't see them marching into the mine."

"The prisoners never come out of the barracks here," he explained. "There's a special tunnel. They go straight from the barracks to the face of the mine."

These guys never saw the light of day—not even an hour of hanging around the yard. They lived like moles. What a miserable existence. I had vowed I would never go underground again. I could still hear those coal carts thundering toward me, out of control, and my body still ached from the broken back. But I knew I had to visit my brothers in this subterranean hell. "I want to go into the mine," I announced.

"You're crazy."

I'd heard that before, but I insisted until they relented.

That night around nine o'clock, Chen was waiting with a prisoner's uniform, boots, shoes, helmet, filthy tool bag, and miner's lamp. I strapped on all the old gear and stuck my camera into my tool bag. I looked too clean for this line of work, so I grabbed some good, honest coal and rubbed it all over my face and hands.

My two other friends commandeered an empty tram, and I hunkered down, *whooooosh*, riding back in time. The opening tunnel was eight feet high, but when we got farther into it, men were crawling on their hands and knees, the only way to attack a three-foot seam. As soon as my eyes adjusted to the darkness, it all came back to me. This was not like the free world, where foremen and miners risked their lives to move coal. This was a jail, long, dark, and dangerous.

The men in the mine were divided into four categories:

First, the police, armed with automatic weapons, to prevent any escape or riot.

Second, the Public Security cadres, unarmed, in uniform, giving orders to the prisoners. Because they knew all the workers, they were the most dangerous to me.

Third, prisoners entrusted to supervise other prisoners, to prevent them from escaping.

Fourth, hundreds of workers, like Sun, Chen, and Hang, forced to remain as electricians, winch operators, gas inspectors.

I held my helmet down over my face to avoid all those watchful monitors. Sun walked in front of me, holding a miner's lamp. If anything unusual were to happen, he would signal by waving the lamp. Hang stayed with me, and Chen stayed outside to watch for trouble, but nobody noticed me. I fit right in. The low roof and narrow corridors made me feel compressed, squeezed, trapped, but I must admit I also felt oddly secure. My life as a prisoner had returned. I remembered Dickens's *A Tale of Two Cities,* in which Dr. Manette could never forget the shoe-sewing technique he had learned in prison. He would always be a prisoner, and so, it seemed, would I.

In this dark three-foot-high tunnel, I had a hideous fantasy: What if I were caught up in a line of prisoners and marched into the barracks?

"But I don't belong here!"

"Sure. Right. Tell it to Deng."

I witnessed another familiar sound and sight: two Public Security officers beating a prisoner with a wooden construction beam. His scream of pain was drowned out by the rumble of the mine cars. In the dark pits, the dust billowed from the face of the mine, where men cut the coal. The floor of the mine was wet, with an evil odor. The prisoners bent forward, knowing they had to work for as long as twelve hours, until they had achieved their daily quota.

I looked for a chance to shoot some videotape, but the lights were never bright enough for me even to dare. After forty-five minutes, I had seen enough. I nodded to my friends—"Let's get out of here."

My pals had the run of the place, including the bathhouse, where the greasy, foul water almost made me pass out. Soon I would be back in California, with my nice shower, the fresh, hot water, the soap, the thick towel, but these guys were condemned to live like this for the rest of their lives. My tears welled up, as if to wash off those scenes. Here, in this one camp, at least six thousand people lived like this, minute by minute, day by day, year by year. This is what party leaders called reform through labor. Where was the reform?

From Shanxi, I journeyed to Qinghai Province. It is a hard place, a region of mountains and desert, harsh winters and brutal summers.

Not many people would choose to live there, but that did not matter to the government. Qinghai is a perfect place for prisoners. In the 1950s, many Catholic priests I had known in Shanghai were sent to Qinghai for the crime of practicing their faith.

I went to Xining, the provincial capital, to Nanshan Street—four miles long, one factory after another: Qinghai Leather Factory, the Plateau Switch Factory, Qinghai Water and Electricity Equipment Factory, Qinghai Construction-Materials Factory, as well as a plastic-foam factory. I knew that some of these factories were operated jointly by Qinghai camps and Hong Kong entrepreneurs. Most of these buildings looked normal, except for the watchtowers. An ex-prisoner who lived there told me that one-third of the 300,000 people in Xining were former prisoners and their families. I was going to do business at one of the factories. There were so many outsiders in Xining that instead of dressing down, trying to look Chinese, I wore a Western-style suit, carried an imported briefcase, and arrived by taxi. That would open the gate for me.

I had chosen to visit the Qinghai Hide and Garment Works, otherwise known as the Qinghai Provincial Number 2 Laogai Detachment, although officials did not go out of their way to tell anyone that. I flashed my Meftech card, and the factory's representatives launched into their sales pitch, proudly telling me of their Hong Kong sales agents and their exports to Japan and Australia. Under the impression I was American, they made me an offer of two hundred thousand square feet of lambskin for $1.49 per square foot, payable in U.S. dollars. I signed the contract, knowing I'd never go through with this deal—or would I?

I did some quick calculations. Lambskin was selling for $6.49 in some places in the world. If I wanted to drop my principles and become a businessman, I could make a million dollars. I considered it—for a second. After I let it be known I was interested, I asked, "How are the prisoners' skills? How do you guarantee your product quality?"

Wan Xiaohua, the manager of the hide division, told me, "You will understand after you see our products." I noticed the prisoners in their blue uniforms, heads shaved, working over sheepskin. He took me to the chief of the detachment, a Mr. Gao. Inside the display room, hanging on the walls, were samples from foreign countries, along with medals and award banners from the government, plus a framed exporting license.

"May I take some pictures?" I asked, bumbling around like a profit-driven Western businessman in an exotic land, without the slightest awareness of the rights of the workers.

"Sure you may. Except this one," Mr. Gao said warmly, gesturing toward one banner I had not noticed on the back wall. ADVANCED COLLECTIVE FOR SUPPRESSING REBELLION AND CEASING CHAOS, proclaimed the banner, from the Ministry of Justice, dated October of 1989. Qinghai Province Number 2 Laogai Detachment had been one of thirty-one camps honored after the Tiananmen Square repression.

"Certainly, I am not interested in that," I replied while snapping pictures of other samples and banners. When Mr. Gao was not looking, I swiveled the camera quickly and—*click*—the outside world would see a manager strutting and preening in front of banners that proclaimed his dual function: suppressing prisoners and making money.

I then was permitted to wander around the back shop. I noticed a prisoner who seemed to be hiding behind a vat of chemicals used to cure the lambskins. Ultimately he emerged and, to my astonishment, began to strip off his uniform. When he was stark naked, he climbed into the vat and began to stir the chemicals with his body. The chemicals were intended to cure the lambskins, and I shuddered to think what they were doing to his skin. I managed to snap a few photographs.

Gao noticed my interest in the prisoners. "Let me explain," he offered. "In the United States, they have their own laws, and they are out to impose them on China." Gao and Wan gave me the name of the Hong Kong company that exports their products. As for me, I couldn't wait to get out of the place. (Months later, after 60 *Minutes* aired my photographs from the Qinghai Hide and Garment Works, there was a rumor that Gao and Wan were punished for letting me in. But in 1995, security police in Wuhan confided in me, saying that both men had been held blameless for following government policy. I know what punishment would have suited them—a day in the vat.)

The next leg of my trip was Wei Jingsheng's old camp, located in the Qaidam Basin, a few hundred miles to the west. An old friend of mine,

Liu Jingqin, was willing to take the chance of accompanying me. Liu had been arrested in 1956 for trying to join his parents, who had emigrated overseas, and was sentenced to eight years, but then, like most of us, he had been forced to stay on after serving his full sentence. In 1971, he had again tried to contact his parents but was sentenced to three more years before he was finally released. Now he is humpbacked from hard work, and even if he tried to stop smoking, he would still be racked by a cough. Two of his daughters had left for New York to seek a better life, and Liu brought along his third daughter, who could not have been more than ten. I was glad to have the girl along; the police just might be a little more relaxed if they saw a child.

Liu had traded some money and cigarettes to borrow a uniform from a Public Security officer—olive slacks with a red stripe, beige shirt with gold buttons. It even came with real badges, which I removed; I did not want anybody to think I was impersonating a police officer. I would fit right in even without the badges because many officers dress informally, and even family members of officers wear uniforms because they are cheap and available—so there is an entire class of people impersonating officers, so to speak.

We hired a driver, telling him we had to travel nearly a week into the desert, well over a thousand miles. I skipped over the fact that we would be visiting six or eight camps. I told him I was a reporter for Public Security, and he was willing to go to the places I named because of my borrowed uniform.

We reached the open countryside, and I thought about my college days, more than thirty years ago, when I dreamed of becoming a geologist, of exploring the remote mountains and wilderness of my motherland. I remembered a song from the old days:

> The white clouds winding around the Qilian Mountains,
> Fresh flowers blooming on Qinghai grassland,
> On the grassland, there are innumerable cows and sheep,
> In the remote mountains, there are countless precious resources.

The sky in Qinghai was bright blue, and there was snow in the mountains even though it was early August. On the boundless prairie, there were a few white Tibetan-style tents of herdsmen and farmers, with cows and sheep scattered on the hillsides. The land was as beautiful as the poems and the paintings had promised, but it is also a land of terror. On April 26, 1990, there had been an earthquake measuring 6.9 on the Richter scale. The Communist press had reported that there were no fatalities at Tanggemu Farm, but when I got there and talked to people, I discovered that the buildings, made of prefabricated slabs of cement, had toppled down on officers and their families, causing many casualties. Because the earthquake hit late in the afternoon, most prisoners were still working in the fields, so probably few were injured. The Communist press boasted that no prisoners had tried to escape, which might have been true. Tanggemu Farm extends about forty-five miles from east to west, and in this vast grassland and desert, with neither trees nor houses, drinking water nor food, where could anybody run?

At sunset, we approached Tanggemu Farm, where Wei Jingsheng had spent four and a half years. We would have to stay the night at the guesthouse at the entrance to the camp. The closer we drew to the farm, the greater became my anxiety because there were no casual tourists, no outsiders, no civilians out here. It was time to put on my security blanket: the police uniform Liu had borrowed.

We took Liu's daughter with us when we went into the office to register. I was hoping the child would bring us good luck.

"I need beds for four people," I told the clerk.

"How many nights?"

"Three."

Liu looked sideways at me, wondering how we could stay three nights, but he observed my rule: no questions.

The clerk asked for my identification, and I pointed at my uniform, but the clerk said, "I need your ID."

I turned to the driver, who was convinced I was an officer because of my uniform, and I said, "I left mine outside. Please give him your ID, so I don't have to go back to the car."

The clerk accepted the driver's papers and registered us. As we headed to the room, I whispered to Liu, "Don't worry, we're not staying three days. I just paid the clerk to assure them. Tomorrow morning we keep moving."

We were put in a dormitory-style room with wooden beds but without a bathroom or running water. As I tried to sleep under the filthy cover, I kept thinking of all the officers nearby. I did not sleep well.

By morning, I was eager to get away. I dressed in my uniform and asked the driver to take us three miles down the road and then hide his car in a ditch and take a break by himself. I put my video camera inside the handbag I had bought in mainland China, to adhere to another one of my rules: Never attract attention by carrying Western goods.

I walked closer to the fence to get a better look at the farm where Wei had lived, and I noticed a tall, red-brick prison building with watchtowers. Perhaps I was too preoccupied by the danger, or perhaps I was too preoccupied with communing with Wei. Suddenly I took one step too far and tumbled headfirst into the ditch outside the fence, no more than a three-foot drop but enough to make me fall on my left arm and feel a severe pain shoot into my shoulder. Holding my left arm with my right hand, I staggered back to the ditch where the car was hidden. Liu and the driver felt the bulge in my left shoulder but were unable to tell whether a bone was broken or the shoulder was dislocated.

"We don't know a thing about medicine," Liu said. "Let's go back to Xining."

"No," I said. "We've come this far; I cannot return empty-handed. Come over here, hold my arm and do what I say!" I was sure the shoulder was dislocated.

I leaned against the car door and asked Liu to turn my left arm. Slowly twisting and pulling, he finally pushed the arm back into its socket. I wiped the sweat from my face and borrowed a belt to tie my left arm to my waist, making a sling of sorts. I regretted having thrown away my Advil a few days earlier, not wanting to have American medicine in my Chinese bag. I had work to do before getting back to Western pain relief. My shoulder throbbing, I picked up my camera bag and trudged toward the front entrance of Wei's camp, trying to blend in with dozens of guards in uniform. I had no cap, but neither did most of them. Some guards were escorting prisoners from prison to the fields while others were reporting for their shift.

The armed police in the watchtower waved at me, which gave me a start, but I recovered and waved back. When we arrived at the iron gate, I saw that all the officers signed in with the gate officer. Their day pass was then tied on a rope and lowered from the watchtower, and then the iron gate was opened, letting one group of prisoners in and another group out. There was safety in numbers here. I slipped in with a large group of officers and prisoners.

I was actually inside Tanggemu Farm, but I had no time to enjoy my audacity. My left arm was useless from the fall, and I had to fumble around with my right hand in my travel bag, letting the camera work through the hole in the side. I followed the prisoners to the work sites, noting their empty eyes, their shabby uniforms, their hard labor in the midday sun. I took some photographs of them, but my pain cut short the visit. (To my amazement, some of this footage from Wei's camp actually came out. In September, it would be broadcast on 60 *Minutes*, proving a valuable link between the government and forced labor.)

Upon returning to Shanghai, I called Ching-Lee in Taiwan; she had not heard my voice for five days. Then I bought some painkillers and took a bath. My shoulder was still aching, but at least nothing was broken.

The CBS crew had arrived: Ed Bradley; his producer, David Gelber; and a cameraman. The 60 *Minutes* people had government permission to work on other stories in Beijing, but they went first to Shanghai as tourists, which gave them cover to work on the real story. Ordinary Chinese did not recognize Ed Bradley as a television star as he walked the streets of Shanghai. He is a decent guy, not full of himself, and he told me casually that he could not walk around freely like this in Hong Kong. For a few days, he could operate as a journalist without his celebrity status getting in the way.

Our first stop was the Shanghai Laodong Machinery Factory, which has been sending goods to the United States for years. I had already made a fifty-dollar mail-order purchase of an adjustable wrench and other tools, just as samples. Now it was time for the big deal. CBS wanted to make sure we got Ed Bradley on camera, so we rented a suite in the Portman Shangri-La and hid three different cameras, including one the size of a lipstick container that had a ten-yard maximum range.

Ed Bradley was waiting in another room upstairs, and our camera-man, Norman Lloyd, posed as my immediate boss as we greeted four officials from the company: the president, a deputy, a sales manager, and a female engineer, who spoke English. I pretended to arrange their seating by status, but in fact I was trying to get good angles for the three hidden cameras.

I told them I was worried about the trade laws involving labor-camp products, but the top official assured me, "We will be exporting indi-rectly," meaning they had found ways around this inconvenient U.S. law. We worked out a deal—eighty-eight thousand dollars' worth of business—and more where that came from.

Now that we were talking money, our cameraman picked up the phone and talked with Bradley for a while. Then, turning to the rest of us, he announced, "Our vice president just arrived. I told him we were signing a contract, and he was very happy, but he wants to be present when we sign."

Ten minutes later Ed Bradley—Mr. Big—entered and shook hands with everybody. With that confident television voice of his, he feigned concern about the quality of the work. He praised me in front of the Chinese, but he added, "Because we want a long-term relationship with this company, we have to be sure about the reliability of the workforce." The officials reassured us: No problem—they'd been running these fac-tories for forty-one years. Bradley was also concerned about quality con-trol, and he asked me, "Harry, have you visited their factory?"

"No, I haven't. I visited their manager, but I haven't visited their workshop."

Bradley looked a bit worried and said, "Harry, according to our com-pany policy, you must visit the workshop. We are looking for potential, and we must go further."

Bradley then left and went back to his room. The Chinese officials seemed to hesitate. They had already signed the contract, but they knew it was not valid unless they followed the American company's procedures. I knew that a visit would be a problem because the trading division and the labor division in Chinese companies were kept far apart—the smiling face and the ugly reality. You meet the general manager of a trading division, but you never get invited to meet the general manager of the production division.

"I feel awkward," I said sadly. "If I cannot get the visit, I probably cannot implement the contract. It's too bad because we want to do a lot of business here."

They tried to call their boss but were unsuccessful. They looked sad, so I invited them downstairs for a buffet. As everybody relaxed, they told us that the general manager of the factory was also the deputy chief of the Shanghai Labor Bureau of Laogai—a government guy, not just a free-enterprise guy. That was the point we were trying to prove, of course. Finally they said they would definitely arrange my visit for the next day. I had to tell them we were moving on, so we could not make it this trip. They kept apologizing, and I kept saying, "Next time, next time."

We would not see the prisoners working, but the audio- and video-tapes of these hotel meetings, as well as the signed contract, were evidence enough of the link between foreign trade and forced labor.

⌒

The next day we flew from Shanghai to Tianjin to visit my old place, Qinghe Farm, where Ching-Lee and I had taken pictures only two months before. I managed to squeeze three *lao-wai* (foreigners)—Ed Bradley, David Gelber, and Norman Lloyd—into the backseat of a small van, whose side windows I had covered with curtains. I told them, "Don't move, and don't shoot without my orders."

We drove for an hour from the Hyatt Tianjin toward the Yonghe Bridge on the Yongding River. I saw two soldiers, so I told the driver to stop and let the *lao-wai* out of the van to walk around. David Gelber was nervous and wanted to keep moving, but I instructed the driver to say hello to the guards. "These foreign visitors would like to see the cable structure of the bridge," the driver said.

While the soldiers were still hesitating, I gave them two Marlboro cigarettes. Sometimes it is that easy. We kept rolling through Qinghe Farm, for fifteen miles, with white patrol cars passing us, one after another, and thousands of laborers digging a canal, repairing roads. I asked the driver to park down the road, and I told the three crew members to get out of the van and walk side by side with the Public Security guards, just as if they belonged. I was taking the chance that the guards were so unprepared for foreigners that we could take some quick footage and leave immediately. To this day, I cannot understand why nobody stopped us.

Back on the road, we spotted prisoners working in the vineyards, which I knew produce grapes for Dynasty wine, made jointly by the French company Rémy Martin and Tianjin wine and sold in California and other places in the States. I invited Ed Bradley to get out and buy some grapes at the vineyard while the cameraman shot the scene through the van window.

"This foreign guest wants to buy some grapes," I told the guard.

"No problem. Our rosé delicious have ripened. They are excellent. You can taste them first."

He gave Ed a big cluster of grapes, and then he actually said, "Wait a moment, I'll ask the criminals to pick some fresh ones for you."

A few minutes later five or six filthy, scrawny laborers appeared lugging two carts of grapes, and they filled a big basket for us, maybe twenty pounds. We ate a few grapes and made a big fuss of saying, "Mmmmm, delicious," and then we paid and drove away before the police had a chance to wonder why a bunch of *lao-wai* were driving around eating grapes. After seeing the prisoners trudging dispiritedly in the vineyards, we did not have any appetite. We left the grapes in the van.

From Tianjin, I took off for Hong Kong while the crew flew to Beijing, where Ed Bradley had an appointment with Tong Zhi Guang, the vice minister of export and import in the Ministry of Foreign Economic Relations and Trade.

Tong obviously had not been warned about the inquisitive nature of *60 Minutes*. With the cameras in full view, Bradley told Tong that people from the Shanghai Laodong Machinery Factory had assured us they could provide exports from a forced-labor camp.

"It is not to my knowledge," Tong said in very good English. "To my knowledge, in the first place, no prison-related manufacturing facility has ever been given the right to engage in foreign trade. They are not allowed."

Bradley waved some documents at Tong. "There it is, right in the middle of Shanghai," Bradley said.

"To me, it is inconceivable," Tong sputtered. "They are not supposed to. . . . If that is true, they are violating Chinese policy. . . . The Chinese government never allows the export of what you called forced-labor product."

"You think this is a mistake?" Bradley asked.

Tong said, "It is either a mistake, or the letter is in doubt."

Bradley waved a copy of a 1988 official government trade brochure that bragged about the 20 percent increase in export from forced-labor products. "It's in print," Bradley said for emphasis.

"I never know it," Tong said, his eyes darting back and forth, looking for support, perhaps hoping a couple of Public Security officers would cart this crew of insolent foreigners off to a distant camp.

The vice minister was just smart enough to know he had run into a buzz saw. Because the Chinese do not have a tradition of free journalism, an official like Tong, no matter how suave and fluent and educated, is totally lost in the face of the Western press. An American public official would know how to smile at the camera and say, "No problem," would know how to lie without batting his eyes. Tong, however, was having a rough time.

"What is your position?" Bradley persisted, giving Tong the opportunity to say there had been a terrible mistake.

"Vice minister of export and import," Tong said miserably.

"That comes from a government publication," Bradley said.

"Government publications can make mistakes," Tong assured him.

Bradley tried to give Tong an out by saying it would be easier if both parties could just concentrate on making the best deal, without other considerations.

"Business is business," Tong said hopefully.

The interview would make wonderful television in September. By the time Ed Bradley was done with him, Tong had lost considerable face. Any foreigner who has seen this *60 Minutes* segment will remember the way Tong had blustered when faced with undeniable evidence.

—

When I got to Hong Kong, I began to plan our last mission: a visit to the trading company representing the lambskin people from Xining.

The CBS crew met me at the Sheraton Hotel. This time Ed Bradley had to stay out of sight because he would be recognized in Hong Kong, so Norman, the cameraman, got to be boss.

With our cameras hidden, we got Mr. Pung, the middleman in the trading company, to tell me he was the leather expert who went to the camps. He told me that a lot of the workers were bad guys, prisoners, who could be kept in line. The only problem was he said all this in Mandarin, which required translation for American television. His assistant, a woman, was mostly quiet. Still, we had it, with the camera running: annual sales, production, shipping—everything.

When we left the Sheraton, I was eager to take a look at the film. The cameraman suggested we return to our hotel, but I said, "No, I want to look at everything right now." Right outside on the street, he rewound the film and tried to play it. Nothing. For whatever reason, the film was blank. The cameraman looked sick. Even though the camera had been hidden, and he could not check it during the operation, it was still his responsibility. He was angry with himself, afraid he would lose his job.

"Let's go to the hotel," I said. "I'll think of something."

When we got back, we ran into the soundman, Ned Hall, dressed in his most casual clothes.

"Do you have a suit?" I asked.

Ned looked at me as if I were crazy. "What's happening?" he asked.

I told him he had just become an importer of lambskin and would need to dress up to play the part. I suggested he take my credit card and rush downstairs and find a tailor in the lobby, which you can find in all good Hong Kong hotels, and get a suit made up for himself in an hour, but Ned is a professional, and he always carries business clothes with him on all trips, just in case.

I got on the phone with Mr. Pung. "I'm very happy with you and your assistant," I said, "but my boss just arrived, and he really wants to meet you."

To my relief, he agreed to meet us again right away. Ned returned, looking terrific in his conservative business suit. On the way over to the other hotel, I taught him everything he would need to know about the lambskin business.

The Hong Kong traders were very impressed with my big boss. It must have been the suit. I pushed a button, started up the hidden camera, and this time it was even better. The assistant, the woman, must have enjoyed her lunch, because she started chattering away in English. Our soundman said he was worried about the quality of the goods, and he asked how the company could ensure quality control, given that the workers were prisoners.

No problem, the man said in Chinese.

The assistant, wearing a long, flowered skirt and a reddish blouse, elaborated in English. "They have their own regulations, and also we send our people to keep on checking the quality of them," she said enthusiastically. "Once we report to them the quality is not up to standard, the prisoners will have the punishment of beatings or some other thing." To emphasize, she waved her right hand in a vigorous chopping motion.

As soon as we got away from the hotel, we checked the film. This time the camera had worked.

I called Ching-Lee and told her to finish up her job in Taiwan and get to America before September 15 because our show would be on *60 Minutes* that night, and there would be a cover story in *Newsweek*. There was going to be a small celebration in New York for the show and the magazine story. My wife was part of the success of the trips, and she absolutely had to be at the party. She flew to America the next day, and we began our new life together.

The *60 Minutes* segment was shown on September 15, 1991; the *Newsweek* cover was great; and my trip was also described by *The Washington Post*, *BusinessWeek*, and a Chinese-language newspaper, *World Journal*. As a result, public hearings were held by the U.S. Congress and the U.S. Customs Service that fall.

The Chinese authorities may not have noticed Ed Bradley when he was walking the streets of their cities, but they noticed him now. On

September 19, the Chinese Ministry of Foreign Affairs' spokesman in Beijing, Wu Jianmin, said, "CBS and *Newsweek*'s articles severely distorted the facts. They are notorious for vilifying China. Due to the ideological and value prejudice, as well as the extreme hatred for the social system which was chosen by the Chinese people, the author confounded black and white, and confused right and wrong." I later learned that the *60 Minutes* show was actually seen at major hotels that cater to foreign trade in the big cities in China. When a country starts allowing modern electronics, it cannot completely control the information that comes rushing in. The Chinese government did manage to ban *Newsweek* that week, however, and later interrupted BBC and the Voice of America, which were broadcasting discussions of the trip.

CBS would later win an Emmy for that show and was very appreciative—except for its accountants. When I got back to California, I turned in a request for reimbursement of eighteen thousand dollars in expenses, itemizing major expenses like plane tickets but listing other expenses as "taxi driver $200" or "police officer $100" or "former inmates $300." I had explained to David Gelber that I would not demand receipts because the police could trace my steps more easily if I did. But now the CBS accountants were demanding my receipts and also charging me for the camera Ching-Lee had dumped when the guards were chasing us on the first trip. I had risked my life for CBS, but apparently that did not mean much to its accounting department. Finally Betty Bao Lord, the writer and wife of the diplomat Winston Lord, a former U.S. ambassador to China, notified Don Hewitt, the boss of *60 Minutes*, who straightened the matter out in much less than sixty minutes. Four years later, when I was released by the Chinese, I would repay Hewitt's thoughtfulness with an exclusive interview.

⌐

Now that I was infamous throughout China and elsewhere because of *60 Minutes*, many people assumed I would never try it again. "Picture this," I would tell them. "On a warm spring day, we go back to Qinghe Farm, to Field 586, and we lay fresh flowers on the unmarked ground where my friends are buried."

12

MEIHUA

There was one other development from my second trip to China: I was back in touch with Meihua. Still unable to accept the way she had rejected me so many years ago, I had gone to see her before I left Shanghai. Ching-Lee knew I was going to see her. Ching-Lee knows she is the love of my heart, the woman I waited for, but she also knows there is a place in my heart for Meihua.

It was seventeen years since I had last seen Meihua, on my leave from the coal mine, when, unable to talk about the past, she could barely face me. I still wanted to know why she had given back the crucifix, why she had broken off with me so abruptly thirty-four years before. What had people said to her? What threats were made? What fears had Chairman Mao struck in everybody? We were older now. Time was short. We should not be afraid any longer. I did worry that my activities would bring trouble to her, but despite my fears of surveillance, the Chinese authorities seemed to have had no idea of what I was up to. Besides, I was not going to confide in Meihua; I was not going to ask her to conceal any tapes. She had always been innocent, and I would never put her in jeopardy, but I just wanted to see her again, this woman now in her fifties, and try to remember the girl I had loved.

I tracked her down through her relatives. Meihua lived in the suburbs of Shanghai now, with her husband, and she sent word that she would meet me at the home of her sister-in-law. I rushed to the home at the appointed hour and saw her across the room, the same face I had envisioned all those years, now framed by graying hair. Meihua wore regular slacks and a sweatshirt and plain shoes—nothing fancy. We were not twenty-five-year-olds meeting in a bar, she with makeup and a fancy hairdo, me with a gaudy shirt and strong cologne, on the start of some grand adventure. Nothing like that. We were old friends meeting casually in a family home.

This time Meihua was not afraid to face me. We walked toward each other and wrapped our arms around each other, cheeks touching, for three or four minutes. I could feel the embrace of a true friend, somebody who still cared for me. And I knew my arms told her the same. I am not good with descriptions, and I can only say that by Chinese standards, she is not a movie star, not a beautiful woman—average size, average features—but I saw her face, and I knew she was Meihua, the girl of my childhood, the girl of my lost dreams.

The sister-in-law bustled about the room, saying she had to run off to the store and would be back in an hour. Meihua made tea for me, and we sat at the kitchen table.

"You are so thin," I said. She was lithe and slender, not the way Chinese grandmothers used to look.

"I practice sword dancing now," she said. "You know, martial arts, like tai chi. Every day I go down to the park near my house, and we exercise. We must exercise. We are almost sixty."

"Not quite," I said. "Several years yet. Are you okay?" I asked. "I heard you had health problems."

"I'm all right," she said. "Back in 1957, they moved me to Manchuria. It was cold up there, and there was not enough food."

She said she tried to get sent back to Shanghai but did not have the right political contacts because her family was considered rightists, just like mine, so she had claimed to have serious health problems, and they eventually agreed to relocate her in Shanghai. "I've got minor problems but nothing serious," she said.

She knew I lived in the States now, and I told her I was a research fellow in California, but I did not go into any detail about my activities, and Meihua knew enough not to ask. I told her about Ching-Lee, the woman I had met on a blind date on a street corner in Taipei, the woman who shared my life. I could see her nodding and smiling, and I knew Meihua was happy for me.

"Do you have grandchildren?" I asked. She said that her Number Two Daughter had given her one granddaughter.

I never asked about her husband, his job, or even his name. Maybe this will sound callous or peculiar on my part, but her marriage did not matter to me. We were not going to see each other again. Our relationship was in the past. All that mattered was that I sat in this room with this middle-aged woman, and we felt the immense weight of the past. I asked whether she had any old photographs of us or the old neighborhood or our friends in those innocent days, but she said most of her family's belongings had been destroyed by the rampages of the Red Guard. Photographs of young lovers had been seen as relics from a bourgeois era, impediments to the new age in which everybody loved Mao the best.

We were all starting over without a past. Now there was a woman a few feet away from me with a smile and a sad look that I remembered from my childhood. I asked myself what there was about Meihua that made me love her so much, then and now, but I could not say.

"We seem to see each other every seventeen years," I said. "I don't know if it will be possible to meet you again in seventeen years."

The political tragedy had produced millions of personal tragedies, but perhaps Meihua and I did not constitute a tragedy. We had parted before we had ever had the chance to be lovers, before we could become engaged, before we could be husband and wife. This loss was pure because neither of us could know whether we would have succeeded together. We recognized that both of us are strong-minded, so maybe we would have wound up arguing and resenting each other, moving apart. We could not know. We were never given the chance to find out.

Fortunately for both of us, our lives went on. I sat there in the room with this middle-aged lady, and I thought of the girl who rode bicycles with me around Shanghai in another life. "I'm happy I came back to see you," I said.

I could not tell her what I was really thinking, that she was my first love, that she was always in my heart. I could not say those words.

Her sister-in-law returned, and I knew it was time for me to go. I wondered whether the party official on the block would report that Meihua and I had been seen at her family's house, but I had done nothing to compromise her. I had kept my secrets. We embraced at the door, and we promised to write, and then I rushed down the street, going home to Ching-Lee in California. It would be a very long time until 2008.

13

I BECOME A FOUNDATION

The phone rings. Mandarin at the other end. "We are going to kill you." *Click.* It happens every so often, just often enough to keep me on my toes. Once I was on *60 Minutes*, strangers knew me, for better or for worse. I would find a message on my answering machine or maybe a note in the mail: "You are a traitor. Lay off China. We know where you are."

But there is no hiding from terrorism. The old feuds cross the borders. Somebody from Taiwan gets knocked off in the United States for what he's written in a newsletter. Somebody from Chile gets blown up in Washington, D.C. Some Bulgarian in London jabs a man with a poisoned umbrella tip. A government official disappears from an embassy, and the body is found. They call it suicide, but you don't know. It's going to happen if they want it to, but I cannot let the prospect frighten me. Otherwise, they win.

I knew I was getting somewhere in 1993 when I went to Geneva for a human-rights meeting and half a dozen Chinese on the chilly sidewalk started accusing me of making mistakes in my book listing all the camps.

"I admit it, some information is incorrect," I said. "Everybody makes mistakes. Are you telling me that even your great leader never made mistakes? I have the right to speak."

"You work for foreigners," they taunted.

"Hey, not all foreigners are bad guys," I shot back. "What about Marx? What about Stalin? They were foreigners. You like them, right?"

"You lie," they said.

I asked where my accusers got their information. I quickly realized they had not read anything; they were just accepting Beijing's propaganda. What annoyed me was that they made a big point about being dissidents who had been at Tiananmen Square, which might—or might not—have been true. Now, in exile, they were frightened, insecure, and perhaps they didn't want China mad at them. Fine, I would be happy to be the scapegoat, to take the heat, to give them cover.

I was no longer some solitary Chinese man roaming the earth, seeking justice. After my first trip to China, I had testified a second time at a congressional hearing and had met Jeff Fiedler, the secretary-treasurer of the Food and Allied Service Trades Department of the AFL-CIO, which had published a map of the *laogai* that had been worked up from my early research. I learned that Jeff had been a U.S. soldier in Vietnam and had later gone back to study there, and his wife was Vietnamese. Later he had worked in Turkey, helping to organize the Kurdish labor movement, so I knew he understood other parts of the world. Jeff also cares deeply about human rights and had worked with a young Chinese dissident who escaped after Tiananmen Square, and soon he became one of my best friends.

Obviously the AFL-CIO does not appreciate having goods coming into the United States that are made by unsalaried prisoners in China, but more important, it opposes slave labor anywhere in the world. My friendship with Jeff went far beyond the union activity on his part, however. Jeff went to China on his own for the first time in September of 1991, to investigate labor-camp production for a large American corporation. He made another trip in 1993 and still has not forgotten being trailed by seven Public Security guards. Once his cover was blown, he decided he couldn't go back.

Jeff began giving me sound political advice, something I had never had before, telling me, for example, which members of Congress might be interested in my cause. Until I met Jeff, I had concentrated only on exposing the Chinese camps, but he urged me to be tougher on U.S. companies, saying they should be penalized for encouraging prison labor.

I was just staying solvent, with my money going for airplane tickets and office supplies, but Jeff had an idea: "People don't give money to individuals. They donate to foundations." With the help of Linda Pfeifer, a woman in San Jose, California, who cared very much about the cause, Jeff and I chartered the Laogai Research Foundation. The two of us are directors, along with Jean Pasqualini, a half-French, half-Chinese friend of mine in Paris who, with Rudolph Chelminski, wrote the book *Prisoner of Mao*, about his own suffering in the *laogai*. Simon Leys, a writer on China, has called Pasqualini's book "the most fundamental document on the Maoist 'Gulag.' "

Much of the foundation's income is derived from my speaking engagements, but we are also supported by some friends and the National Endowment for Democracy. For security and political reasons, any gifts are earmarked for domestic expenses and research rather than for my expeditions overseas. I also began issuing papers about the specific abuses of the system, sending five hundred or a thousand copies to opinion makers around the world. I included maps of the camps and lists of products reaching the West.

One of the first U.S. policies I criticized was President George Bush's "Memorandum of Understanding Between the United States of America and the People's Republic of China on Prohibiting Import and Export Trade in Prison Labor Products," signed August 7, 1992, in which Beijing agreed to comply with a number of human-rights standards and with international law in order to retain its trade privileges.

Although I am far from articulate in English, I have my moments. After Bush signed the MOU, I went around the country telling people that the initials stood for Meaning of Useless. Jeff liked this so much that he kept repeating it to everybody.

The longer I am in the West, the more I appreciate just how deeply many Western people agonize over what they do and how they appear. "America has millions of people in prison," people will say. "We have chain gangs. Many of the incarcerated are political prisoners, in jail because of their beliefs or the color of their skin or the place where they were born."

I reply, "Would you really compare a chain gang in Georgia with the Russian gulag or the Chinese *laogai*? The Communists take people thousands of miles away and hold them for decades just to get more work out of them. In China, if you say, 'Down with the Communist Party,' you go to jail, but in the United States, if you say, 'Down with the Democrats' or 'Down with the Republicans,' no problem."

China is not a country or a civilization that believes in explaining itself, but to my amazement, on August 11, 1992, China actually issued a white paper to spell out its policy on labor camps. I am totally convinced that our activism prodded it to issue this unusual explanation:

> China is the most populous country in the world. Its crime rate is nevertheless much lower than the world average due to a series of measures adopted by the political power of the people to stimulate growth in the economy and maintain social stability. . . . China's basic goals in criminal reform are to turn offenders into a different kind of person, one who abides by the law and supports himself or herself with his or her own labor, and to reestablish these people as free citizens in society.

Beijing's principal goals are easily summarized:

1. People can be reformed.
2. According to Chinese law, a criminal's due rights during his or her prison service are protected and may not be violated.
3. It is especially important for criminals to engage in productive and socially beneficial behavior.
4. Since most criminals are young, without much education, and ignorant of the laws, an important part of the work of reform through labor is helping the prisoners to become better educated or to acquire more legal, moral, and cultural awareness and working skills.
5. Means of persuasion include libraries, books, dramatic productions, lectures by former prisoners.
6. Prisoners are handled humanely, in accordance with the law.
7. Criminals are punished.
8. Convicts are employed, resettled, educated, and protected.

The white paper raised many more questions than it answered: How many camps? How many prisoners? How many are common criminals, and how many are so-called counterrevolutionaries? The paper noted that more than forty thousand appeals had been heard by Chinese officials, a number we found unbelievably high, given the lack of due process in China. The paper claimed that "the criminals have the right to live a normal life" and insisted that prison meals had a protein level close to the average for the country, which I find incredible, having sampled the cuisine. The paper spoke of freedom to correspond and freedom of religion, both of which I knew to be nonexistent. It went on to mention a two-year reprieve granted to prisoners subject to the death penalty, "during which time they are to undergo reform-through-labor to see if it will be effective." Was that true, or were the authorities just keeping prisoners around until their kidneys were needed for transplants?

Elsewhere the paper insisted that "in China, the products manufactured by the detainees serve above all to satisfy the needs of the work-reform system." But if that were so, then why did they put phony names on their prison-camp factories, as if trying to conceal the profitable use of forced labor?

Finally, the paper claimed that goods from prison factories and farms constituted "about 0.08 percent of the nation's total industrial and agricultural production output value" in 1990. That sounds low—until you remember how huge China is. The government was talking about millions of dollars derived from slave labor. And my focus is always on the individual, that one person laboring for decades, perhaps for political reasons. Even 0.08 percent is a huge figure if you are part of it.

Eventually Jeff convinced me that we had to monitor the U.S. companies that do business with the Chinese. I soon began to suspect that Wal-Mart was bringing in goods made by Chinese prisoners. I managed to get my name on the list of people who could address the fifteen thousand stockholders at the company's annual meeting in Fayetteville, Arkansas. When we got to the meeting, the company goons running security took a video camera away from Ching-Lee, something the Chinese authorities had never done on our trips. Fortunately Jeff had arranged for two other people—wearing Wal-Mart T-shirts and baseball caps—to enter the meeting carrying video cameras. They came away with a classic piece of film of Rob Walton, the son of Sam Walton, the founder, cutting me off after exactly three minutes, my allotted time, and fifteen thousand shareholders hooting at me.

Jeff was afraid I would be offended and frightened, and he asked me, "Have you ever been in a hostile crowd like that?"

"I've seen rallies like this, where they use children and flags to stir up emotions, and they do not allow debate," I said leaving the Wal-Mart meeting. "It was in Communist China."

Once the foundation was running, I was seized with the idea of collecting photographs and histories from survivors. It is easy to get people to talk in the West, but in China people do not want to recall the decades they spent in the camps. They are afraid and just want to get on with their lives.

I decided to have other people work for me in China, an idea that led to a *laogai* survivor named Feng, who was living in Hong Kong and working as a photographer. In March of 1993, Ching-Lee and I went to Feng's place: just a tiny, squalid room, no bathroom, no kitchen. I almost cried because he had suffered so many years and had so little. I offered him four thousand dollars to interview people, so he quit his job and traveled to China, taking photographs of survivors. I also gave him the names and addresses of six or seven labor factories located in the middle of major cities. I warned him not to use false identities, not to trespass, but if he happened to buy inexpensive material from these prison factories, I would reimburse him.

In the end, Feng would produce not one picture of significance, not one record of a survivor. He was sixty years old, too fearful to be effective. He also told me he had left some film at a friend's house, and the police had confiscated it. I was not happy, but still, through a third person, I helped Feng get his wife safely out of China, and I asked friends

to help him get a better life in Hong Kong. To this day, I am not sure
what his agenda was, but I do know that my relationship with Feng
would surface at my trial in 1995. He was only one of many people who
worked with me inside China, and even if this one did not work out, at
least we helped him survive.

⌒

China was changing. Even I had to admit that. Back in the 1950s, the
leaders believed in their system, believed in brainwashing, believed they
could make everybody think and talk the same way. In my time, most
people said, "Communism is our future; there's no way we can resist." If
someone escaped from camp, he had no place to go. If he loved his parents, he didn't go near them because they would be forever branded if
they gave him a place to sleep for even one night. If he didn't have a
food coupon, he just starved. As for finding a job—forget about it.

But brainwashing did not work. The next generation produced its
rebels, its dissidents, its thinkers, an electrician named Wei Jingsheng
writing bold essays about democracy. By the early 1990s China's rulers
were not bothering as much with brainwashing. Forget ideology. Deng
opened up the country to commerce, to telephones, to travel. Soon
there would be talk of going global, of getting on the information highway. It would become harder to maintain a closed society.

So the regime changed its tactics. In 1983, Deng made every camp
become an individual financial center, just like a corporation or a factory. In bottom-line China, the operators had to pay for the uniforms,
salary, benefits, and education of their police and skilled workers. If,
however, they covered their expenses, their workers received more benefits. The old-fashioned warden was now a production manager. His
margin of profit was derived from the amount of free work, the number
of free products he could squeeze out of his prisoners. If somebody
from a human-rights organization or a foreign government or the
World Bank was coming, the police would behave a little better that
day and ladle out a better brand of soup. China was changing, not necessarily for the better.

14

NEARLY CAUGHT

My new project was an entire country turned into a prison camp. The rest of the world knows it as Tibet, with its own language, its own people, its own history, but the Chinese have ruthlessly turned it into an "autonomous region" without much autonomy.

I first became fascinated by Tibet when I was in college in Beijing in 1959 and the government loaded us onto buses and brought us to a rally against Tibet. We were shown photographs and documents that allegedly depicted Tibet as a backward nation, terribly primitive and cruel, where the monks possessed great wealth and could have any woman they desired and would cut off a person's hands as punishment or bury him alive. Tibet badly needed correction by China, we were told, and in fact was really part of China. By March 31, 1959, when the Dalai Lama scrambled over the mountains to India, I was having my own difficulties with Chinese authority.

China's crude bullying backfired. The Dalai Lama became one of the most respected people on earth, known for his interest in science and for his gentle, open manner. Thirty years later he was awarded the Nobel Peace Prize and today is a spiritual and political leader of all Tibetans, exiled or captive. I had the pleasure of meeting the Dalai Lama in Washington in 1992 at a peace conference. He signed one copy of our foundation poster, kept another copy for himself, and later wrote to endorse our foundation, although he has no connection to us.

～

The Communists began sending Chinese prisoners and other settlers to Tibet to increase the ethnic Han population, a minority in Tibet but the majority in China. In 1993, I heard reports of as many as twelve new labor camps. I have to be blunt and say that Tibetan human rights is not a popular subject even for the courageous Chinese who demonstrated in Tiananmen Square. Most Chinese consider the Tibetans "others," not worth thinking about.

If ever there was a perfect location for a prison camp, it is Tibet, "the roof of the world," as it has been called. With the Himalayas to the south and the Taklimakan Desert to the north, Tibet is a perfect place to house prisoners, political or otherwise. The natives' resentment of Chinese rule runs so deep that hardly any Tibetans would help an escaped Chinese prisoner.

I decided to expose the labor camps of Tibet and Qinghai province to the north, but in February of 1993, my visa application was turned down in Hong Kong, no reason given. We saw that the young woman at the Chinese consulate in Hong Kong wrote on Ching-Lee's visa application, "Harry Wu's wife. Forbidden entrance."

I started all over again, contacting several Tibetan exiles and telling them I needed a Tibetan escort, a special permit to travel to Tibet, and help getting across the border from Nepal. This was to be the most secretive of my trips, with codes scrambled three ways, contacts that involved three people before reaching me—anything to ensure safety. After several months of preparation, the exiles were ready, so in August of 1993, I flew from San Francisco to Hong Kong to Bangkok and on to Kathmandu, the capital of Nepal, fifty miles or so from the Chinese border. I met my guide, named Katuga; a young Tibetan who also speaks Mandarin; a Tibetan woman who would pose as my wife; and Katuga's brother. To protect them, I told them only my first name. Also part of the entourage was a businessman named Capu, who had agreed to provide free passage across the Nepal-China border. I did not feel comfortable about the way Capu had just materialized, so I asked whether I could take his photo, knowing that exiles do not like to be identified. He hesitated, but finally allowed me to, which I took as a sign of trust.

The next morning Capu took off by himself, claiming to have business to conduct. Undaunted, Katuga and the Nepalese guides and I got into the car and took off toward the border. On the four-hour drive, it rained so hard there were landslides and small floods, and we had to get out and push the car through the muck. Around three in the afternoon, we arrived in Tato Pani—"hot water" in Nepalese—a small village of about twenty or thirty families, less than three miles from the border with China or Tibet, whichever you want to call it. We passed through three checkpoints and were in a neutral zone, where the Chinese seemed to move freely. It was not easy to go unnoticed, but I was so exhausted and covered with mud that I took a chance and had a bath in the natural hot springs on the hillside.

Something was not right. I was outside when I heard a jeep chug over from the Chinese side of the border and stop by a fountain. A man jumped out and started taking pictures, and I noticed that the white Toyota jeep had 00868 stenciled on the side and a license plate that said GA, the initials for Public Security in Chinese. The man had a definite pattern to his photo taking. He would snap something in some other direction but would always return to the front of our hotel. Then I noticed that the driver was wearing a police uniform. They were after me, I realized. Right away I slipped off to my room.

We were staying in a combination general store, saloon, and hotel, where my modest room had a ceiling not much above my head and a window facing the main street, with Nepal in one direction, Tibet in the other. There was no electricity in the room, and it was quite dark in there, which gave me an advantage: I could see out but could not be seen from outside. In a few minutes, the man got back into the jeep, and it took off and headed into Nepal. With Katuga's help, I set up our cameras. I wanted to make a record of them, the same way they were making a record of me. I was positive they would come back for me.

I knew it was a forty-minute trip from Tato Pani to the next village, so when I spotted the jeep returning in less than twenty minutes, I suspected the men had simply driven off to discuss their plan to get me. The car drove directly to our hotel and stopped in front.

I got very nervous. I had been accosted by police officers during my first two trips, but this was the first time I had encountered aggressive surveillance. Either the men were trying to intimidate me, or they were going to haul me back to a Chinese jail. Even though I had an American travel document, I was not an American citizen. I feared the Chinese could still claim me as one of their own, and the border between Nepal and China hardly seemed a deterrent.

I activated the video camera on a tripod at the window and started snapping pictures with my still camera. Villagers poked their heads out of doors and windows while others scrambled away from the main street. The police were looking for someone very specific. Perhaps I was paranoid, but I was sure it was me they were after. I counted five men, two taking a post across the street from the hotel while the others barged into the store right below my room. I had no way out. I stuck my ear against a hole in the wooden floor and listened as they demanded information from the old innkeeper. "Ask him! Has he seen any strangers in the hotel?"

A translator repeated the question in Nepalese, and to my great joy the owner played stupid, stuttering and mumbling and saying nothing. I could do nothing but sweat it out. After getting no answers from the old man, they left. When I went downstairs, I asked the owner what the police had asked him. He was as inscrutable with me as he had been with the police.

One of the Nepalese guides assured me it was safe to go into Tibet that night, and I thought of the twelve Tibetan labor camps and how badly I wanted to get across that border. Maybe if it had been just me, I would have ridden in on horseback disguised as one of the local cowboys who rustle yaks and bulls and horses through the Himalayas, but it wasn't just my life that was at stake. I decided it would be best if Katuga crossed the border to meet Capu and find out what was happening. After about an hour, the Nepalese escort came back and gave me a written note. In my line of work, you never put these things in writing, but Katuga's note said everything was all right, that I could try to cross the border in the morning, or if I did not want to cross, I could send the camera equipment to Katuga via our escort, and he would attempt to document the existence of the camps. I agreed and gave the cameras to the Nepalese escort to deliver to Katuga.

"Just come back," I had told him. "If they ask for a confession, confess. If they ask for money, give them money. Throw away the equipment. I just want you back. If you come back with no footage or information, I won't complain at all."

The next morning, in an attempt to divert some suspicion from Katuga and the escort, I made a big production of walking halfway across the so-called Friendship Bridge, acting like a typical tourist, putting one foot over the red-painted line marking the border, having a friend take my picture, and chatting up the guards. Then I made an even bigger production of getting onto the bus and leaving the border, just to show the border guards that I was not going to Tibet.

There was nothing to do but go home to California. I worried about Katuga as I made my way back to Kathmandu. He did not have any secrets to give up, but still I was afraid he would be caught, and I did not want anybody's life on my conscience. I did not hear from him for weeks. I was so worried that I called my contacts among the Tibetan exiles and asked them to check on him. Sometime later I received a report that Katuga was all right, but I could not relax until he was out of Tibet.

A few weeks after that, I received a phone call from Lhasa. "I bought a pair of sport shoes for you," said the voice on the other end.

"What size?" I asked.

"Seven."

"Thank you," I said almost prayerfully as I hung up the phone.

Katuga was safe. The number seven was our code for "all clear." Katuga had returned safely to Kathmandu and had gone to all the places and gotten everything I wanted. I was so excited that I grabbed Ching-Lee and flew out to Kathmandu to meet this man whom I now considered a hero. I was even more in awe of him when I saw he had been to nearly every place I had mapped out. He had videotapes, still photos—everything. I bought a small video screen and played the tape off the camcorder, asking him to identify each frame by date and location. He had gone to at least ten camps, and it took us two days to get through it all, picture by picture. We now had almost everything we needed to make a first-class documentary on the captive nation of Tibet. The only thing lacking was film of Katuga crossing the border, just for effect.

"No, I cannot go near the border," he said.

"Why? It's safe," I said. "It's the last thing we have to do, and we're finished. I have an American green card and travel document; I'll escort you."

There was so much torment in his face—he was so adamant about not going to the border—that I knew something had gone wrong.

"Please," I insisted, "tell me the truth."

He admitted that he had been arrested in Lhasa and that the Chinese authorities had confiscated all the videotape and the film, which the police developed. They threatened Katuga with jail if he did not divulge the identity of this mysterious man known only as Harry. Because Katuga did not know my full name, he felt free to tell them all he knew. Thus, his life was spared. But why had they allowed him to go free? Who had turned him in? Apparently when the Chinese security men took him from Lhasa to the border, Capu was waiting with Chinese agents. But they had let Katuga go, and they even gave him back the original film and the photographs, after copying them, hoping he would take them to me at the border. But Katuga was faithful to me. He warned me against going near the border.

I realized I owed him a favor. I knew I couldn't use the film Katuga had shot because his family in Tibet might be hurt if I did. I called the exiled Tibetans and told them they, too, were responsible for this man's life, and I said I would talk to the Dalai Lama and put in a good word for Katuga. Even now, every few months, I call to be reassured he is safe in Nepal.

But I still think of all those captive people in Tibet—not just the Chinese prisoners but the Tibetans themselves, cut off from their spiritual history. The Dalai Lama speaks darkly of being the last in the line of Tibetan leaders, and there is no doubt the Chinese intend to meddle in the future of Tibetan Buddhism. The irony is that a regime that brags of its disdain for any religion wants to help choose the next generation of Tibetan Buddhist leaders. Beijing seeks to appoint the next Panchen Lama, second only to the Dalai Lama. The tenth Panchen Lama died in January of 1989, and the Tibetans awaited the discovery of his reincarnation. By whatever mystical process they use, the monks found a six-year-old and submitted his qualifications to the Dalai Lama, who then verified the child as the eleventh Panchen Lama.

But the Chinese government promptly whisked the boy and his family away and declared another six-year-old as the rightful reincarnation, creating a major schism among Tibetans. Should the Dalai Lama, who is now in his early sixties, die before the rightful Panchen Lama is reinstated, the Chinese will probably be able to secure their own candidate as the Panchen Lama. The Chinese Ministry of Foreign Affairs has insisted that the Dalai Lama's choice is "neither missing nor in custody." The government plays rough in that part of the world.

I also feel bad because many Chinese dissidents fight so hard for their own human rights but do not consider the Tibetans deserving of the same freedoms, the same choices.

Maybe I should have taken the adventure in Nepal as a warning about crossing the border, but all I could think about was my failure to help Tibet. I was determined to succeed next time.

15

KIDNEYS AND CORNEAS

Evidence was starting to roll in that made me glad I had gone through the camps when I did: The Chinese government was now apparently executing prisoners to harvest their organs for transplants.

Human Rights Watch/Asia was a major source of this information, estimating that between two thousand and three thousand organs, "(mainly kidneys and corneas) from prisoners each year are used in this manner, with government officials reportedly receiving priority in their allocation." According to Amnesty International, 90 percent of Chinese transplants are from executed prisoners. Human Rights Watch, magazines in Hong Kong, and Japanese television all had detailed information, even some eyewitness reports.

I was not totally surprised. Just before I got out of China in 1985, I obtained a confidential government document describing the first wave of organ transplants. At first, I thought it was a throwback to the ancient Chinese practice of devouring an organ for its supposed powers of healing—eating the dried penis of a tiger, say, to cure impotence or feeding the scooped-out brains of an executed prisoner to one's elderly father whose mind is wavering, as Captain Li in my coal mine had done. But this was different. This was modern Chinese science at work.

It was outrageous. A man is an enemy of the government, or so the government says. It keeps him alive, gives him a limited amount of food, a limited amount of freedom, makes him work to bring wealth to others, maybe brainwashes him. And then it kills him to give the organs in his body to somebody of standing in the party or to make a profit for the country. Has there ever been another country with a policy for the removal of organs from executed prisoners?

We began accumulating testimony from many sources. Ma Po, a former reporter for the *China Legal Daily*, had settled in the United States in December of 1989 and told about a female dissident in Jiangxi Province who had been sentenced to death in the spring of 1986 for writing DOWN WITH HUA GUOFENG on a wall. At the same time, Ma said, a pilot at the Field Hospital in Nanchang needed a kidney transplant. The hospital had arranged with the local police to delay the prisoner's execution until an army surgeon could treat her with anticoagulants. Then she was shot and taken to a surgical van parked at the execution site, and her kidneys were transplated to the pilot's body.

Stories about the widespread transplant business began piling up from many different sources: a human-rights activist in New York in 1988; the *South China Morning Post* in Hong Kong in 1988; the Associated Press in Hong Kong in 1991; *The Lancet*, an international medical journal, in 1991. It was, apparently, a booming business. *The Hong Kong Standard* reported in 1991 that a wealthy Hong Kong man, Deacon Chiu, had made a one-million-dollar donation to the First Affiliated Hospital of the Sun Yat-sen University of Medical Sciences in Guangzhou after receiving a kidney. The same paper claimed that a source at the hospital had verified that the kidney came from an executed prisoner.

Other patients paid more standard but still significant fees. Writing in the *Transplantation Reviews* in July 1992, Dr. Ronald D. Guttman of Canada wrote that through 1989, 4,596 kidney transplants had been performed in China, and he charged, "Executed prisoners have become a significant source of donors." Dr. Guttman added, "The kidneys are used in a major hospital in which the foreigners, usually Overseas Chinese, pay approximately $30,000 (U.S. equivalent) or 'three times' that charged to a local Chinese work unit."

By 1993, the issue was being debated around the world. The United Nations Committee Against Torture petitioned the Chinese government, demanding to know "whether the death sentence might not constitute a form of cruel and unusual punishment . . . (and) whether the bodies of persons executed could be used for the purpose of organ transplants." The British government sent a human-rights delegation to China, which later urged the government to produce "a code of conduct for executions which prohibits . . . the use of organs from executed prisoners for spare part surgery," according to a "Report on Visit to China" by a delegation led by Lord Howe of Aberavon in July of 1993.

After the flurry of reports in 1993, the Chinese government made extravagant gestures of banning the export of organs to everyplace but Hong Kong. But every day desperate people looking for transplants were still flying in from Hong Kong, Macao, Singapore, the nations of the Persian Gulf, Japan, and America.

This was not a matter of bootleg operations or private clinics. You hear rumors in some countries that people are murdered for their organs, which is a crime, or maybe desperately poor people sell one of their kidneys to support their family. Chinese law forbids the selling of organs, but Deng Xiaoping's economic progress had enabled modern hospitals to give miraculous help to ailing patients who could afford it or who had political clout, with obvious danger to prisoners.

The part that really bothered me was that doctors were involved in this terrible practice. Doctors were saying, in effect, "We are using the waste products of society to help other patients"—just what Nazi doctors had said about Jewish prisoners during the Holocaust.

I wanted to find a doctor who had taken part in these executions, and in November of 1992, I went to Hamburg, Germany, to visit a Chinese doctor now living in exile. Not wanting him to feel I was zeroing in on him, I invited twelve or fourteen other Chinese exiles out to dinner, and I arranged to sit next to the doctor. We started chatting. He told me how he had been sent by the government to Thailand for a United Nations medical program, but after Tiananmen Square, he had stood up in Bangkok to protest the massacre, and when the Chinese embassy wanted him to return, he had received political asylum in Germany. I told the doctor I wanted to do a documentary on why people left China. The other dissidents were sitting around talking, drinking, eating, giving me information. One man said, "I was a police guard. I beat people and tortured them"—until he realized he had to escape.

It was the doctor I really wanted to interview. The following year I was preparing for some work with the BBC and visited the same doctor in Hamburg, trying to persuade him to go public, but he was cautious. "My family is still in China," he said. "They have a kidnap policy and will come get you. Or they will get your family."

I told the doctor I was planning to study the boom in kidney transplants in China, and I asked him whether he could supply some details as to how the transplants worked. Apparently he had been a recent graduate of medical school when he was told to accompany two older doctors on a mission. "I was sent along with three other surgeons to remove kidneys in Xindu County, about fifteen miles from Chengdu," the doctor told me. "Only upon arriving at our destination were we told that we were inside a prison. In a special ward lay an anesthetized prisoner. We did not know his name, nor could we see his face. Quickly we cut open the prisoner, removed his two kidneys, and placed them in a special container. We handed the container to a staff worker, who immediately boarded a military helicopter. . . . We stitched the prisoner back up. . . . On our way back, traveling in the same car, I was told by the lead surgeon that the prisoner had been sentenced to death and would be executed the next day."

The doctor said that eight kidneys were removed by four surgical teams, and eight transplant operations were performed all in the same night. Obviously, taking two kidneys from a person is tantamount to execution. He said he had been told that the intended recipient of the first two kidneys he removed was a high-ranking military official.

I told him I would like him to go public with his experiences, but he said he could not.

I wondered how China justified this shocking practice. I soon discovered that the government was doing it the normal Chinese way: Do something first; then make a rule about it. In most places in the West, the law comes first. Not in China. The government already had taken away around two million people before it began writing its reeducation-through-labor regulations, which were issued in 1954.

This kind of retroactive policy also apparently applied to transplant regulations.

Transplants in general had begun in 1979 with Dr. Xia Shuisheng of the Tongji Medical University, but it was not until October 9, 1984, that government agencies recognized them legally. Six years later the document authorizing the practice was finally made public. It was entitled "On the Use of Dead Bodies or Organs from Condemned Criminals," and it allowed the removal of prisoners' organs under three conditions: first, if the body is not claimed; second, with the consent of the prisoner who is about to be executed; and third, with the consent of the prisoner's family.

There were other rules: "The use of corpses or organs of executed criminals must be kept strictly secret. . . . A surgical vehicle from the health department may be permitted to drive onto the execution grounds to remove the organs, but it is not permissible to use a vehicle bearing health department insignia or to wear white clothing. Guards must remain posted around the execution grounds while the operation for organ removal is going on." These clauses betray the government's desire to conceal from the public any knowledge of what the doctors are doing. It seems clear that police and doctors work closely together, supply and demand intertwining, as it were, with drastic results for prisoners who happen to be in the wrong place at the wrong time with the right organ and the right blood type.

According to the criminal code, which took effect on January 1, 1980, sixteen crimes are punishable by death, including corruption, embezzlement, and drug trafficking; nine of them are listed as counterrevolutionary. How many of China's prisoners are rapists and murderers, and how many of them are simply workers who raised their voices in complaint against corruption or inefficiency or stupidity? The government refuses to say. Amnesty International counted actual executions at 750 in 1990; 1,050 in 1991; 1,079 in 1992; and 1,419 in 1993.

The number of executions was rising at the same time the number of transplants was rising. Human Rights Watch/Asia would describe, in a report in August of 1994, two reasons the transplant programs were flourishing: "First, the commencement of a series of 'crackdown on crime' (*yan-da*) campaigns, held every year since 1983, which greatly

Harry Wu in Room 611 of the Karamay Hotel in Horgas, China, on June 21, 1995, the third day of his detention.

(*All photos from author's collection*)

Wu standing just inside the border on Friendship Bridge between China and Nepal, after his Tibetan colleague had entered the country.

ABOVE: Chinese security officials looking for Wu in the Nepalese village of Tatupani in August 1993. Wu took this photo from his hiding place in a small inn. BELOW: A duty prisoner holding a warning banner in the tea field of a *laogai* camp in Zhejiang Province in April 1994. A prisoner who goes beyond the warning banner will be shot.

One of the watchtowers of Zhejiang No. 1 Prison (April 1994).

The new signboard for Hangzhou Shenda Tool Factory, which in reality is Zhejiang No. 2 Prison (April 1994).

ABOVE: Prisoners in a lineup being counted after working in the Hangzhou Shenda Tool Factory (April 1994). BELOW: A *laogai* survivor demonstrates how he ate when his hands were cuffed behind his back twenty-four hours a day. He is wearing his father's *laogai* jacket. The father committed suicide in the camp, and the jacket was his only possession still in existence.

A Jinma diesel engine manufactured in Yunnan Provincial No. 1 Prison and imported into the United States by a company in San Diego. The U.S. Court of International Trade ruled, after a lengthy trial, that it could be legally imported.

Ching-Lee speaks out in San Francisco on July 16, 1995 at "Free Harry Wu Day," which coincided with a visit by the mayor of Shanghai. Linda Pfeifer, a friend active on behalf of Chinese and Tibetan human rights, is at her left.

Chain hoists made in Zhejiang No. 4 Prison. The CM brand (*left*) was sold in the United States, and the FELCO brand (*right*) in the United Kingdom.

Harry Wu dressed as a policeman, along with the *laogai* survivor Liu Jing Qin in August 1991, at the remote Qinghai No. 13 Laogai Camp. Liu, who obtained the uniform, was forced to give testimony (but did not tell the true story) against Wu at his trial in 1995. Liu, his wife, and his youngest daughter left China and came to the United States in July 1996, with help from the Laogai Research Foundation.

Left to right: Ed Bradley, Harry Wu, David Gelber, and Norman Lloyd on the bridge leading to Qinghe Farm, also known as the Beijing No. 1 Laogai Camp, in August 1991.

Ching-Lee and Harry Wu at their wedding on February 11, 1991, in Taipei, Taiwan.

BELOW: The BBC reporter Sue Lloyd-Roberts in the Taklimakan Desert during the visit to *laogai* camps in Xinjiang in early April 1994.

Father Wang, a priest who spent thiry-three years in various *laogai* camps because of his religious beliefs. Wu interviewed him in the United States in 1992 as part of the Laogai Research Foundation's oral history project.

ABOVE: Jeff Fiedler and Wu meet formally after testifying before a House subcommittee in September 1991.

Wu just after getting off the airplane in San Francisco following his release from China on August 24, 1995. His wife, Ching-Lee, is to his right; Jeff Fiedler is just behind him, to his left.

increased the number of criminals sentenced to death and hence the potential supply of transplantable organs; and second, the introduction to China of cyclosporine A, an acknowledged 'wonder drug' which greatly raised the success rate in transplant operations."

The Chinese government was sensitive about criticism of prisoners' organs being removed for transplants, but it did not deny that the practice existed. The United Nations Committee Against Torture paraphrased the remarks of Ambassador Jin Yongjian and his delegation in 1993: "Removal of organs without the permission of either the person or his family was not standard practice. There were, however, cases in which permission had been given to remove organs from the bodies of persons executed."

One thing I knew was that Chinese people traditionally do not donate their organs the way thousands in the United States and many other countries do. I've got a pink donor card in my wallet, so my organs can go on living in six or eight people, but Chinese tradition is that the body must be buried whole. Even cremation has been a drastic but necessary step, because so many people are living in crowded cities, and not everybody can afford to have his or her body returned to a native village for burial with his or her ancestors. Still, Chinese people on the whole cling to the desire to be buried in a natural state.

This tradition goes back to the old days, when the royal court had a select group of functionaries who could be trusted with the women of the household because their genitals had been removed when they were young. The body parts of the court eunuchs were preserved and guarded with great diligence, and when the eunuchs died, their families made sure their body parts were buried with them so they could enter the afterlife as complete individuals. Such beliefs do not die easily. Even forty years ago most rich people still chose to be buried in a private cemetery. Now, though cremation, like organ donation, is relatively new in China, it does have an appeal to most people, whereas organ donation does not.

The doctors know they are not going to get organs from people who die in car crashes or hospitals, because most families would not allow it and time is against it. So they go after the prisoners, testing their blood first, with the prisoners usually unaware of the reason for the test.

In February of 1994, I traveled to Toronto to work with a Chinese-born man with the Canadian Broadcasting Corporation. He placed a call to an administrator named Li who worked at Zhengzhou Number 7 People's Hospital, in the city where I had witnessed the forty-five executions in 1983. Telling Li that he needed to arrange a transplant for his boss, the Canadian man got Li to talk about the transplant business, and we taped the conversation without informing him.

Li said that more prisoners were being shot in the head than in the back because corneas are more readily available from other sources these days. "We can get them from patients who die," he said. But if kidneys or other internal organs were wanted, the doctor said, "you blow off the head, the brain is dead."

Li said he had been sent to Anyang to pick up kidneys from an executed prisoner. He said he was always warned that information about transplants "should be kept secret from foreigners. They all come from prisoners, death-row prisoners. . . . We buy the corpses. . . . Everything is approved."

Li then explained how the executions worked: "We drive the surgical van directly to the execution site. . . . As soon as the prisoner is executed, upon completion of necessary procedures by the Public Security Bureau and the court, the body is ours. . . . We buy the whole body. . . . From the legal point of view, once a prisoner has been shot, he no longer exists as a human being. He has no mind; he is only a corpse, only a thing."

He added that executed prisoners are labeled brain-dead, which means that legally doctors can extract the organs, but of course the prisoners are brain-dead on demand, with help from the police and the doctors. The corpses are then cremated, Li said. "What the family gets is an urn of ashes." He said that officials with the police and the court system were given gifts, like dinners and cigarettes, because "we need their help in lifting the corpse into the surgical van and to guard the execution site longer than usual so the van is not in public view. . . . We also give them gifts on special holidays."

This was the first time I had heard somebody talk about the concept of brain-dead prisoners. My stomach turned. An entire segment of Chinese society was being turned into grave robbers, desecraters of the dead. Naturally police techniques had to keep pace with the latest medical techniques. Back in the old days, they just blew away the back of the prisoner's head, the way I had seen done in the executions in Zhengzhou, but later the government needed photographs to document which prisoners had actually died, so it was sloppy to shoot prisoners in the head. Now, depending on what organ was needed, they were even more careful about how they killed their hapless prisoners.

I met Gao Pei Qi, formerly a deputy commander with the Public Security Bureau in Shenzhen, who had defected and lived in Hong Kong but was now in London. Gao said he had worked ten years for the bureau and had never heard of a prisoner giving his permission before the state removed an organ. Gao spoke of the new technique of shooting the prisoners in the back of the heart: "It may appear a bit more civilized because the face is left intact, but if one misses, the prisoner does not die right away. I saw some videotapes in which a prisoner was not hit in the heart and was left rolling around and yelling in great pain. A second shot had to be fired to end his misery.

"So for fear of missing the target, the criminal's back is either marked with chalk, or a knot is placed where the heart is so the executioner can aim. Even with such precautions, executioners do miss, in one case even hitting the hand of a Public Security officer who was propping up the criminal from the side. Sometimes after the order to shoot has been given, the executioner will poke the criminal with a bayonet to make him stand still, then promptly shoot him." Gao said that in Henan Province, he had watched as a prisoner who was about to be executed was propped up by two police officers and then shot from behind by a third officer. The prisoner was then given three kicks on the back and pushed into a pit, where his abdomen was trampled on to make sure he was dead. After this prisoner had been shot in the head, a forensic officer poked his brains with a pair of long tweezers placed through the bullet hole.

Still, some things remained the same: Executions were still taking place before major holidays, thus competing with movies and soccer matches as public spectacles.

Some hospitals advertised their kidney-transplant operations in Hong Kong and other cities. You could even express interest by answering by fax. I could hardly wait to try it. I wired the hospital at West China University of Medical Sciences and was sent a fax with all the details about transplants. The hospital boasted that its one-year survival rate for kidney-transplant patients was generally 82.35 percent, but in the most recent year, 1991, the rate had improved and was now 90.20 percent. The three-year survival rate was 70.33 percent, the five-year rate was 61.54 percent, and the longest survival, at that point, was thirteen years, seven months.

The Chinese authorities celebrated their success. I did not. The practice struck me as the ultimate human-rights violation. Somebody had to go behind the bamboo curtain and get more evidence. If not me, who? But how would I get there?

At the end of 1993, I was qualified to become a naturalized citizen of the United States, but usually the procedure takes a year from the time one first applies. After filling out some forms on January 5, 1994, I was stunned to be sent directly to the chief of the local Immigration and Naturalization Service, who walked me right into the judge's chambers. I found myself raising my right hand and swearing my allegiance to the United States of America. *Bam.* They put the seal on it, and presto, I was a U.S. citizen—in one day. The only trouble was I had not expected it so soon, so nobody had come with me. No friends, no witnesses, no photos, no celebration.

Twelve days later my passport came in the mail. When asked what name I wanted on the passport, I had said, "Peter Hongda Wu," remembering my alternative Western name from childhood, but when it arrived, it said, "Peter H. Wu." Better yet. Beijing still did not have the computer facility to check all the details and one's name and face, so I applied at the consulate in Chicago for one more legal visa, and it was approved. Maybe Peter H. Wu could get some information on organ transplants.

16

THE WILD WEST

Having failed to get into the captive nation of Tibet, I now decided to visit another subjugated region, the Xinjiang Uighur Autonomous Region in the northwest corner of China.

Xinjiang was fast becoming the home base of the *laogai* industry, with huge deposits of uranium, coal, gold, and graphite, and, according to the Chinese, seventy-four billion barrels of oil in reserve. No wonder Beijing wants to control these six hundred thousand square miles of mountains and desert as well as the indigenous people, Turkic Muslims known as Uighurs. After Mao came to power in 1949, he started stuffing Xinjiang with defeated Kuomintang soldiers and their families. My Number Three Brother, Wu Hong Dao, was sent there to teach in 1959, and I have not seen him since. It would be too compromising for me to see him now, but I wanted to feel close to him, maybe just walk down his street.

I had never been to Xinjiang, but I had been following its huge growth, from four million people in 1952 to approximately sixteen million people by 1994, divided between roughly 41 percent Han Chinese and 45 percent Uighurs.

The Chinese government admits to keeping more than 150,000 prisoners in Xinjiang, but I would multiply that number by five. In 1990, the *Xinjiang Legal Journal* said, "Xinjiang is one of the provinces where our country's *laogai* system plays a comparatively important role. They opened the desert to make farmland, planted trees to make forests, built roads and bridges, made bricks to build buildings, explored mines to extract coal, and manufactured goods." The journal made the workers sound heroic, like pioneers or settlers, but I knew better: These people performed their labor at the point of a gun.

To this day, the World Bank skips over the fine point that slave camps are big business, and it continues to fund major projects in Xinjiang. There was more than enough danger in Xinjiang for a roving troublemaker, and I wanted to share it with somebody.

As it happened, I had gotten a call from a journalist in London named Sue Lloyd-Roberts, who often works for the British Broadcasting Corporation, the best international news agency in the world. Her specialty is human rights, and she has been to some pretty rough parts of the world and was looking to visit China and Tibet. Did I know anybody who might want to travel with her?

Soon after that, I was in London, and we met at dinner. At one point, I reached into my jacket and pulled out my new blue American passport and said, "Look what I just got. The Chinese don't know I'm an American citizen. I'll go with you." She seemed surprised that I would take the chance, given my exposure on *60 Minutes*, but I told her the new passport would give Peter H. Wu the chance to do what Wu Hongda had done. We arranged a deal in which the BBC would pay for the trip and even finance a camera, and starting with the camps in Xinjiang, we would investigate the boom in organ transplants. This time, though, I could not pose as a businessman or a normal tourist since the region was closed to foreigners, so I altered some letterheads and business cards and became Peter Wu, professor of anthropology at the University of Oklahoma, and Sue became my assistant. We obviously had no connection to that school, but I felt we were not hurting anybody with these false credentials.

Our stated purpose was to study the Silk Road, the old trade route between Asia and Europe that Marco Polo had used to bring fabrics, spices, and other goods back to Venice. There are actually three routes called the Silk Road, and we chose the middle way, along the Tarim

River, just north of the Taklimakan Desert, because that's where the majority of prison camps in the area are located.

~

I met up with Sue Lloyd-Roberts in Frankfurt. She had had the BBC create a special bag for a hidden camera, with one-way translucent plastic covering the lens. We flew to Almaty in Kazakhstan and then to Ürümqi in Xinjiang and on to Aksu, near the border. We had no trouble at the border. Inwardly I heaved a huge sigh of relief.

Technically we were in China, but I had the feeling I was in a different world, a Muslim world, where the indigenous people looked at me as if I were a foreigner. We saw brightly dressed women, some covering their heads and faces with flashy silk veils and scarves and shawls that only called others' attention back to themselves. The men wore dark jackets. Some of them rode horseback out to the long, green valleys leading up to rugged gray hills. There, nomadic shepherds lived in felt tentlike homes, called yurts, their horses hitched outside, sheep wandering around, camels doing the heavy work. One had a sense of freedom, a sense that the people felt this land would once again belong to them as soon as they could get rid of these temporary visitors, but the visitors had no intention of leaving.

Our first step was to hire a private taxi. We knew that if the authorities hauled in the driver, he was going to talk, so we paid him a lot of money and hoped he wouldn't pay too much attention to what we were doing.

I was inclined to hire a Uighur on the theory that he would never divulge information to a Chinese official. But we met a Han, an ethnic Chinese, and he was not only a driver but a mechanic, a skill that would come in handy where we were going. I had some questions about his temperament since he had wrapped a bandage around his ear and across his forehead. He said he had gotten into a street fight with a Uighur and that five or six Uighurs had beaten him up pretty badly. "If there's a fight, you'll get a lot of Uighurs jumping in," he said. "But other Chinese people won't support their own people. They just stay away."

No matter what the official Chinese propaganda says, the Uighurs resent the Chinese, seeing them as intruders. The Uighurs have their own religion, their own language, which most Han Chinese (including me) do not understand, and strong ties to the predominantly Muslim states across the northern border in the former Soviet Union, so the Chinese are understandably nervous. There were pro-independence riots in Kashi in the 1980s, and the occasional bomb still goes off.

Because the Uighurs have a tradition of large families, the Chinese allow married couples to have two children rather than one, the legal limit everywhere else in the country. Judging from what I saw on our trip, most families are larger than that, which is explained by the old Chinese saying, "The mountains are high, and the emperor is far away."

The modern-day "emperor" has taken major steps to bring law and order to the mountains and the desert. There are approximately two million people in the quasi military in Xinjiang, over 90 percent of them Han Chinese. Simply put, Xinjiang is a colony, a colony with minerals and a captive labor force.

Even though he had been in a brawl with the Uighurs, our driver said he still hired Uighurs to work for him, and he even offered us a Uighur driver for a short trip. "You see, I don't have anything against Uighurs," he said. I sized him up as a man who would not go out of his way to turn me in. I told him that I was a professor studying the Silk Road and that I wanted him to follow the route just north of the desert. I knew that the labor camps were located along the river, which is useful for its water supply and as a dumping ground for all the camp factories' chemical waste.

"They used camels to travel back in the old days," I said. "Camels need water, so maybe there is a river just south of here. I'd like to see where they went for water."

We headed east from Aksu, driving through little towns where people dressed in the local costume, rugged country people, often waving or smiling or joking with one another. We saw cute little children who had to travel five or ten miles each way to school, dozens of Uighur men out in the middle of the day, shooting pool on outdoor tables. The Chinese are always saying there is no unemployment in the workers' paradise, but we saw an awful lot of men standing around at outdoor labor markets, looking for work.

Not far out of Aksu, we saw a labor camp, so I started filming.

"Why are you filming?" the driver blurted. "This is a labor camp."

"What is a labor camp?" I asked, playing dumb. "I'm an American scholar. I've never heard about it."

We got some pictures and kept heading east. The road was brutal. It was April, past the snow season, but ugly, cold, and dark. The first time it rained, Sue and I were astonished. Brown rain, windblown sand mixed in with rain, and great big gobs of mud falling from the sky, splattering on our windshield. Sand in your nose, your mouth, your throat—a desert storm.

When I wrote my first book, cataloging all the *laogai* camps, I listed the site of Talimu Farm, a major source of cotton for the clothing that is exported to the West, as unknown. Not too many things in this world are unknown anymore, but I could not pinpoint the location of Talimu in the vastness that is Xinjiang. This time we tracked it down.

When we got close to Talimu Farm, we told the driver to go south, but he balked. I reassured him that it was our idea, not his, and that we would take the responsibility, and besides, we were just studying the Silk Road, but he was not reassured.

"You should not go south. There are *laogai* camps down there," he said. "They will take my license away."

"We'll say we are lost," I assured him. "Can we try?" It was both a request and a command. He dutifully turned south, but he was nervous, and so was I.

We drove on the inner path of the farm for around five hundred yards, until we got to a dead end of cotton fields behind a grove of trees. The whole place was cold, dismal, bleak. I spotted prisoners in the cotton field, and soldiers with weapons, about a quarter of a mile away. My heart started thumping, a familiar adrenaline rush of anger and fear. The driver wanted to back up and get the hell out.

"Wait," I said.

Sue and I got out, walked eighty or ninety yards into the field, the video camera rolling. We walked to a clump of bushes and a dry ditch, hoping to get close to the prisoners. Suddenly a prisoner jumped out of the bushes, no more than two feet from me.

"Captain!" he shouted, making me jump.

I recognized the type: an older prisoner in the blue uniform, clearly trusted to act as a lookout. I had done this line of work myself years earlier. If a prisoner is trusted to keep an eye on the others, he has the freedom to snag a few vegetables from the ground or get first crack at the corn buns. Sometimes it means the margin between life and death. I had nothing against this man. He was struggling to survive. I only wished he would shut up and let me continue filming.

"Captain!" he shouted again.

I knew what this guy needed: a dose of authority. "Shut up," I hissed. "I'm looking for the captain myself."

Hearing me speak urban Mandarin with imperiousness, the watchman faltered. He was no longer so sure of himself. Instead of being the temporary master, he was back to being the slave.

A police officer approached and seemed agitated to see two civilians out in the field. I said we were lost, and he started to give us directions, and I dragged them out with plenty of questions while Sue spotted the prisoners moving toward us.

"Let's go," the officer said. "Where are you from?"

"America," I said.

To gain time for more filming, Sue chatted up the officer, smiling and flirting, trying to charm him. Finally he smiled and relaxed. Somehow, while she made small talk, she managed at one point to turn her back on the guard, whip out the camera, and shoot some tape of dozens of men in prison uniforms trudging through a cotton field out in the middle of nowhere. When she had enough tape, Sue charmed the officer again, and we got back into the car with our wonderful new directions.

Back to the Silk Road, we said. Our driver looked vastly relieved.

That afternoon we were driving through the Tanan Laogai Farm, where we noticed a single prisoner working next to a shed near the road. Not seeing anyone around, we decided to stop, figuring we could always say we were lost if questioned.

On my first two trips, I hardly had the chance to speak to a prisoner because of tight security. Because prisoners work in factories or on farms with guards all around them, I could only observe them from a distance and maybe take photos. Still, I always tried. I would put on my police uniform and try to mingle, but I knew that in these remote camps, all the guards knew everybody. This was a rare opportunity—a prisoner standing by the side of the road, alone.

We began to talk. He appeared weak, listless, defeated. He said he was from Shanghai, my hometown, so right away I felt an extra wave of empathy with him. He had gotten involved in a fight at the wrong time, just after Deng Xiaoping had announced a crackdown on street violence, and the authorities were throwing people in jail to please the chairman. At age eighteen, he had been sentenced to life, but after eleven years he came down with stomach cancer, and his jailers told him bluntly they were not going to pay for an operation. As a sporting gesture, they reduced his sentence to fifteen years; he had only four more years to go, if he lived that long. Still, he had probably outlived some of his pals from the streets of Shanghai. He told us this very openly. There was nobody around—and in his condition, what did it matter? He was too sick to work with the gang on the farm, so he had been assigned to the storage shed.

Sue took out her camera. I was trying to be dispassionate, telling myself it was my job to investigate human misery, but this poor kid really got to me. I was the same age when I got in trouble. Maybe he had made some mistakes, done some violent things, but unlike me he was almost sure to die young. I could feel my tears well up as he talked. His whole life—just down the drain. He let us look around the grubby little shed, with its tiny cot, no water, and two miserable wheat buns, hard as a rock, in a tiny bowl.

I reached into my backpack and began handing him the freeze-dried noodles and chocolate bars and biscuits we had brought to sustain us in the dismal outback of Xinjiang. I could see Sue's eyes widening, as if to say, "What are we going to eat for the next three weeks?" I even gave him the packs of lethal-smelling Marlboro cigarettes we had brought along as bribes for the heavy-smoking Chinese. But the way I saw it, at least we had money, at least we had hope, at least we had passports to get us out of here. This poor guy was going to die young in the wasteland of Xinjiang for what—a street fight?

He seemed lonely. Probably nobody had spoken a kind word to him since he was a boy. I had a strong desire to stay and protect him. But I saw Sue packing up her camera and gesturing to me. From the shed's open door, we could see a huge tractor pulling a truckload of prisoners, accompanied by officers, at the other end of the field.

"Let's get out of here," Sue said.

I knew it was crazy, but I didn't want to leave the kid.

"Harry!" Sue said.

I got into the car. This time we didn't have to tell the driver to roll out of there. He was already in gear, the motor running. But fifteen seconds later I said, "Go back! Go back!" They both said I was mad, but I insisted. We pulled back in front of the shed—the guards moving ever closer—and I jumped out of the car.

"Hey, give me back those cigarettes," I told the kid. "I'm not giving you those damn things. They are bad for your health."

I know it sounds bizarre, my taking back cigarettes from a sick prisoner, but I was acting on my emotions, wanting to protect him.

He handed me the packs, and I shoved some more candy bars and tins of food at him. "Hide this stuff under your bed, so they don't steal it," I said, nodding at the approaching guards.

"Harry!" Sue yelled at me.

I wanted to do something more for this kid. I reached into my pocket and found a business card, the phony academic's card with a real American phone number on it. "I know you can't contact me from here," I said to him. "but if you ever get near a phone and need help, you try to get in touch with me."

Sue was leaning out the open car door, filming the approaching tractor. If they caught us, we'd be working right here alongside the kid. I jumped into the car, and the driver peeled away.

I can still see the kid sitting by the side of the road, my business card hidden somewhere in his dusty uniform.

⌐

We kept heading east, through the desert, which sometimes rolled like the sea. The road was barely visible, blocked by reeds sticking out of the sand, just like on a beach. There were rivers or washes from the snow melting on the mountains to the north, flowing down to the Tarim River. The yellow-brown sands, always shifting, made for very difficult walking, except by camels. When the sun came out, it was exhilarating, but it was depressing when it rained because the car's tires would get stuck in the rutted mud, and we had to wait for a large truck to come by and haul us out. We ruined two tires and had to fix them in the mud. And sometimes, because of the occasional sandstorm, we just couldn't see at all and had to wait for the storm to end.

We stayed in nasty little places disguised as hotels. We didn't shower because there was no running water; we didn't have proper food, just chocolate, nuts, bottled water, stuff from tins. Sometimes we tried a meal in one of those small towns, but my system had long since adjusted to sanitary, appealing Western food, and I didn't want to take a chance of becoming sick by eating the unwashed, uncooked food.

Sue and I began to grate on each other. I have a temper and a strong will and the need to be the boss; as a journalist, she fits the same profile. One day we were taking some footage in front of a hospital, and she was doing what is called a stand-up, talking into the camera, risky for two people with foreign passports. I was getting better with a camera, but Sue would instruct me between takes: "Hold the camera still!" or "Move closer." Naturally I had my own ideas.

That night Sue looked at the footage from the day. "Rubbish, sheer rubbish," she muttered. She told me that while I had my field of expertise, hers was television, and I should listen to her and not try to push her around. "Harry, I was in Romania when Ceausescu went down," she said. "I was there a week, and I was arrested all seven days." She had been in enough tough places to know how to survive. She was not afraid of anything—including me.

We snapped at each other for a while, but we agreed to work together even if it meant that we would have two generals on this trip.

~

We approached the giant camp of the Thirteenth Regiment of the First Division, one of these half-military, half-production farms out in the middle of nowhere in Xinjiang. This was where my Number Three Brother, Hong Dao, had been living for more than thirty years as an exile because of his counterrevolutionary family. He was now the principal of a high school, and although he was never a prisoner, it was unlikely that he would ever be able to leave Xinjiang.

I knew I could not afford to be seen by him, but our driver just happened to park right outside the school, and I could hear the chatter of teachers and students. Somewhere in there was my brother. Would he recognize me after our not having seen each other since 1955? What would he think of me? After all, it was partly my own prominence as a "rightist" in college that had tainted him. Part of me wanted to seek him out, shake his hand, say, "Look, no matter what, I am your brother. I think about you, I care about you. Your daughter is my daughter." And part of me knew that would be the kiss of death, certainly for me, maybe for him. Suddenly I felt the need to get away, to leave him alone to live out his life here, without any more trouble from his meddlesome, wayward brother.

"Let's go," I told the driver, putting on my dark glasses so nobody could recognize my face or see my tears.

＿＿

We kept heading east, hoping to visit Lop Nur, the great dry lake at the edge of the Taklimakan Desert, but the road was closed. Our driver seemed relieved, because he knew his car was not rugged enough to test the washboard texture of the desert road.

In this desolate area, we began to notice that people had hideous white patches on their skin. We would ask what had happened, and many of them called it "my own personal disease," but Sue and I knew better. People said there were no fish left in the ponds and rivers and that the special Xinjiang fragrant pears, which they used to sell as a delicacy to the Japanese, were now being refused. The Japanese were not rejecting the pears because they were concerned that the people who picked them were little better than slaves. No, the Japanese did not want pears that glow in the dark.

This region is where the Chinese began testing nuclear devices in 1964, without adjusting for minor details like prevailing winds—or maybe such details didn't matter to them. Not surprisingly, the Soviet Union, just to the north, became upset about the nuclear clouds drifting toward it, and the two countries, ostensibly united in Communist brotherhood, bristled on the brink of war.

We met one man who said he had been forced by military police to go into the test area under the pretense of rounding up missing sheep. The Chinese authorities had brought in special doctors and divided people into control groups, using prisoners and their families for scientific tests. One witness, a medical technician, insisted the authorities had known exactly what they were doing. "They knew we were in there. We were just looking. We saw the yellow in the sky, golden colored, burning. The next day there was a big story in the newspaper that China had made a nuclear test."

This was considered a great triumph for Mao and communism—even when many people later developed white splotches on their skin. By 1986, a few brave people had actually protested the continuation of nuclear testing, and the regime put down this insurrection. Most people we met did not seem to understand what had been done to them, and I did not have the heart to tell them. Part of the world is becoming more responsible about nuclear testing, and the Russians even stopped unilaterally, but there is no predicting what the Chinese overseers will do to prisoners, to Uighurs, to Tibetans, to the environment.

We drove back to Korla, where we would take a train north to Ürümqi, and we said good-bye to our driver with the bandaged ear. He had done a great job, taking chances even when he sensed we were up to no good. I hoped he would be all right.

The capital of Xinjiang has a Mongol name that means "beautiful pastureland," but there is not much pastureland left. The city, located in the center of oil fields, resembles one of those boomtowns in the American West in the nineteenth century, but it also boasts a Holiday Inn that makes you think you're back in twentieth-century America—fifteen stories high, topped by a disco-restaurant, on a tree-lined boulevard with skyscrapers in the background and then the mountains. Ürümqi is a city of nearly 1.5 million people, with Han leaders, Han wheeler-dealers with contacts in Taipei and Hong Kong and Los Angeles and Vancouver. It's not a backwater anymore.

At the train station, Sue and I tried to buy tickets with yuan, the national currency. The clerks tried to charge us the higher foreigner rate, and they also wanted to charge us a 15 percent rate for not using foreign exchange notes. Figuring the clerks were indulging in a little personal capitalism, I argued my case. Meanwhile Sue was filming the station, the people on line, the people buying tickets, and when I turned around, I saw two female police officers closing in on her. They ordered us to the second floor of the station, lecturing us about taking photographs in a restricted area. I said I had not seen a sign forbidding cameras. A male officer demanded my passport, and I knew that if they scrutinized it too long, I risked big trouble. He glanced at it, saw it was American, and I snatched it back with no resistance.

"I want to see your chief," I shouted. I knew that if I were a Chinese citizen, they would have been beating me by now.

Sue was used to this kind of fracas, and she started shouting, "Don't touch me!" to attract the attention of police supervisors.

Pretty soon the chief and another officer arrived, and I began vigorously complaining about the "surcharge" on the tickets. "They're cheating me," I said.

Another officer told me, "The money isn't going into anybody's pockets; maybe it's a misinterpretation."

I continued to bluster, saying I was very disappointed in this behavior and threatening to complain when I got to Beijing. Mere mention of Beijing made them nervous, and the officer apologized.

Sensing that I was winning this round, I asked the officer why they were bothering Sue about the film, and he said, "Oh, okay, you can go."

But I could not leave well enough alone, and I could not resist twitting the two female officers who were following us out of the station. "I have a suggestion for you," I said. "I respect the Chinese government, I don't want to break the law, and you really ought to have a sign warning against picture taking."

They had had enough of me. "Okay, okay, have a nice trip, thank you."

When we were around the corner, Sue and I smiled at each other. In the land of the bully, you have to be a bit of a bully yourself.

17

HOSPITAL WATCH

On the train between Ürümqi and Chengdu, Sue and I changed our cover story. Instead of posing as researchers, we would now pose as an American couple who had come to China on a mission of mercy. We were hoping nobody would pick up on Sue's obviously British accent—and nobody did.

The story was that my uncle needed a kidney transplant *immediately*. I had brought along a letterhead from another major American university, on which a knowledgeable American friend, a doctor, had written down the proper medical language to describe my uncle's condition. His signature, like most doctors', was illegible. I've got to be honest and say that I had no qualms about using these made-up credentials. We were not using a real person's identity, we were not causing problems for anybody else, and our cause was just.

Our first stop was First University Hospital at West China University of Medical Sciences in Chengdu, where the doctor I met in 1992 in Hamburg had worked. This was hardly the first time the hospital administrators had seen Westerners, and they were extremely accommodating, letting us wander around by ourselves, even letting us take films.

The transplant wing was not your typical Chinese hospital wing, what with its private rooms, private bathrooms, private nurses, cleanliness, heating, modern technology, and wholesome food. Few questions were asked, particularly if a visitor seemed to have money.

We were the ones with the questions. We described how urgent my uncle's condition was; we asked about the nature of the conditions in surgery, the location of the operating room, always steering the conversation back to the quality of the organ that would be used.

"Don't worry," they said. "We guarantee good quality."

I asked to speak to a specialist in the urology department and was introduced to Dr. Yang Yuru, a professor of urology who had worked in New York in 1992. Dr. Yang positively glowed as he described the progress since the first kidney transplant in 1979. "We have performed over four hundred operations, ranking first in the country in the number of transplants performed," he said. "We can revive the kidney fast and at the appropriate time. We can guarantee the kidneys are working. The key point is the sooner the kidneys are removed, the better the chances are for a successful operation. As far as I know, there are too many legal procedures involved in kidney removal in the United States. The distance poses another problem. Sometimes it takes twenty hours, but here in China we are close to the donors, and it never takes longer than ten hours. Surgical vans are used in most cases." Dr. Yang said that kidney failure in postsurgical patients was 10 percent in China whereas it was 30 to 40 percent in the United States.

I had learned from the exiled doctor in Germany that Dr. Yang's hospital sometimes used helicopters to deliver the kidneys. If true, this was strong circumstantial evidence that the government itself was involved in the business of transplants, since civilians and private businesses are not permitted to operate helicopters in China.

Dr. Yang and his fellow doctors conceded that the hospital had used helicopters but that they did not need them anymore because special surgical vans are less costly and more convenient. Still, they insisted, the quality of the kidney to be used is just as good.

During the conversation, I slipped in a question about the donors of the kidneys.

"The organs come from brain-dead people, but our policy is we're not allowed to talk about it," Dr. Yang replied. "The patient and the patient's family are not allowed to have contact with the donor or the donor's family. But we guarantee it's good."

"But who is the brain-dead person?" I persisted. "Is it a worker? A peasant? From a man? From a woman? Did he die in a car accident? Did he die in surgery?" I wanted to go slow in introducing the concept of prisoners, because I could see their defenses were up. We talked to three doctors and one hospital official, a woman named Wu Jingping, the head of international relations for the hospital. They all steered us away from a discussion of the donors. I even suggested that my uncle might want to make a donation to the family of the donor, as a gesture of thankfulness, but the doctors were not going for my story.

I asked about the method of payment and was told bluntly, "We prefer cash—dollars." What about the waiting list? Two or three weeks, they assured me. The kidneys usually came from elsewhere in the same province in which the hospital was located, and they were always of good quality, always from "brain-dead people."

But where exactly did the kidneys come from? From whom? And how? The doctors pleaded ignorance. A Dr. Li, who said he had done 120 kidney transplants, told us, "We doctors only know the number of kidneys available and their arrival time. There is a unit [within the hospital] called the Scientific Research Department, which is responsible for contacting the kidney sources. . . . The source is confidential. . . . We remove from brain-dead people. . . . By state regulations, we are not allowed to talk about this at all."

I asked Wu Jingping to define *brain-dead.*

"I can't say exactly," she said. "Each country has its own standard, and therefore the definition is different. There exist some political differences between our country and the United States. In the United States, even the minute of death and trivial matters all seem to be tied to the issue of so-called human rights. It's very difficult. . . . We act according to our laws and reality."

Obviously there is a worldwide debate in medicine: When does death begin? When you stop breathing? When the heart stops? Are you truly dead if the brain still has measurable activity? While scientists and ethicists studied the problem, doctors all over the world sought to transplant vital organs to save the lives of patients. And here, in China, Sue and I were being offered a kidney from a donor, identity unknown, who, we were assured, was safely brain-dead.

I decided to be direct: "Is the kidney from a prisoner?"

"I'm not talking prisoners at all," Wu said.

I acted as if my family were squeamish about who the donor might be, but Wu remained vague. "Things in our country are different from yours," she said. "We can do what is impossible from the legal point of view in your country. As to contact with the kidney donors, it is impermissible. But we do guarantee that our kidney donors are healthy and that the organs are of excellent quality." (She was speaking English, which was very good for Sue's hidden camera.)

"In two or three weeks, we can get a living kidney," Wu continued. "A team of surgeons will be sent for removal and delivery of the organ at a fee of of between eight and twelve thousand U.S. dollars, cash preferred. We receive customers from Hong Kong, Taiwan, the United States—from all over the world."

I persuaded Wu and the others to let us film an operation so we could reassure the folks back home. They were not nervous about the camera because they seemed to accept us as potential customers with money, trying to document China's high medical standards. I asked to see a kidney transplant, but they said they would let us film a heart operation to show off their excellent facilities. Fine. The next day we returned and shot footage of the surgeon placing an artificial valve on a heart, knowing full well it was not a kidney operation.

Sue and I both felt good about the visit to the hospital at West China University of Medical Sciences. We were sure their evasiveness, most of it in English, would show up on television. And it did. (Later, when the BBC documentary was aired, it included footage of the operation, but never once did the narrator claim it was a kidney transplant.)

⚯

Outside Chengdu, Sue and I went to Xinkang, the largest asbestos mine in the world, with its ten thousand people, approximately six thousand of them prisoners. We saw prisoners in chains being led out to dig asbestos—with their bare hands—and only a few wore masks. This lack of protection is totally unacceptable in the West because it is known that inhalation of asbestos can lead to cancer. For many of the prisoners we saw at Xinkang, no matter what their official sentences were, their real sentence was the same: early death.

This was the end of Sue's journey with me. We had spent eighteen days together, and I hoped she would not have any trouble leaving the country. I was worried that somehow the Chinese authorities had gotten wind of our trip. This was a source of constant anxiety. After all, after my appearance on 60 *Minutes*, I could no longer take my anonymity for granted. Sue left for Guangzhou and passed through customs without incident.

On April 18, Ching-Lee arrived, traveling with Shannon Ramsby, a friend of ours who worked with Jeff Fiedler at the AFL-CIO and often helped us with the foundation. I had shocked him by asking whether he would travel with Ching-Lee and also provide security for us on the trip and then take film and documents out with him. He had never been to China, but he had an American passport that would provide some help if we were spotted. Even with her American green card, Ching-Lee was still a Taiwanese citizen and would not have full political protection should anything untoward happen.

Shannon's role was to stay in the same hotel, keep an eye on us, but not travel to the camps with Ching-Lee and me because that would call attention to all of us. My orders to him were that if we disappeared, he should get out of the country as quickly as possible and let my friends know I was in trouble.

One day in Chongqing, we told Shannon we would be back by one in the afternoon, but we got delayed and did not return until six. When we saw him, he had a wild look in his eye, and I know he was thinking of packing and getting out of there. "This was my first real taste of fear," Shannon said later. "You know what it's like when you're a kid and you're walking in the dark alone? That's how I felt the whole time."

After a few camps, we decided to take a three-day excursion on the Yangtze River through the Three Gorges area. We figured this might be the last time we could see what is often called China's most beautiful natural region. In Chongqing, engineers were preparing to dam up the river at Sandouping to end the dreadful flooding downriver and create a gigantic lake that would change the face of China forever.

We took the best accommodations possible, called second class, which meant Ching-Lee and I had a room together and Shannon had to share a room with another man.

On the ferry, as we churned downstream toward the proposed dam, I noticed two People's Liberation Army soldiers in their informal uniform of slacks and a sweater with the army emblem. I did not think they were looking for me, so I decided to chat with them and discovered they were heading to their next post, near Wuhan. I decided these guys could help me find a place in Wuhan for Shannon to stay while Ching-Lee and I explored a few camps in the countryside. I thought Shannon was going to hyperventilate when he saw me chatting with these two soldiers, who had already noticed that he was the only Westerner on the ferry. They were friendly enough, but they declined to help Shannon, saying it was too much trouble. I knew I was on China's most-wanted list by then, but I did not figure these two young soldiers would be looking for Harry Wu on the Yangtze.

We got off the steamer at Shashi, and the three of us were forced to spend the night in the same hotel room because of overcrowding. The next day we went on to Wuhan, where Ching-Lee and I visited another organ-transplant hospital, Tongji Medical University. We had heard a great deal about the pioneering work at the Research Institute of Organ Transplantation and about its chief surgeon, seventy-two-year-old Dr. Xia Shuisheng, who was attracting patients from all over the world. This time I really would be married to my companion as we inspected the hospital.

Business must have been good. Just outside the ninth-floor elevator, we saw a huge mirror with a little plaque saying it was a gift from a Thai businessman named Wang, who had received a new kidney there in February.

We were received graciously by the hospital's officials. Ching-Lee and I explained our visit, saying that my uncle needed a kidney. I wanted to observe recovery conditions so I could tell my uncle exactly what to expect. We would have to await his approval before making arrangements.

The next day a young assistant escorted us around the recovery area of the transplant wing. Suddenly he was stopped by a colleague who needed to discuss something. The young doctor asked us to sit and wait a few minutes, and he disappeared into a nearby room. It was too good a chance to pass up. As soon as he was gone, we rushed down the hall. Nobody stopped us, and so we started looking for a patient.

In a room off a corridor, we spotted a man sitting up in bed, looking healthy, eager to talk to somebody. The man, who said that his name was Li and that he worked in the financial bureau of the municipality of Wuhan, told us the doctors had said the kidneys came from executed prisoners. "Five of us had our kidney transplants done on the same day. There were six kidneys available that day. One was sent to another hospital. . . . All from young prisoners, all under twenty-five and very healthy."

Ching-Lee whipped out the camera from the bag strapped over her shoulder and kept an eye on the door while I chatted with Li and other patients in the room listened to the conversation. We were taking a big risk.

Li told us that the prisoners had been executed in the Dongxihu district of Wuhan, forty minutes from the hospital. "They were executed at eleven in the morning, and we had our operations at two in the afternoon," Li said. The other patients confirmed with their nods and smiles that they, too, had received prisoners' organs. These people were all grateful, glad to be alive, proud that modern Chinese medicine can give them a second chance at life. For a moment, I felt a tremor of remorse for fighting this system, but then I remembered where these people's kidneys had come from—from people just like me.

We must have had ten profitable minutes talking to these patients before a doctor passed by the ward and noticed Ching-Lee and me chatting with the patients and filming the conversations. Suddenly the hospital's chief doctor, Xia Shuisheng, appeared and began to shout, "Who allowed you to come here? This is a private ward. Let's go." He started giving us what is called the bum's rush in English while asking me who had given us permission to enter the ward. I told him that other doctors had arranged for my visit, and he calmed down a little, but he and several other doctors continued to hustle me and Ching-Lee down the hall. I neither complained nor resisted. All I wanted was to get out of the hospital with my film and my camera intact, without getting into an argument or being grilled by hospital security and the police. We hustled down the hall, past the elaborate mirror, the gift from the Thai businessman, and into the elevator, straight down nine floors and out into the street. I did not mind. It's amazing what you can learn in ten minutes.

From Wuhan, Ching-Lee and I set off for Jingzhou, on the outskirts of the city, to get information on Jingzhou Number 3 Prison, which exported eighty-five million dollars' worth of textiles to several countries, including the United States, in 1989 alone. While we were filming in the town, we noticed a poster on a brick wall outside the Judicial Bureau and also on the message boards at the railroad station, describing the execution of three prisoners on April 19, the same day the transplants at the Tongji Medical University took place. The poster did not specify where the executions were held, but anyplace around Wuhan was certainly within reach of surgical vans or helicopters servicing the hospital.

Of course I have no proof linking the poster announcing the three executions with the six kidneys, but the fresh kidneys came from somewhere—from healthy prisoners who were conveniently brain-dead. The time and proximity of the executions in Jingzhou meshed with the operations on the patients in Wuhan, making me suspect these were the sources of the kidneys. I had heard enough to convince me that organ transplants were a new menace to prisoners.

Now it was time to get back to visiting the camps. On April 26, we all flew from Wuhan to Nanjing, but Shannon flew on to Shanghai, where he had an adventure on his own. At the Shanghai Airport, he was standing in line waiting for a taxi when a modern sedan pulled up directly in front of him and a Public Security man leaped out wielding a camera. The man took a quick photograph of Shannon, then turned around, took a few other quick snapshots, and leaped back into the car. Shannon knew that he, as the only Westerner on that line, had been the target, and he wondered whether the police were already on to him. He had to sweat that out while Ching-Lee and I took a bus south into Anhui Province on a personal mission.

A friend of mine in Los Angeles named Liu Xing Hu had given me the uniform his father had worn at Baimaolin Farm when both had been imprisoned during the Cultural Revolution. Although they were on the same farm for ten years, they saw each other only twice. The son survived by working in the crematorium, a job given to the healthiest young men, who were fed better so they could work harder. Finally the father committed suicide, and the son inherited his tattered dark-gray uniform, with at least forty individual patches on it. The son eventually escaped to the West and asked me to pay homage to his father at Baimaolin Farm. I did more than that. With the help of a former prisoner named Zhang, I took some photographs of the factory there, where they make tables with English-language labels on them.

Our next target was the Wuyi Machinery Factory in Zhejiang Province, just south of Shanghai, where they make chain hoists for export to the West. Here we got lucky. We were standing at a bus stop, discussing Wuyi, when a man said to me, "Are you looking for the old place or the new place?" It turned out the old factory is out in the countryside while the new factory is right in town, with a couple of thousand workers, including prisoners. I asked the man how he knew that, and he told me his sister worked in the new building, and he gave us directions. Ching-Lee and I found the new place, where I noticed an office still under construction. I walked in and looked out the window and took some footage, and nobody seemed to pay any attention.

Our next stop in Zhejiang was the tea plantation at Nanhu, a joint venture with the Japanese. We found the farm, and we spotted prisoners across the field, so we walked straight toward them so I could launch into my "lost tourist" routine, asking for directions while Ching-Lee took more footage. On our way out, we noticed a company store, which was selling bags of tea marked in English, obviously for export. I bought a package to use as evidence and stuffed the bag in my knapsack.

Unfortunately when Ching-Lee and I got off the bus in Shanghai, I left the knapsack behind. I was frantic, and we rushed off to the bus depot, trying to find the bus, but it was midnight, and everything was closed, and nobody would help us. I worried that somebody would find the tea and figure out what we were doing.

Our paranoia level was pretty high as Ching-Lee and Shannon prepared to leave from Shanghai on May 2. Shannon had negatives of thirty-five-millimeter film, probably six inches thick and six inches long, distributed in his socks and in a case strapped around his waist, and I knew he was suffering because, as he said, "I am not a smuggler; this does not come naturally to me." I waited near the departure gate as a clear signal in case the police were tailing us. Probably they would want to catch me leaving the country, so they would not stop Ching-Lee and Shannon, and the photographs and other evidence would get out safely. They got on the plane, and I turned around to let the officials know they still had me if they wanted me, but nothing happened.

I left the international airport at Shanghai and quickly took a domestic flight to Qingdao, the hilly coastal city the Germans had helped build during their imperial days. Now the Chinese did their own colonizing, using their own people.

I had a few more courtesy calls to make. First, some background. In November of 1991, the good folks from the Laiyang Steel-Pipe Factory had been kind enough to visit California for the Shandong Province Trade Fair in San Francisco. Their brochures bragged about selling to the Middle East, Europe, America, but they also listed the manager's name and the factory's address, which matched information on documents I had showing a prison camp at the same address, with the same man as police manager. In one picture, the big shot is wearing a suit, and in the next picture he is wearing a uniform.

Bob Windrem, a producer with NBC, had gone along with me to the fair, posing as the marketing manager of my company. We had placed an order for more than two thousand tons of vulcanized steel pipe and received more documents proving the factory is a prison camp. But the officials at the show noticed the camera and jostled the NBC cameraman to try to spoil the footage. I asked one official whether the pipe was made by prisoners, and I showed him a document listing the factory's camp name. He took out his pen and crossed out the name of the camp and wrote down another factory name. The Chinese just take for granted that the average American businessperson does not care and will not ask questions. When I went back with George Lewis, an NBC correspondent, we asked the people from Shandong about the change of name, and they insisted they had just learned of it.

Three years later I thought it only good manners to go back and visit the friendly folks from Laiyang. I quickly took a taxi from Qingdao out into the countryside, into Shandong Province. I was taking a chance by going to Shandong, way up north, all by myself, because there was nobody to watch my back. If I was caught, I could disappear.

The front entrance to the Laiyang Steel-Pipe Factory was rather pleasant, like a regular office; the prison entrance was at the rear of the building. I wanted an overview of the prison, so I found an accommodating civilian who allowed me up on the roof of a tall building across the street. In addition to the main factory building, I could see a prison farm with corn and wheat fields. I took some photographs of the entire facility and of gangs of male prisoners doing farm work, others lugging steel pipes.

I decided to take a closer look. I walked around the facility and saw family members visiting prisoners through the back door, which obviously one does not see at normal factories using free workers. Noticing a guard tower, I hid in a nearby ditch for about half an hour, to make sure I was not being observed. I wanted to film the men working inside, maybe 150 yards away. All was quiet and peaceful, so I climbed out of the ditch and started walking toward the wall, right under the watchtower.

Big mistake. The minute I pointed my camera, I heard a voice shouting, "Hey, you over there. Stop!"

The guard must have been inside the watchtower the whole time, napping, eating, reading—whatever. Now he wanted to do his job. "What are you doing?"

"Nothing," I said.

"Stay there."

He disappeared into the guard tower, rushing down the stairs. I figured I had maybe fifteen seconds to save my life. Instead of running away, I noticed that the door had a clasp, where a lock could be inserted. I did not have a lock, but I did pick up the sturdiest-looking stick on the ground and inserted it into the clasp. Then I jumped into the ditch for cover and started running.

For all I knew, another guard in the watchtower was pointing a gun at me. I hoped he would shoot into the air first, as a warning. "They wouldn't shoot me right away," I reasoned. "They want to catch me first." But I could not be sure. If they found my passport, at the very least they would confiscate my film, but more likely I would never get out of China.

I kept running. I was no longer the rugged little infielder who played baseball in Shanghai and Beijing. I was a fifty-seven-year-old troublemaker who suffered from a bad leg, a bad back, bad food, and bad beds—and I was trying to run some film back to America. I could not outrun my bad dreams. Now I was trying to outrun a bullet.

I sprinted down the ditch, sprinted away from the steel-pipe factory, and kept running for two hundred yards, until I reached the highway. I was afraid the guards would catch up to me, so in desperation I tried to flag down a passing vehicle, knowing that hitchhiking is not common in China. For whatever reason, a truck driver stopped and gave me a lift out of the area. Nothing happened, nobody came, nobody caught me. I was lucky—that time.

⁓

Jeff still says my last mission to Liaoning Province, in the northeast corner of China, sandwiched between North Korea and Mongolia, was the most dangerous one I ever made. I was totally alone, with no backup, no nothing, far from anybody who would even think about diplomatic niceties if I got caught.

My goal was Shenyang, to visit what I call Laogai Boulevard: a collection of terrors on one street, five major prisons right in a row on New

Life Path, just quivering with guards and police. I walked down that street with my video camera running inside my bag, and I estimated that 90 percent of the people were guards or police officers or very official-looking men in civilian clothes. This was the home base.

At one factory, the prisoners make rubber accelerators for Western vehicles, and another factory produces rubber boots for a prominent retailer in the United States, using shady dealers as middlemen. Jeff has a photograph of an unidentified American business official visiting this camp, and he vows one day he will put a name to the face.

I was interested in one specific camp on Laogai Boulevard. In my zeal to expose prison-camp conditions, I had not especially focused on women prisoners, who constitute perhaps 3 percent of the camp population in China. But I wanted to document the Shenyang Women's Prison, with its estimated three thousand inhabitants, who make perfume and clothing.

I found the women's camp and sat down on the sidewalk, drinking some water and scouting out the neighborhood and planning my next move. I noticed a vantage point from the hospital across the street. I walked in and told the receptionist I was visiting a friend, paid the two-yuan admission charge, and worked my way upstairs, past a few floors of operating rooms and a few floors of wards. Still looking for the best angle from which to photograph, I opened a door on the top floor and slipped inside. From the window that opened onto the street below, I got a great view of the camp. Then I turned around to scan the room itself and saw jars and vats of body parts: hands, feet, arms, legs—all preserved in alcohol. The room did not appear to be a working classroom for medical students. It was just a dusty storage room for body parts. I felt my stomach turn over. "Just keep looking out the window," I told myself, but then I would turn my head, fascinated by this chamber of horrors.

I forced myself to take long-distance shots of the women prisoners and their guards milling around in the yard across the street. I worried about getting caught but somehow convinced myself that not many people in the hospital would be likely to check out this particular room. I got my pictures, and then I willed myself not to look again as I left the room and slipped downstairs. The women's camp was my twenty-seventh separate camp in the past month. It was time to go home.

———

My friend Jeff Fiedler says of my trips, "The two most dangerous times are entering and leaving—just like the takeoff and landing of an airplane." And it's true. That's when one is most likely to be nabbed. I was all by myself, didn't have anybody else to take the film, so I had to do it myself. I made a reservation for a direct flight to Hong Kong, to throw the authorities off the track, and at the last moment I veered off my plan.

After securing my luggage at the airport, I took a taxi back to the hotel. I had already taken my stuff out of my room, but I had paid for another night just to confuse anybody who might be following me. I took the elevator up, promptly went back down, and took a different taxi back to the airport, where I took a domestic flight from Shenyang down to Shenzhen and then a ferry across to freedom.

As Jeff and I had previously agreed, I went to his room at the Prudential Hotel in Hong Kong and knocked on his door. It had been a week since anybody had heard from me. He opened the door, and we both cried.

"You look terrible," he said. "Promise me one thing," Jeff said once he had recovered. "Promise me you will never do this again."

"Okay," I promised.

18

HOLOCAUST

I went home from Hong Kong in May of 1994, but after gaining a sense of the transplant business, I realized I had some unfinished business with the Chinese doctor in Hamburg. In August, I joined Sue Lloyd-Roberts in Berlin, and we arranged a trip to Auschwitz, to strengthen my connection with the Holocaust, with all people who have suffered.

When I was a young student in China, I had heard of the German campaign against the Jews, but after I had lived in the West for a year or two, I realized just how cold-blooded and methodical the Nazis had been. They systematically exterminated some six million Jews and another five million Catholics, Protestants, Communists, Gypsies, homosexuals, dissidents, people of conscience, people who had spoken out, people like me, inconvenient people, troublemakers of one sort or another.

I read how Adolf Hitler carefully used euphemistic phrases like "final solution," how only later did the world discover what he had meant, and how his assistants interpreted and carried out his orders. The photographs of Hitler, that terrible sneer on his face, his eyes bulging out, were a warning to the world that he would kill anybody in his way. One never saw Mao with an ugly expression on his face, but in my opinion he ranks right up there with Hitler because of the way he methodically damaged an entire people, in this case, his own. Mao killed just as many people as Hitler, maybe even more. He intentionally sought to destroy the traditional Chinese family system because it is inherently subversive of the collective Communist utopia he wished to build. With a sweet smile on his face, he was responsible for millions of deaths from starvation as a result of his lunatic agricultural policies; he was responsible for millions being banished to camps, for many thousands being executed.

My office in California is cluttered with tapes, books, manuscripts, videos, and letters, but I always know where my personal Chairman Mao book of quotations is. Not his book of sanitized sayings, but the one describing his ugly words and deeds that crippled an entire people. I still study Chairman Mao. In his public documents, he used terms like "suppression" and "purge," but in his internal documents he often used the word *sha*—the Mandarin word for "kill." On January 17, 1951, he issued the following instructions to his accomplices, including Deng Xiaoping: "In 21 counties in west Hunan, over 4,600 bandit chieftains, local tyrants and Kuomintang agents were killed. Another batch are planned to be killed by local authorities. I think this disposal is very necessary." On May 16, 1951, in another confidential memo, Mao said, "Talking about the number of counterrevolutionaries to be killed, a certain proportion must be set; in rural areas, it should not exceed one thousandth of the population, while in urban areas it should be below one thousandth of the population: 0.5 thousandth seems appropriate. For instance, among the two million population of Beijing, over 600 were killed. Another 300 are planned to be killed. A total of 1,000 will be enough."

Mao often had a political motive for his killings. He would advise his people to wait for the appropriate moment in a campaign. Kill to prove the point. Kill to show he meant business. "Kill the chicken to frighten the monkey."

Of course our friends the Russians had shown us the way with Stalin's gulag system. Mao had invited Soviet gulag experts to China. I have seen the Chinese documents saying that the first Chinese labor-reform laws were worked out with the help of Soviet experts. At that time, the Chinese people were proud to say they learned from the Soviets. There was a grand link of military, cultural, judiciary, public security. We learned from the experts.

When I came to the United States, I realized that China was not always the center of the universe, certainly not for mass tragedy. I became engrossed with the Holocaust, reading books, watching documentaries, asking questions. I learned about Kristallnacht in Germany in November of 1938, the destruction of the synagogues and more than seven thousand Jewish businesses, ninety-one people killed nationwide, and about thirty thousand Jews delivered to the concentration camps of Buchenwald, Dachau, and Sachsenhausen.

In Beijing, Mao called for the Red Guards to "take revolutionary action," which they did on the day and night of August 18, 1966, rampaging through the city, killing whoever displeased them, 1,741 people in all. They did not kill for reasons of religion or ethnicity but for politics. "My neighbor is a capitalist? Torture him, kill him." It was the same all over China. I felt a terrible link with the Jews whose lives were destroyed on Kristallnacht and during all the other official pogroms.

The first Nazi camp I visited was Dachau, in November of 1992, on a depressing, rainy day. I went in through a side door and noticed a dormitory, where the prisoners had slept, crowded together, five or six hundred people who were given five minutes a day to use the so-called bathroom and then get out. Just a sink and water. Hundreds of people waiting for dirty water. For a moment, I found myself thinking, "These conditions are no worse than ours were." But then I remembered that this was a work camp for prisoners of the Nazis, and I felt sickened.

When I left Dachau, I went out through the front gate, where I noticed the slogan on the iron grillwork: ARBEIT MACHT FREI. I asked somebody to translate it and was told, "Labor makes (you) free." I was stunned, and I asked, "Are you sure?" and my friend said yes. I said, "In China, the slogan for our camps was 'Labor makes a new life.' "

I left Dachau more confirmed in my belief that the Chinese and the rest of the world must respect the Jews for what they have suffered. I had come to the West to find kindred spirits, common bonds. From my reading, I knew that during the Second World War, the United States had information about the Nazi camps, the British knew about them, the Vatican knew about them, but they did nothing. The International

Red Cross and other groups had to know, but they would say, "It is wartime; what can we do?"

In August of 1994, I had to see Auschwitz. One hot day, Sue and I took the train from Berlin. I was going to see the gas chambers with my own eyes, to try to imagine what it was like to be herded into that room. I needed to connect myself with the ghastly piles of hair, the mountains of clothing, the nearly two million people who perished there, so I asked Sue to take my picture in front of the displays. I think she was a little put off by my posing as a tourist, but I had no qualms. I had to link myself with this other culture. They suffered; we suffer.

I closed my eyes, and I imagined myself in Germany in 1944. The Nazis had their own doctors, not political people, just ordinary citizens doing their job. Every day those doctors saw hundreds of people going to the gas chamber. Tortured. Burned. Killed. But that wasn't all. These doctors had research programs. All in the name of science. Maybe they were studying how long it would take for a pilot to lose consciousness if his plane was disabled and he lost oxygen. The doctors did not want to experiment on their own airmen, so they would talk to the camp commandant and say, "Hey, can I have someone?" This was not a medical experiment on a mouse or a dog. They needed a human being to experience this terrible pain. And so the doctors would take a Jew and perform experiments on him. Maybe they would even promise a prisoner good treatment, good food to produce a healthy body for the experiment. And maybe the prisoners thought, "At least I will survive today, enjoy better food, and tomorrow I'll die. I'll take it." The Nazi doctors would check the color of the subject's eyes, his hair; their geneticists became involved in documenting details of people who were one-quarter-Jewish, half-Jewish. It sounded familiar to me. The Chinese had economy "doctors," political "doctors." They documented what one's grandfather did for a living, one's class. If someone married a woman of a poorer class and then lost his property, he was still part of the landlord class, he still had tainted blood. It was like being one-quarter-Jewish. Obviously there was a difference. The Germans did not regard the Jews as part of their race. When the Americans and Russians were coming, the Nazis followed through on Hitler's final solution.

Would it have happened without Hitler? I don't know. I visit Germany frequently and have many friends there. The Germany I know has many fine people who care about human rights in their own country and around the world. Could there have been another Hitler? Could there have been another Mao? Why not? In China, we did not have Hitler's gas chambers, but in a racial sense, we do put Tibetans and Uighurs and other minorities in a special category. And we put our own troublesome people, our class enemies, in camps and make them work. I have no doubt that if war came, the Chinese would kill the people in the camps if they could not use them. The Chinese have created an enemy, a separate class, a prisoner class.

History shows that the Chinese will not hesitate to kill one another. The Kuomintang was not innocent—let's start with that. After the war against Japan, the Communists came down from their base in the northwest, marching, invading, attacking, setting up local systems. After the Long March in 1934–35, they already had prisoners in labor camps. In 1948, when the Kuomintang counterattacked, the Communists withdrew, killing their prisoners.

After the war, the defeated Nazi soldiers and doctors would say they were not responsible for the killing. Hitler and Heinrich Himmler had ordered it. They were just following orders. They were experimenting with human lives. Eventually some of the Nazis were tried and convicted for their crimes against humanity and were executed.

After posing for my photograph that day in Auschwitz, I knew it was time to visit the Chinese doctor in Hamburg. Sue and I went to his house and were received graciously. His wife cooked us a nice dinner. But I was still tortured by what I had heard in China—and what I had seen at Auschwitz. My emotions were high as I led him back to the subject of the transplants he had seen as a young doctor in China. "Let me ask you something," I said to the doctor. "If you take two kidneys out of a human being, how long can he live?"

"Probably less than twenty-four hours," he said. "Some people last just a few hours; then they die."

That was enough for me. The doctor had saved the lives of unhealthy patients, and he had risked his own life to criticize the Chinese government, but he had also participated in taking both kidneys out of prisoners, prisoners like me. I stood up, and I told him, "Doctor, you are a murderer."

His wife looked stunned. "What are you talking about?" she asked.

"You and your colleagues killed them. You took away their organs. The next morning they were executed, but that doesn't matter. You executed them."

"I am not a murderer," the doctor said evenly.

"Yes, you are," I insisted. I was thinking to myself, "You call yourself a doctor, but you are a killer. You are no different from the doctors who worked for the Nazis. You use words like *mercy* and *charity*, but you are a killer."

Although the doctor spoke some English, this exchange had been in Chinese and was so calm that Sue was not aware of what I had said. To her, the doctor seemed shocked, depressed, frustrated rather than mad.

He could not deny that I was telling the truth, but he was not ready to face it either. The concept of human rights was so far beyond his mentality that he could not change even though he had been in the West for a while. He had to tell himself, "I save lives." There I was, now a free man in a German city, accusing a Chinese doctor in exile of once having behaved like a Nazi. He had to think, "I did it in the name of medicine. I'm not responsible. It wasn't my fault. They made me do it. It was the other guy."

Sue and I left his house. Up till then, I had resisted the BBC's desire to use footage of the doctor because I did not want to tarnish him, but now that I had heard his weak rationalizations, I no longer objected. "Go ahead and use the footage," I said, and the filmmakers did, although when the documentary was put on the air, the BBC did blur out his face from the scene at the dinner, where he had admitted helping to take kidneys out of doomed prisoners. I vowed that the world would know what we Chinese had done to one another.

～

While I was in Europe in 1994, I also went to the Anne Frank House in Amsterdam. I felt a strong kinship with this Jewish family, hiding in a room, trying to avoid the Nazis. I know Chinese who have hidden other Chinese at grave risk to themselves.

Many people have seen the movie *Schindler's List*, about one German-speaking man (a Czechoslovakian Roman Catholic of Austrian descent) who helped many Jews escape deportation to death camps. The same things have happened in China. We must honor the good people who resisted, the good people who gave water or food or shelter or safe passage. Even if money changed hands, helping Jews was always dangerous. We must remember our Schindlers as well as our Anne Franks. It was too late for Anne Frank and her family and millions of other Jewish people, but I stood in that little house in the middle of Amsterdam, and I thought, "At least they have their place now. People remember Anne Frank. We Chinese are human beings, too. Who will remember us?"

In 1993, the AFL-CIO mounted an exhibition of photographs in conjunction with the opening of the U.S. Holocaust Memorial Museum in Washington, D.C. My friend Jeff Fiedler and I went down to the lobby of his office to see the photographs, and I found myself seething with anger at the images of gas chambers and death-camp dormitories.

Two officials of the Holocaust Museum happened to be in the lobby, and we got to talking, and they invited me to the museum. Not only does it have a haunting display of photographs of the death camps, but it also has a huge database of hundreds of thousands of names. You can type in a name or a place, and the computer gives back information: more names, ages, places of birth, when persons were sent to the camps, their approximate date of death. You touch another button, and information about survivors pops up on the screen: their words, their faces, a vivid picture of suffering and survival.

I was transfixed. I stayed in front of those computers for as long as I could. I understood why the Jewish people repeat to themselves, "Never again." The Jewish people do not forget their own. The rest of the world must never forget them either. I dared to confide in one of the museum officials my dream that someday the word *laogai* would be as well known to the world as *Holocaust* and *gulag*. I was hoping the museum official would not think I was downplaying the horror of the Holocaust, but he understood my emotion and encouraged me to protect the memory of my own people.

While walking back the few blocks to Jeff's office, I began to dream that someday there would be a *laogai* museum to tell the story to our children's children. After all, I was already collecting information on the Chinese people in the *laogai*: who went, who survived, what happened to them. By 1993, I had already collected audio and video interviews of two hundred people. What about the millions of others who disappeared? Who speaks for them?

Today in America, you hear ignorant people say, "Oh, the Holocaust was exaggerated. Maybe it never really happened." I have heard the same thing said about the *laogai* system. I want to expose the system. I am the needle in the heart, the bone in the throat. Truth is on my side. I went back to China and came out with evidence of evil. This is just the beginning. I want to compile the evidence and put it in one place, the *laogai* museum. I want to say, "Yes, it happened. Here is the proof."

19

WIN ONE, LOSE ONE

Maybe it was because diesel engines don't blend into the scenery, like artificial flowers or shoes. Whatever the reason, there was a smashing victory for the good guys in 1994: For the first time, labor-camp products from China were legally denied entry by a high court.

I take a modest share of the credit for stopping the Jinma (Golden Horse) engine. Having Ed Bradley talk about slave labor on worldwide television in 1991 was an embarrassment for the Bush administration, which was clearly squeamish about enforcing the rules against importing prison-made goods. Bad for business and all that. As a result of the 60 *Minutes* story, I was invited to Congress for the first hearing ever held on slave labor in China. Members of Congress were calling up U.S. Customs officials, pressuring them to enforce the laws against importing prison-camp goods.

I learned a long time ago that righteous indignation goes only so far. Many Europeans and Americans care about human rights, but somebody has to remind his or her government of the existence of laws banning slave-labor products. Otherwise, the government tends to forget. The United Kingdom, for example, has had a law since 1897 banning the import of goods made in prisons, but to my knowledge it has never banned any *laogai* product. Where would the British be without a cup of tea every hour? We have a Chinese-government document that says one-third of all Chinese tea comes from places like the Guangdong Province Red Star Tea Company, where prisoners work in the fields not far from salaried workers. It is impossible to determine the source of each individual tea leaf, of course, but governments should try.

The United States banned forced-labor products in one of the nation's most controversial laws: the Hawley-Smoot Tariff Act of 1930. From what I understand of the English language, the names Hawley and Smoot have a funny ring, particularly together, but there is nothing funny about their place in history. Hawley-Smoot raised tariffs on imports primarily to save American jobs as the Depression put people out of work by the millions. Many critics blame the resultant high levies for cutting international trade, forcing European countries to suspend debt repayments, worsening the Depression, and bringing about the Second World War, which is a lot to say against one act of Congress.

Other historians and economists say Hawley-Smoot should not be blamed for the powerful forces of depression and war that were then loose in the world. The tariffs themselves have long since been amended or dropped, but the act remains in force, including the provision that forbids imported goods made by forced labor: " 'Forced labor,' as herein used, shall mean all work or service which is exacted from any person under the menace of any penalty for its nonperformance, and for which the worker does not offer himself voluntarily." This is the bill's final paragraph.

The early 1930s were not a time for caring about the human rights of "foreign" workers, but the U.S. Customs Service has used the banner of human rights on occasion to block the entry of goods made by forced labor. And after I testified at the congressional hearing in 1991, Customs was under pressure to enforce that wonderful old Hawley-Smoot Act. As often happens with China's rulers, they respond to a show of force. On October 10, 1991, China notified the U.S. government that it would adhere to its own regulations banning the export of forced-labor products. Also in October of 1991, the Customs Service ordered its agents to impound certain wrenches and steel pipes that I had testified were produced by forced labor.

The next month the San Diego office of the Customs Service found invoices for hand tools imported from China. The exporter and importer had "forgotten" to mention the name of the manufacturer, which is supposed to be listed on the invoice. Customs agents wanted to know who was making these hand tools, and they called Washington, and somebody called me. My friends in Congress had suggested to the Customs agents that a well-known troublemaker like Harry Wu might actually have some information that could help them enforce the laws of the land.

I quickly discovered that the hand tools on the invoice were actually spare parts for fifty diesel Jinma engines that had been brought in from China. The engines, used to generate electricity in rural homes and on farms, were brought in by China Diesel Imports, located near San Diego. This company, owned by a man with the wonderful name of Hardy Day, listed only three employees and one million dollars in annual sales, and it had been importing machinery from China since 1977.

I promptly informed Customs that the model X195 engine was produced by Yunnan Provincial Number 1 Prison, which is also called Yunnan Jinma Diesel Engine Factory. It's located in Wangda Qiao, outside Kunming in Yunnan Province, in the south-central portion of China.

My work was paying off. I had been keeping tabs on this camp for years. It was established in 1957, and according to Chinese records the workforce in 1991 was more than twenty-five hundred people, including one thousand prisoners as well as hundreds of workers undergoing "reform" or "reeducation." The prison assembled at least fifty thousand engines a year for domestic use and export. Yunnan is a model region for the new Chinese economy, which stresses "horizontal economic coordination," a euphemism for integrating prison labor into broader economic structures. A pamphlet published in 1989 by a school for prison officials observed that *laogai* production has "two properties: the place and means of reforming criminals . . . and commodity economic development." It also boasts, "Yunnan Provincial Number 1 Prison has already developed into a 'dragon head' of economic coordination. . . . Both production and reform are lively."

The pamphlet continues: "The Yunnan Provincial Number 1 Prison produces Jinma (Golden Horse) brand internal-combustion engines. It has 98 factories manufacturing and supplying parts, components, and assembling them into final products. The annual total output grew from 26,000 to 60,000 engines after the coordination. The quality has been awarded a Silver Medal for three years. Because labor costs were lowered, the price of each engine is 100 yuan cheaper than the same product from other factories."

I shared this information with Bob Windrem and George Lewis of NBC, both of whom had accompanied me to the Shandong Province Trade Fair in San Francisco just a month before. Lewis called the home of Hardy Day, the owner of China Diesel Imports. Day was not home, but his wife volunteered that he had been to the factory in China at least twenty times. When NBC finally reached Day by telephone, he hung up. But the information was already in the hands of the Customs Service.

On March 18, 1992, the *Federal Register* included section T.D. 92-27, entitled "That Merchandise Imported from the People's Republic of China Is Being Produced by Convict, Forced or Indentured Labor." It went on to say, "This document advises that the Commissioner of Customs, with the approval of the Secretary of the Treasury, has determined that certain diesel engines manufactured by the Golden Horse Diesel Engine Factory . . . are being manufactured with the use of convict labor and/or forced labor and/or indentured labor." It said the importation was found to be in violation of the Hawley-Smoot Tariff Act of 1930 and that importations of this type of engine shall be "prohibited."

Hardy Day's goods were seized. In turn, he sued the U.S. government. The Chinese government tried to mollify Washington. On August 7, 1992, there was a memorandum of understanding between the United States and China, with both countries agreeing to adhere to their national rules against exporting and importing prison-labor goods and promising to exchange information and visits in case of allegations of abuses.

On October 29, 1992, a representative of the U.S. Customs Service tried to visit the Jinma Diesel Engine Factory but was "denied access to certain areas," according to the official report, and therefore could not be sure that prisoners were actually manufacturing the banned engines. Another attempt was denied on November 4, 1992. The Chinese asked the Americans to put their request in writing, which they did on January 28, 1993, only to be turned down the same day.

Later that year a group of Chinese officials visited the United States and asked to view the confiscated Jinma engines. On March 20, the Chinese government denied that any *laogai* products had been exported to the United States. Two days later I went to a Los Angeles trade fair sponsored by the Yunnan Province Economic Trade Delegation. Wouldn't you know it? The Jinma diesel engine was still featured in its company's sales catalog.

The U.S. government pursued the San Diego case all through the courts. Finally, in December of 1994, Judge Jane A. Restani of the U.S. Court of International Trade in New York ruled that the engines were indeed made at the factory outside Kunming, which relies mostly on prisoners for manual labor. The judge also found evidence linking the hand tools to prison production. As a result, the diesel engines have never been released for sale in the United States. The judge's decision should be a guideline for U.S. Customs to apply to all goods coming in from China.

Of course, it is easier to track diesel engines than tea leaves. And to be blunt, many American businesspeople do not know—or do not want to know—the implications of purchasing forced-labor products. In May of 1993, operating on a tip from me, Bob Windrem and Bob Kur, also of NBC, visited the Columbus McKinnon Corporation in Amherst, New York, on the morning NBC was to air a report on forced-labor goods. Kur asked Herbert Ladds, Jr., the president of Columbus McKinnon, whether his company's chain hoists might have come from labor camps in China.

"Well, I don't think they would, . . ." he said hesitantly, adding that "there's no sign of guards. There's no sign of any forced presence."

"Do you think the Chinese could be somehow fooling you on this?" Kur asked.

"They could possibly be fooling me, yes," Ladds replied. He then reached into his desk and pulled out six photographs of Chinese workers and showed them to Kur and Windrem, to prove that he would never dabble in forced labor. But Windrem spotted the blue uniforms and shaved heads and prison caps.

Windrem tried not to get excited, and he said, "Hmmmm, could I borrow these to show my people?" And the man let him have the photographs. Windrem and Kur flew to Washington immediately, and Windrem rushed to Jeff Fiedler's office, where I was that day, to show me the photographs, asking, "Harry, are these prisoners?"

My knees nearly buckled. The men were wearing the same blue uniforms I had worn during my nineteen years in China's labor camps. When I regained my powers of speech, I said, "Yeah, prisoners," and they put it on the six-o'clock news, along with charges I made at a press conference that afternoon.

"Today's report says China not only sells chain hoists but a variety of items made by prisoners in forced labor: rubber-soled shoes, boots, kitchenware, toys, tools, and sporting goods—things Americans use every day," Kur said on the evening news.

One of the great things about the government of the United States—all the civics textbooks say so—is that it is divided into three branches. I had reason to be happy with the legislative and judicial branches in 1994, but I was quite disappointed in the executive branch. I got back from risking my life in China only to watch the United States give up its best weapon in the struggle for human rights. President Clinton renewed China's most-favored-nation (MFN) status and openly admitted he would not use tariffs to pressure China to improve its behavior on human rights. He announced he was going to trade with China as if it were a first-world democracy and not expect any improvements in human rights. I had always looked to America as a country that spoke out—and acted against—dictators. But not this time.

The MFN status is a powerful weapon in the arsenal of diplomacy. Technically almost all nations are annually classified as "favored," which means they get favorably low tariffs on imports to the United States, but there is a long and honorable tradition of withholding the status. For example, the United States withheld it from South Africa until that country abolished its system of apartheid. The threat of withholding it has kept some Eastern European and Latin American countries on better behavior. And the United States did not hesitate to put up blockades and declare boycotts against pariah nations like Cuba and North Korea. Why couldn't Washington show the same courage toward China for its treatment of dissidents and the Tibetan people?

The thing that really bothered me was that in 1992, candidate Bill Clinton had criticized President Bush for being too lenient in regard to China's human-rights behavior. Yet in his first year as president, on May 28, 1993, Clinton renewed China's trade benefits for another year. To be sure, he did make a gesture by insisting China meet two "must-do" conditions the next time: end restrictions on emigration and comply with a 1992 agreement banning the export of prison-labor products to the United States. China was also supposed to make "overall, significant progress" on a number of other issues, ranging from easing the crackdown on the Tibetan pro-independence movement to accounting for political prisoners.

The Chinese sensed that President Clinton would not be tough with them. They have a nose for such things. Look, I'm Chinese. Everybody knows you have to be strong with them. You have to threaten them and take strong actions, and they will respect you. But if you try to show a good example and expect them to follow, they will walk all over you.

With the annual renewal coming up in May of 1994, President Clinton was under pressure to take stronger action, but he was also under pressure from the business community to renew the most-favored-nation status. Knowing the Chinese had not enforced the previous year's "must-do" conditions, Clinton agreed to new terms. According to published reports, China's exports to the United States were $3.8 billion in 1985 — about equal to its imports from the United States. But by 1994, China was exporting $31 billion worth of goods and business to the United States while the United States was exporting only $9 billion in goods and business to China. The Chinese were sending the United States almost three and a half times what the United States was sending them. If the United States raised tariffs, American business would be hurt. Businesspeople complained that the tariff on sweaters and shoes imported from China to the United States would have risen from 6 percent to 60 percent, and the levy on Christmas-tree lights from 8 percent to 50 percent.

Some of Clinton's advisers argued that the United States had nothing to gain from standing alone against China on human rights: The policy would not work, and a huge world market would be diminished. The president heard American corporations say they needed ongoing business with China. He got the message and made a decision based on economics rather than ethics. He did ban the importing of Chinese guns and ammunition — only two hundred million dollars in business a year. He also said he would continue a few minor prohibitions on the export of American weapons and military goods to the Chinese. He did not claim it was much. "To those who argue that in view of China's human rights abuses we should revoke MFN status, let me ask you the same question that I have asked myself: 'Will we do more to advance the cause of human rights if China is isolated, or if our nations are engaged in a growing web of political and economic cooperation and contacts?' "

I've watched President Clinton on television as he interacts with many Americans and foreigners who have suffered. He has a real feeling for them, the way he embraces them and looks them in the eye. I just wish he would show some of that same empathy with the millions of people in the Chinese camps. To me, the president's remarks of May 1994 sound as if he did not want Deng Xiaoping and his followers to be mad at him. Instead, he has made some Americans mad at him. In *The New York Times* on May 31, 1994, A. M. Rosenthal concluded, "Politically, the Chinese Communists have taken a new prisoner—the President."

As for me, I was particularly disappointed because I could predict what would happen next. The Chinese government had delayed the trial of fourteen dissidents until the decision about tariff privileges. Now that the heat was off, in late July, China staged a trial of the fourteen people who were linked to pro-democracy and labor groups. It was the first large political trial in three years, and the timing was obvious.

By the end of 1995, China's trade surplus with the United States would leap to $36.8 billion. The imbalance was so high partly because China does not pay royalties on pirated items, like compact discs.

China's rulers, however, were learning the slippery ways of U.S. public relations experts. They tried to change their image. In December of 1994, the government officially stopped using the word *laogai*, which implies reform-through-labor camps. Now it was calling the system *jianyu*, which refers to prisoners. The government officials wanted to suggest they were dealing solely with hardened criminals, but it was all semantics. In their own literature, they suggest the change in terminology will go over better with those concerned about human rights. Still, the authorities grab people who stand out—troublemakers—and throw them into camps, forcing them to work for free.

It is this habit of theirs that I had determined to denounce and to break—or die in the attempt.

20

CALIFORNIA, JANUARY 1995

How did I come to live this well? I've gone from the camps to the comfortable sprawl of Silicon Valley, outside San Jose, but I still live in a world with all-Chinese shopping centers, where not just the restaurants but every type of business has signs in Chinese—the new California. The foothills of the Sierra Nevadas are just to the east, brown most of the year but bright green in the early spring. Sometimes I dare to take thirty seconds to gaze at these hills, so far from the slopes of my native land.

My house is at the end of a quiet cul-de-sac in a development like thousands of others. There is a newspaper lying in the driveway. My two cars are parked out in front. The houses are close together but private. The neighbors are a typical Silicon Valley mix: American-born, Korean, Chinese, Japanese, Spanish, Indian. I look out the window of my study on the second floor and see children in the other houses and realize that my time to be a father has probably passed, but sometimes Ching-Lee and I talk about adoption. I find myself wishing I had more time to play catch with the kids on the block. Ching-Lee says that when I play, I am like a little boy myself.

Today I am working at home, in sweatpants that say COUGARS and a gray sweatshirt and socks. A dozen pairs of shoes arc lined up, Asian-style, by the front door. Ching-Lee's father and mother—now my father and mother, too—are sitting in the den downstairs, watching Chinese programs on cable television. They moved from Taiwan to California in the summer of 1994, two months after we moved into this house, and I feel fulfilled having a house filled with family again.

My mother has not been writing since she moved to the States, but she puts her creativity to use in the kitchen, which I greatly appreciate. She recently gave up smoking, on her doctor's orders, and fusses that she has gained a few pounds, but I say it's better this way.

My father is a strong man in his eighties. He retired from the Taiwanese air force when he was about sixty and began hiking in the mountains right in the city of Taipei for an hour, an hour and a half every day. He wears blue jeans and flannel shirts and has the physique of a fifty-year-old. Every day he goes to the porch behind the house and works out on the exercise machine, standing up, pushing down on pedals, pulling on handlebars, rising high in the air—three hundred repetitions a day.

They still visit Taipei, and even with the tensions between Taiwan and the mainland, they would like to visit China one day. They know they are Chinese. We are all Chinese. Because they are our parents, they are entitled to the master bedroom on the second floor. They are independent and respectful of us. My father stays in his bedroom for many hours every day, doing calligraphy—graceful, strong strokes with brush and ink.

Because I am often on the road, he monitors our little swimming pool in the back, scooping up all the dead leaves that the electric filter misses. The branches of orange and grapefruit trees extend over the wall that divides our property from our neighbors'. Our neighbors tell us, "Take all you need," and sometimes—not very often—I take fifteen minutes off from work and stand in the yard and bite into an orange. For nineteen years, I never tasted fruit.

January can be nippy near San Jose, but most of the year I am tempted to take a quick dip in the pool. People who see me in my bathing suit exclaim, "You don't look your age, and you look pretty healthy for somebody who has suffered as much as you have." What can I say? Should I give myself more scars or starve myself? I look better than I feel. I have to remember to go to the garage and hang upside down on a machine that stretches my back, forces the bad disk—my souvenir from the mine accident—back into place.

I walk upstairs to the large front room facing the street. Ching-Lee is already sitting at her desk, working. I know how fortunate I am that she was willing to change her life around, to live with this driven man. Sometimes when I am traveling, making speeches, I hear her voice on the telephone, and I know she is lonely for me. I miss her, too, but I cannot stop.

When I am home, Ching-Lee listens while I talk on the phone. The Mandarin language does not distinguish between *he* and *she*—the listener is assumed to know the reference—so it is common for Chinese people to confuse genders in English. I will be discussing a woman, yet I will say *he*. From across the room, Ching-Lee will whisper loudly, *she*. She is my eyes and ears. In all the lost years, I never thought this could happen. Sometimes we flirt like teenagers because we are still new to each other, and sometimes we argue just because we like to argue. We are still getting to know each other. But mostly we work, Ching-Lee at one desk, I at the other, and sometimes we have assistants working at a third desk.

The shelves on two long walls are already filled with books and tapes, including several good hardcover copies of *Les Misérables* and the tape of the musical, which we saw in a theater in San Francisco. Sometimes I pop the tape into the machine and sing along with it. There are rows of videotapes, copies of my second book, *Bitter Winds*, in German, Dutch, Chinese, Japanese, French.

The office is packed with dozens of filing cabinets and machines: a mobile phone, a fax, two large personal computers, a VCR, a machine that rewinds videotapes, a copying machine, a shredder, and—perhaps most important—a coffeemaker. Then there are tools and supplies: scissors and rulers, staplers and tape, stacks of paper goods. There are bins: one for recycling paper, one for waste.

On the walls are plaques, from the World Federation of Hungarian Freedom Fighters, from many civic groups that have honored me, and a photo of me with the Dalai Lama.

The phone rings, and I speak in Chinese. The phone rings, and I speak in English. The phone rings from Washington. The phone rings from California. The phone rings from Germany, where somebody wants to talk about Wei Jingsheng.

Now that the Chinese have lost their bid for the Olympic Games in 2000, they will soon pop him back into jail. I know that Wei does not want to be exiled to Germany, where his sister lives, but he cannot keep silent. We do what we can to put pressure on Beijing: Leave Wei Jingsheng alone.

The morning goes fast, with calls from the East, calls from Europe. At noon, Ching-Lee disappears downstairs. By her own admission, she never learned to cook very well, but now she cooks with her mother's help. I sit at the telephone and smell strong spices floating up the stairway. There were nights in the camps when we would sit around and discuss our fantasies of a normal life. Some men would talk about going home and making love to their wives, and others would say, "No, no, don't talk of such things. It is too personal, too painful." But we all would hallucinate about the best bowl of rice we ever tasted, about noodles, vegetables, beef, soup, corn buns, fish. Now these wonderful odors are wafting into my office in a quiet cul-de-sac in the state of California.

"Harry," Ching-Lee calls. "Lunch is ready."

I pad downstairs in my sweat clothes and stocking feet.

The kitchen is bright and sunny. I reach into the refrigerator and pour myself a small glass of red wine. I raise a deep bowl of fish soup toward my mouth and eat with a dainty ceramic spoon. I take my time, no longer having to wolf down my meager ration to protect it from marauders. I help myself to beef with vegetables, rice, broiled shrimp. I pick up chopsticks and begin to eat.

"Put red sauce on your beef," Ching-Lee tells me.

It's a family joke. Ching-Lee's parents lived in Sichuan, and they keep half a dozen jars of spicy sauces—peppers and chilis and onions—on the table. They know I don't eat very spicy foods, and they love to tease me about it.

I have become a good American who will eat almost anything— except Mexican food, with all the beans. When I am traveling, I eat lightly, one big meal a day and a snack here and there. But in my home, with these succulent meals at midday, I know I am a lucky man.

For dessert we have sticky buns with plum paste inside. There is a bowl of grapes. We discuss the politics of Taiwan. Ching-Lee's family lived through the early days, when dissent was suppressed, but now there are three political parties in Taiwan, and the government will hold free elections in 1996.

Lunch over, I go upstairs to check the answering machine. I return some calls. Then I go to the bedroom for a fifteen-minute nap. How I longed for sleep in the days of the *laogai*. I would be standing in a field, shoveling huge hunks of mud, and fall asleep on my feet. If the guards noticed me resting, they would kick me in the ribs, hit me with a shovel, to set an example for the rest of the workers. Back in those days, I slept fitfully at night, on a raised stone bed, called a *kang*, with a coal fire underneath. Now in the California winter, I pull a blanket over my body and close my eyes. I allow myself to nap. Only fifteen minutes. Just fifteen.

21

I BREAK MY PROMISE

When I completed my third trip in 1994, I promised Jeff Fiedler that it would be my last. Let's not say I lied. Let's just say the situation changed. I was so used to living in danger that it was hard for me to live a normal life. I would be working in my house in California, comfortable and happy, but something would start twisting inside me, a voice whispering, "Harry, they need you. You've got to go."

Enough voices were telling me not to go back: Ching-Lee, Jeff, even a few people at the State Department. In May of 1994, the Chinese government put out a blacklist of its top troublemakers. America has its ten-most-wanted list, but China, being bigger and older, has its forty-nine. There were three categories:

Category 1. Mainly persons who left the country without passports following the Tiananmen Square uprising in 1989. The police had instructions to arrest them if they tried to return to China.

Category 2. Mainly persons who left China legally but later became active in dissident groups overseas. The party gave orders to deny entry to these persons.

Category 3. Persons who left China legally and later became active in dissident groups overseas. The police had instructions to detain or arrest them if they tried to return. (According to Human

Rights Watch/Asia, "Border authorities are to seek immediate instructions from above on how to handle the case, while presumably keeping their charges either in isolation or under close surveillance.")

Among those in Category 3 were Fang Lizhi, the physicist, and his wife, Li Shuxian, also a physicist, both of whom had taken refuge in the United States embassy in Beijing for a year after the Tiananmen Square massacre and were now living in Arizona. I was also in Category 3.

The terms were somewhat murky. If we were caught, we might not be shot on sight or tossed out of the country. The authorities might treat us with caution and detain us for a very long time. I took it as a challenge.

After the two BBC documentaries came out, later in 1994, the Chinese were really unhappy with me. They had protested to the BBC about a few alleged inaccuracies, like the shot of the heart operation in the segment about organ transplants, but they could not refute the vast majority of the facts or the general thrust of the exposé. The only thing they could do was make it difficult for BBC correspondents to work in China for a while.

Because the Chinese authorities had tracked Sue Lloyd-Roberts's path in China, they could determine that I had traveled legally as Peter H. Wu. I could not change my legal name, but I wondered whether I could sneak one over on them and get another visa.

I asked Jeff to test the waters, so he had some friends deliver my application to the Chinese consulate in Chicago. For some reason, they sent my papers to the consulate in Houston for processing; on February 1, I got them back with a six-month visa for Peter H. Wu— nothing tricky, nothing illegal about it.

"Okay, great, you got your visa," Jeff said. "Now forget about it. Just don't go."

I told him it didn't work that way. I had to look upon this as one extra, unexpected chance to expose China's cruel system. My luck could not hold out forever, and the authorities would eventually find a way of keeping me out. I had to make this trip really momentous.

My cause this time was a possible link between the World Bank and the Xinjiang Production and Construction Corps (XPCC), the quasi-military organization that has been a towering presence in the area since the change in government in 1949. When Sue Lloyd-Roberts and I had traveled across the northern edge of the desert in Xinjiang in 1994, we had noticed many irrigation and drainage projects in the Tarim River basin. Upon my return, I had received suggestions that the World Bank supported some of the water-control projects in that area and that some of these projects just might be supplementing the forced-labor camps in Xinjiang.

I do not believe the World Bank exists to support forced-labor camps. Also known as the International Bank for Reconstruction and Development, the World Bank was established in 1945 and is based in Washington, D.C. Its funds are used to facilitate investment, encourage foreign trade, and lower the interest on the international debt of developing nations, and it has an admirable reputation for trying to raise the standard of living in emerging nations.

By 1995, according to Reuters news agency, the World Bank had "committed to China a total of $23 billion for 159 projects, with annual commitments of around $3 billion. China became its largest customer in 1993." But did any of these projects actually support forced-labor camps? And did any of the projects allow the Chinese to divert their own money to the camps? My instincts told me to investigate Xinjiang myself, to use my own eyes and ears, my own two feet, to take videotape, ask questions, swim like a fish in the ocean.

Jeff Fiedler tried to dissuade me, saying, "Harry, you don't have to do this anymore. You've got contacts and sources of information now. You've got people who can research this." Jeff had a point. The Chinese bureaucracy puts a great deal of information on paper, perhaps operating on the theory that it is the center of the universe and the rest of the world does not read Chinese or have the patience to monitor China's reports and records. The Laogai Research Foundation was starting to accumulate information, but I wanted to do things my own way. I wanted to return to Xinjiang.

My first target was the relationship between the World Bank and the XPCC, often called the Corps. In 1994, while working with Sue Lloyd-Roberts, I had taken a photograph of the Corps's headquarters in Ürümqi. One sign, on the left side of the gate, says XPCC. The other sign, on the right side, says, rather awkwardly in the English translation, XINJIANG AGRICULTURAL RECLAMATION AGRICULTURE, INDUSTRY, AND TRADE UNITED ENTERPRISE CORPORATION. The World Bank prefers the shortened version of this more benign title, whose initials are XAITC. But the XPCC and the XAITC are one and the same: the Corps.

The Corps has been a major force in Xinjiang since 1949. It was originally formed from demobilized Kuomintang soldiers and their families who remained in the remote northwestern corner of China, protecting the border with the Soviet Union and stabilizing the Uighurs of Xinjiang. The XPCC began as an ethnic Han organization in a largely Muslim province, and it remains so to this day. According to a 1993 XPCC bulletin, the Corps is 88.2 percent Han.

The Corps has been active in every major aspect of life in Xinjiang, particularly in the military. On October 10, 1994, Xinhua News Agency reported on the fortieth anniversary of the Corps. The article, originally aimed at a Chinese readership, was translated into English by the BBC. A segment:

> In the early 1950s, with the purpose of restoring and developing Xinjiang's economy, maintaining Xinjiang's social stability and consolidating the border defense of the motherland, the central authorities decided to transfer most of the People's Liberation Army men stationed in Xinjiang to civilian work and then organize [the] XPCC to execute the historical mission of stationing troops to open up wasteland and garrisoning the frontiers, thus opening a new page in the annals of stationing troops to open up Xinjiang. Through forty years of construction and development, the XPCC has become a special political, economic, military and social organization, embracing a population of 2.2 million, a large number of Corps-run farms and enterprises, and a complete educational, scientific, research, cultural and medical system.

During the early 1960s, the Corps was essential in border skirmishes with India, according to a 1986 edition of the *Xinjiang Agriculture and Reclamation Economy*, a magazine issued by the XPCC. The writer says the XPCC "not only has a rich material base, but it also has suitable military qualities: to serve as support forces for the People's Liberation

Army; to be able to immediately rise up when called; to fight when risen; and to win when fighting. At the same time, when the motherland is needy, if it needs grain, it has grain; if it needs men, it has men."

The U.S. Defense Intelligence Agency issued an unclassified report (*Handbook of the Chinese People's Liberation Army*) in 1984, calling the Corps a "paramilitary organization under joint government, party and military control which has the missions of land reclamation, agricultural production, and economic development in remote and unproductive frontier areas and border defense."

Right into contemporary time, the Corps has been active. During the Tiananmen Square movement in Beijing, on May 19, 1989, many protesters demonstrated in Ürümqi, the capital of Xinjiang. According to the January 9, 1990, issue of the *Xinjiang Military Reclamation*, another one of the Corps's journals, "In the course of spring last year during the counterrevolutionary chaos that occurred in Beijing, the Corps enlarged its staunch militia position . . . and threw itself wholly into the struggle to oppose chaos and prevent riot."

The more I studied the Corps, the more I felt the World Bank had glossed over its military and penal aspects. In a 1985–86 review of its projects in Xinjiang, the World Bank issued a staff appraisal report noting that the XAITC had 171 state farms. In that same period, Xinhua issued a report, in English, which the BBC transmitted on September 11, 1985. It said, "The 171 state farms under the Corps are considered semi-military organizations."

In my opinion, the World Bank concealed its relationship with the XPCC by referring to it only as the XAITC. On March 13, 1984, the World Bank described a forty-million-dollar Seeds Project in twelve provinces and two autonomous regions, including Xinjiang. The bank's own staff report said the local agriculture, industry, and trade corporations would implement the projects. The 1988 Corps yearbook described a "seed development project with a loan for $12 million, with domestic involvement of 18 million yuan, and having a construction period of five years." The 1991 Corps yearbook said, "The high quality cotton seed plant at the regiment was newly constructed using World Bank funds."

The World Bank is often praised for raising the quality of life in remote areas, but it was also clear to me that the XPCC uses prisoners in its economic system and that the World Bank invests in XPCC projects. What had Sue Lloyd-Roberts and I really seen in 1994? How much did the World Bank know? Before I made any charges, I wanted to see for myself. As long as I had a visa, I might as well take advantage of it.

First, though, I needed to expand the capabilities of the foundation. Jeff hired David Welker, a bright young man who had learned to speak Mandarin, first at Longmeadow High School in Massachusetts and then at the University of Massachusetts, where he was a lacrosse player. David loves the language and the Chinese people and has visited Taiwan and Hong Kong and even spent a few days in Shenzhen and Guangzhou during college. The day David was hired, I asked, "Would you like to go to China?"

Also in 1995, Maranda Shieh, a Chinese-American woman who runs her own computer company in the Washington area, started working with us.

Now that I had much more backup, I planned an extensive intinerary. The first step was to check out possible World Bank–supported camps in the desert. Luckily for me, Sue Howell agreed to accompany me for the first week or so, when we would be posing as academic researchers in Xinjiang.

The second step was to investigate the underground Christian church in Hubei Province, where many believers had been persecuted over the years. More than forty years after the Communists came to power, religion was flourishing all over China. The government had tried to suppress a million student dissidents, but it also had to contend with four million to six million Catholics and another six million to eight million Christians of varying denominations plus an extensive Buddhist revival, to say nothing of the thriving Muslim corridor in the north. For this part of the trip, David Welker agreed to "shadow" me while Ching-Lee accompanied me.

The third step was to examine the large ethnic unrest. I wanted to document the mistreatment of the Uighurs and other Muslim groups.

The fourth step was to confront the reality of population control. This was still a high priority in China; at its peak, in 1983, there had

been twenty-one million sterilizations, eighteen million IUD inser-
tions, and fourteen million abortions, many of them involuntary,
according to John S. Aird, a demographer and specialist in coercive
population control, who testified before Congress in 1995. Not only
were women being forced to have abortions if they already had a child,
but the aborted fetuses were being sold for use as medicine, an abhor-
rent practice to many Westerners. Still, many Chinese continue to
believe that a ground-up fetus, or liquefied fetus, is good for fertility or
sexual strength. People go to hospitals and either bribe officials for a
fetus or steal one.

The fifth step was to look into the large amount of graphite I had
learned was flowing from a labor camp to a company in New Jersey.
While I was in Germany waiting to meet Sue Howell, a German journalist asked me to investigate a particular camp. I could not resist the
challenge. I agreed to try to meet the German or one of his colleagues
in China, or maybe I would meet one of my undercover Chinese or
American supporters. Since there was some doubt about who would be
seeing whom, the German arranged for a signal of matching Chicago
Bulls caps he had bought in Bonn. (The translation of the team's name
is Red Oxen.)

The planning took place in the early months of 1995, long before any
public announcement of Mrs. Clinton's proposed trip to attend the
United Nations Fourth World Conference on Women in Beijing in
early September. I was deliberately vague about my plans, even in conversations with sympathetic politicians of both parties in Congress. I
saw some of them on May 4, 1995, when I testified at a Senate hearing
about organ transplants, conducted by Senators Jesse Helms of North
Carolina and Charles S. Robb of Virginia.

Gao Pei Qi, the former Public Security Bureau official who had
defected and now lives in London, also testified. He explained how
prisoners were shot either in the head or in the back, depending on
what part of the body was hot on the market that day. Gao was blunt
and candid: "Basically they look at the prisoner's body as whatever they
want it to be. They would take the prisoner's skin if necessary." For my
part, I testified that the Chinese government was sensitive about bad
overseas publicity on the transplant issue but, on the other hand, had

not blushed about staging public executions since Tiananmen Square, sometimes with fifteen thousand spectators gathered in a stadium or an open field. "It's a big show," I said.

While I was in Washington, I chatted informally with friends on both sides of the House, like Frank Wolf and Chris Smith, Republicans, and Nancy Pelosi, a Democrat, as well as Senator Jesse Helms, a Republican. They urged me not to go back again, but I was vague, saying only, "I'm going, but I don't know when or how."

While I was planning my trip, relations between the United States and China became touchy, particularly when the United States allowed the president of Taiwan, Lee Teng-hui, to enter the country to attend his class reunion at Cornell University. The State Department had previously refused visits by Taiwanese officials, but it relaxed its ban this time because this was to be a private trip to Lee's old college. The Chinese reacted furiously, deeming it a clear signal that Lee was an honored guest and claiming that this was a way of strengthening his bid for reelection in 1996. So Beijing was already annoyed with Washington as I prepared to enter China through its back door.

Unfortunately the back door was protected by modern electronics. In the twinkling of a computer chip, they caught me and then transported me clear across China, to the villa in Wuhan. Instead of my investigating the Chinese, they were now investigating me. It was not what I had had in mind.

22

ROOM 104

I almost had the illusion of being on vacation. Here I was in a pleasant two-story building in a quiet lake area, in a private room with air-conditioning and a private bathroom, just like a Holiday Inn, Wuhan-style. Reality sank in when I noticed three couches in the room. Three guards would be stationed in my room at all times, even when I was asleep. I also noticed a bar on the window, but I did not worry about niceties—not at two in the morning after the long, exhausting trip across China. They could have put the entire People's Liberation Army in the room with me, and I still would have slept.

At noon, I woke up. Sure enough, three young guards, silent and watchful, had arranged themselves around Room 101. I supposed they were under orders to intimidate me with their discipline. I was back in captivity; it was as if I had never left. There was no time for soul search-ing, no time to ask myself, "Fool, why did you let this happen?" I could not afford the luxury of introspection. I had to remember all my sur-vival lessons from the camps. My captors would be looking for weak-ness. Perhaps they hoped I would cry or talk in my sleep. I had to be tough and hard if I was to have any chance at all.

One of my "hosts" was Liu, a well-fed officer who smoked expensive 555 cigarettes, the British-made brand so popular in Asia, and wore expensive Italian loafers and modern civilian clothes. Liu tried to act as if he were my best friend in the world, but after a few minutes of his unctuous manner, my skin crawled and I wished he would leave me to the hard-staring young guards. Instead, he told me lunch was ready, which turned out to be a pretty decent meal, soup and chicken, brought right to my room. After finishing, I waited — and waited. A few police officers popped their heads in to check out this curiosity, the troublemaker from across the sea, but they were clearly waiting for orders, just keeping an eye on me every second, noting everything I did, not letting me out of their sight, even while I relieved myself.

This indignity brought me back to the old days, when the so-called toilet was a hole in the floor, when everybody in the barracks had only a few minutes to go through his most intimate agonies with everyone else. Because of the inadequate diet and no medical care, some prisoners would have such terrible diarrhea that giant hemorrhoids literally slipped outside their bodies, and they would have to push them back, whereas other men were so badly constipated that they had to claw the waste material out of themselves. I've done both, and I've seen people die from both.

We had to be beasts to survive the camps, but now my modesty had returned. I thought it was rude of the guards to stand alongside me while I sat on the Western-style bowl. "You don't care about my smell?" I asked them.

They just gave me the blank "good soldier" stare. It was still early in the game.

~~

During that first day in Wuhan, I was too busy gauging my circumstances to think about Ching-Lee, but at night I found her image surging into my heart. I could see her sweet face at the desk across from me in our study. I could hear her soft voice in my ear. For the first time, I knew it would be easy to break down. Had I thrown away my marriage for an expedition to my own personal heart of darkness? What did I love more, trouble or Ching-Lee? "Forget it," I told myself. "Put her out of your mind." I could not afford to be sentimental or weak and expect to survive.

The next morning, June 30, right after breakfast, I was summoned to Room 104, just across the hall. It was an ordinary hotel room but with a table and some bright lights instead of beds. I was greeted by a man sitting at a table—confident, clearly in charge, about my age, wearing a crisp olive-colored uniform. His secretary was next to him, her nimble fingers, without benefit of a court-recording machine, ready to scribble furiously. A couple of colonels in uniform, named Dao and Duan, sat in chairs at the side. I was directed to sit opposite the man in charge. The room had air-conditioning and a curtain but no bars on the window. In earlier interrogations, I had seen worse.

The leader—N412221, according to his badge—introduced himself as General Wang and said he had been working for the police for forty years and had successfully rehabilitated over 90 percent of the counterrevolutionaries he had handled.

"Even if they die, are they rehabilitated?" I asked.

He said yes. He did not seem to think the remark was funny. Wang said he had once interrogated a British spy who was later expelled, and he was obviously experienced with important prisoners. He did not start off with the nasty, blustering posture I remembered, but he did get right down to business. "According to Article 38 of Chinese law," he said, "we have issued a house arrest for you, to put you under surveillance. Would you sign this paper acknowledging that?"

"No."

"Are you refusing to sign?"

"No, I'm not refusing, but I do have some questions."

He motioned for me to continue.

"First, what is my status? I am a U.S. citizen. How come you have taken me to the middle of China? For what? Am I a tourist? A student? A businessman? Or are you arresting me? What is my legal position today? Also, I want to contact my consul. Second, this is not my house," I said. Being held in this villa did not square with my vision of house arrest: living in one's own home, under surveillance. Could I make a phone call? Could I buy newspapers? Could I cook? Could I watch television? Could I take a walk? Would they follow me? "What can I do; what can I not do? What are the conditions? If you tell me, maybe I'll sign." I tried to let him know I was flexible but not a man to be easily taken advantage of.

"If you sign this, we can inform your family," the general said.

He and his assistants started asking questions—name, age, where I live, simple stuff—but I'm not a soldier and am not required to give my name, rank and, serial number. "I told you, I refuse. I am an American citizen. I demand to know my rights."

When General Wang was out of the room, Colonel Duan told me, "You can trust Wang; he's got a great reputation for interrogating people."

When Wang returned, I suspected from the crocodile grin on his face that he had worked out his act with his assistants. I knew never to trust a Chinese officer who says he can be trusted.

After a break for lunch, more questions began. It was very important for me to grasp the subtlety of where they were going with all this.

"We knew sooner or later you'd come back," one of them said, implying they knew exactly who I was and what I did.

"Here I am, like meat on the chopping block for you," I replied. "Whatever you want, you can chop."

"You are a big troublemaker for our government," he said. "You are stubborn."

Since I would not answer specific questions, Wang and his assistants demonstrated they knew about my life. They had a paper in my file from 1981, submitted to my party committee after I had settled in as a teacher, in my handwriting, saying I wanted to go abroad to improve my knowledge of geology.

"You promised to return to your socialist motherland to do a better job. You lied."

"Sure I said I'd come back. Otherwise, you would not have given me a passport."

"You lie a lot."

I thought to myself, "No, you people lied to me. I learned to lie to survive. I've heard big lies and small lies. I remember the lie in 1957—

from your Chairman Mao. 'Let a hundred flowers bloom.' When I tried to bloom, however, I was labeled a counterrevolutionary." Instead, I said, "What about the biggest lie of all? Communism—it cost me nineteen years of my life."

It is hard for me to explain this to Westerners, but the Chinese totally accept that they will lie when it is to their advantage. The general understood me, he may even have agreed with me, but he had a job to do.

To get my attention, Wang told me that during my 1991 trip to Beijing, Ching-Lee and I had visited a place called the Wu Family Gardens.

"How did you know that?" I asked, impressed.

"We know everything," he told me proudly.

It was true. A man I knew at the Hoover Institution, Wu Yuan Li, who came from a wealthy family that escaped to Taiwan after 1949, had asked me to make an excursion to his family villa, which dates back to the Qing dynasty. Now it was used by the government to house "special guests," like a former defense minister, Peng Dehuai, who had been held under house arrest in 1959, before he was tortured to death during the Cultural Revolution.

How in the world did they know Ching-Lee and I had gone sightseeing at the Wu Family Gardens? Later, back in my room, I figured it out. On that trip to Beijing, I had visited an old friend from the camps named Zhang, whose daughter had died of cancer. He had given me directions to the Wu Gardens, but he was friends with my first wife, and he must have told her that I was in Beijing, and the authorities must have gotten the information from her. No harm. No problem. But I was impressed with their diligence.

Most of the ghosts in my past started to tumble out. Wang and his staff brought up the fifty yuan that my friend had stolen so many years ago and had led to my original sentence. "You are a petty thief," one of them snapped, but I urged them to check their records.

My college rightist friend Wang had confessed the theft in 1978, and Colonel Li in the coal camp had told me to ignore the old charge because it was obvious I had been held as a rightist. "I am not a thief," I told the interrogators.

The next old business was my second wife, Diana. They knew we had met when she was a twenty-year-old student and that we had married in China and divorced in the United States. They did not discuss this as a moral issue of my love affair with a student, just as a fact, a way of making me feel they could pry into every corner of my life.

Next they hauled out a Chinese-language version of my first book, *Laogai: The Chinese Gulag.* "Why do you link the *laogai* to the gulag?" they asked, offended that I would dare to compare the Chinese penal system to the Russian system.

"I've got information that Stalin sent gulag experts to China in the early fifties," I said. "Your laws were changed to be more like the Soviet Union's laws. Look it up."

They also knew about my three old friends who had taken me through the coal mine twice in 1991, but they did not offer details, and I did not volunteer any.

I felt that I got through these early sessions untouched. The stuff they told me was either on the public record or harmless. They had not smoked out my Chinese friends who helped me anonymously, they had not forced me to confess anything that could be used against me in a trial. But it was early. I had to stay calm.

As soon as I was taken back to my room, I took out the ballpoint pen I was allowed to keep, and I took a piece of blank paper they had issued me, and I wrote in elegant Chinese calligraphy the characters from an old Buddhist saying: "The rain falls in the ocean, neither increasing nor decreasing." It means that no matter how heavy the rain is, when it falls in the ocean, it does no harm. It doesn't fall in a pond, it doesn't fall in a river, it doesn't fall in a small creek, it doesn't fall in a large lake. It falls in the ocean. The calligraphy reminded me, "Stay calm. You can take it."

I took the paper and made some glue of rice and water and taped it against a wall. Duan did not object to my hanging the calligraphy. He could read the words but did not understand the meaning, so he asked me to explain. I explained it to the officer, who was less than half my age, from a vastly different culture. "Now I understand," he said. I think he respected me more after that, knowing I lived according to underlying beliefs and philosophies that went far beyond communism. He knew that no matter what they might do to me, they could not break me.

The next day I went on the offensive, haranguing them about contacting the U.S. embassy in Beijing. I told them I would not talk until they respected my legal rights, and they knew I was within my rights, so they did not force me to give information.

~~

I settled in for the long haul. I would wake up around seven o'clock and at seven-thirty have breakfast: a container of food at the table in my room. Around nine-thirty or ten, I'd be summoned to Room 104 for interrogation. Sometimes they would stay for twenty minutes and sometimes two hours, and then we'd stop for lunch. The afternoon interrogations would start around three o'clock, sometimes lasting an hour, sometimes more; dinner was at seven.

The food was adequate, the same as the officers got. Breakfast was rice soup, maybe sautéed vegetables and boiled peanuts, a Chinese muffin. Lunch and dinner usually included a small piece of chicken or beef or eggs, steamed rice, soup, sometimes fish. At first, I complained because the food in Wuhan tends to be spicy, but either I got used to it or they laid off the hot stuff.

Because it was summer, the air-conditioning ran twenty-four hours a day. Although there was a radio in my room, I was not allowed to use it. No newspaper appeared on my doorstep in the morning. For several weeks, the only reading material I had was one book that Sue Howell had left behind, *Political Institutions in Traditional China: Major Issues*, edited by James T. C. Liu of Princeton University. The essays covered different aspects of Chinese life, most of them familiar to me, but I read the book cover to cover, and then, for lack of anything else to read, I translated it into Chinese.

Every evening at eight o'clock, hot water would be available, and I would sink into the bathtub and try to relax. Exactly one hour later, General Wang would come back and interrogate me again, sometimes just making small talk, sometimes laying off the questions I would not answer, sometimes appealing to me as a man of reason.

Wang did not deny China's history. Sure, he would say, we know you suffered. Hey, some of the boys got carried away, but why hold grudges? Wang would remind me of the unexpected comeback of Zhu Rongji, who had been labeled a rightist for speaking his mind during the hundred-flowers campaign of 1957. Zhu had luckily escaped the camps but had spent the next twenty-one years in disgrace, at paper-shuffling jobs, before Deng Xiaoping rehabilitated him in 1978. Now, miracle of miracles, Zhu had gone from the post of mayor of Shanghai to being one of the great economic gurus, known in the West as China's Gorbachev, which is a compliment everywhere but in Russia and China. Wang seemed sad that I could not find it in my heart to be a good sport like Zhu. I was supposed to feel guilty about letting Wang and China down. "Sorry, boys," I would think, "I just can't do it."

After I complained about the close monitoring of my toilet habits, a peephole was installed in the bathroom door. That way I could have some privacy, but they could still peer in at me if they wanted, just to make sure I didn't kill myself or whatever it was they feared.

As soon as the lieutenants were gone from the bathroom, I was able to resume one of life's great pleasures: singing in the bathtub. Chinese music is both patriotic and emotional, and I also have come to love Western classical music: Bach, Schubert, Haydn, Tchaikovsky—all music I find very strong, very moving. I would recall the Russian folk songs I had learned in high school, in the old days of solidarity, when the Chinese had been enamored of Russian songs and poetry and movies. Eventually Russian culture fell out of favor, but not with me. I was especially fond of one Russian song called "A Small Path," about a lonely soldier's family in a snowy field. There was another, called "The Old Cart Driver," about a man far away in Siberia who knows he is dying and asks his friend to go home and sing to his wife: "Tell my wife not to be sad. Tell her to find a good man and marry him."

I also sang American songs in the tub. In Shanghai before the Communists took over, we were exposed to Western music: jazz, Dixieland, pop, the songs of Stephen Foster. Now in the tub, I sang my personal favorite: "Love Me Tender" by Elvis Presley. How did this become my favorite American pop song? It dates back to 1984, when President and Mrs. Ronald Reagan visited China for the first time and the Chinese wanted to be good hosts and play familiar music at the big state banquet in the Great Hall of the People in Beijing. Somebody seemed to think Nancy Reagan loves Elvis Presley's music. Whether or not this is true, I do not know, but that's what they understood. An army band learned to play "Love Me Tender," and thus we saw Mrs. Reagan on television, wearing a bright-red gown and improbably being serenaded by Chinese musicians playing the old hit song.

Many students at the time took the position that if the army band was permitted to play Elvis, it would be safe to sing something from the forbidden West. My students were all going around singing "Love Me Tender." For once, nobody could criticize decadent American music, because it had been played on the order of Deng himself.

Now, in my bathtub, having come full circle to Wuhan, I sang just like Elvis. Corny? Sentimental? Maybe. But it was a way to express my homesickness for Ching-Lee—not knowing when, or if, I would see her again.

After my bath, I told the guards, "Hey, you know, I'm not singing to you guys." They were not allowed to speak to me, but Liu had somehow heard me, and he even said, "Your singing's not so bad; it comes from the heart." I guess that should have been a tip-off that they could hear every sound I made.

⌒

I started to add up all the people keeping an eye on me: three young guards at all times on three-hour shifts, twenty-four hours around the clock. I counted up eighteen lieutenants and four supervisors, not to mention the armed soldiers posted outside the building. I would lie on the bed reading and remember the three guards staring at me. The guards would not use their names, but I tried to get a feel for them as individuals. One day I saw a few in their lieutenant uniforms, and I told one guy, "Hey, you look great dressed in uniform," and he kind of smiled. I could look into the eyes of another chubby, strong lieutenant and know he sympathized with me. One day I tried to borrow a nail clipper, and two of them just shook their heads, but the chubby guy came back later and gave me one. I said, "You won't get in trouble?" and he just shrugged it off. Another officer, tall and thin, confided that he did not want to be a policeman forever. "I want to become a businessman," he said, and he told me he already had a driver's license, which is like gold. Anybody who has access to cars can make all kinds of money in China.

The guards were sizing up the monstrous Harry Wu and deciding he was a human being. And I was chatting them up, partly out of a need for friendship, partly to see whether I could manipulate the system. All prisoners need games to keep their minds occupied. Mine was taking notes when the guards were not looking, not easy to do in a small room. I would sit at the lone table and pretend to read the thick English-Chinese dictionary that my first guardians had bought for me at the start of the trip.

From time to time, I would peek at my three guards in the mirror hanging on the wall over the table. They were supposed to be watching my every move, but very quickly they realized, "Son of a bitch, the prisoner is watching us," so they had the mirror removed from the room, which was exactly what I had hoped they'd do. Now I could hunch over my dictionary and surreptitiously scribble notes, holding the book at such an angle that they could not see my hand near the binder.

They had given me twenty sheets of plain paper for my written requests and letters, and they tried to keep track of every sheet. But I would rip sheets of notepaper into quarters and jot down some notes and hope they would lose count, which sometimes they did. Then I would slip a sheet into the flyleaf of the dictionary or fold a sheet around the inner barrel of my ballpoint pen or crumple up the paper and hide it in my shoes.

Later I got the idea of writing in the inner margins of the dictionary itself. But what if they decided to riffle through the book? I again concocted glue by mixing rice and water and used it to seal the inner edges of the pages together so the authorities could not find the entries. I coded the pages according to the date. For example, on page 704, July

4, I wrote, "Got fresh air for the first time," a reminder that they let me outside for a few minutes.

I was curious to know whether they were spying on my writing, so I would always leave a pen or a piece of paper touching the cover of the book. The book was never disturbed, but one day I awoke and put on my shoes and discovered they had taken my balled-up notes in the middle of the night. I figured they had observed me fiddling with the shoe while I was in the bathroom, but they never mentioned it to me and I never mentioned it to them.

I would write down whatever happened that day: the kind of sounds I heard, the push-ups I did, the sunshine I watched, the parts of my life I reviewed, the old movies I replayed in my mind, the words I read in the dictionary.

Ever since I was a boy, I have been fascinated by insects. I used to pass up a meal just to put ferocious yellow ants in the same bottle with the less aggressive black ants and watch them fight. The yellow ants were always more powerful, and the black ants were slow, so sometimes I would try to equalize things by putting in more black ants.

Here in my villa, I had to devise my own entertainment. I would stand in front of the window, looking out at a wall across the way and the one magnolia tree, twenty feet tall with large leaves. The longer I looked out, the more I noticed the spiders in the window casing, producing one successful thread, waiting for the right breeze, and swinging out to catch hold of something else. Two contact points and the spider made a whole web. Just one filament was enough to snag a mosquito or a fly, but the amazing thing was the spider was able to walk on his own thread and not get stuck. Spiders also have a kind of radar that people have yet to duplicate or even to understand fully. The spider, I realized, was more powerful than any human—maybe smarter, too.

I also watched ants coming up through a crack at the bottom of the window, and I fed them anything I could find: a dead fly or cracker crumbs. If the morsel of food was small, a few of them would arrive to carry it, but if it was larger, like a cracker, an entire division would show up, bigger ants, soldier ants and worker ants. How did they know? One day I found a dead dragonfly, and I put it in the window casement and watched as a whole army of ants lugged this giant body back into their hole.

The guards were softening up. One day I pointed at the yard, where I could see a lot of black ants congregating, and asked a guard whether he could bring me some, so we could watch them fight. He came back with a stick covered with dozens of ants, which we added to the ants in the window, and we watched silently while they fought.

A few days later the same guard handed me, without comment, a matchbox with several dead flies and mosquitoes inside. He pointed to the window as if to say, "Be my guest."

⌒

I spent hours trying to expand my little universe. Very early I gave the officials twenty dollars to buy me a Chinese lawbook, but it didn't materialize until I no longer needed it. Having brought only enough clothes for the three weeks I had planned to be in China, I gave the guards money to buy shoes and pants, specifying the international brands I knew were sold in China—Nike and Levi's—because I wanted to see whether I could identify them as being made by prisoners. The guards came back with Chinese-brand clothes, however, which I refused to wear, saying they were of poor quality. When I left, I gave them to the female nurse who was on duty at the villa.

As a product of their system, I knew I was being given the blue-ribbon treatment. In the past, I'd had my arms twisted behind my back until the circulation stopped, heard voices shouting at me from the darkness or from behind bright lights. I knew these people did not have to search hard for electronic torture devices, like the cattle prods they hold against a prisoner's face, genitals, or feet, but they were taking a far softer route with me. "You are lucky you are an American," Wang said one day. "We treat you like the special of the specials."

His admission made me sad because I knew he was right. If I had still been a Chinese citizen, they would have taken me directly from the border to one of their camps in Xinjiang, put me to work on a road gang or maybe dipped me up to my hips in tanning acid in a leather factory. They still might do that, but first it sounded as if they planned a show trial to prove I was an enemy of the people. "You are a native Chinese," one of my interlocutors said. "You know how we defeated America in Korea and Vietnam. You know how the Singapore government caned that American criminal and the American government protested but couldn't do anything. Well, we are much stronger than Singapore. We can do what we want to you, and the American government cannot respond."

I was told they had informed the U.S. embassy but there was no response, which I did not believe. I knew that my wife and Jeff Fiedler and my friends in Congress would be making noise, but a statement like the one they made does stay in your mind. What if nobody else cares? One really doesn't know. Maybe that pressure changed my outlook a little. I was told that if I signed the paper agreeing to house arrest, then they were bound to inform my family. So on July 4, I agreed, and two days later they produced the paper, and I read it, but they never asked me to sign it. They seemed elated that after six days I was behaving rationally, but they could not resist rubbing it in. Henry Kissinger was in China, they said, with a group of American businessmen. "They want to make business deals," my captors told me. "They don't care about you."

On Saturday, July 8, nineteen days after being taken into custody, I was formally arrested. I was escorted to Room 104 and saw several people with video cameras filming my entrance. I wasn't used to all this attention, so I put my hands in the air and gave the two-finger peace sign. My captors did not think it was funny. "Come on," one lieutenant said. "Come on." An official read from a piece of paper, saying, "I represent Wuhan Public Security, and I arrest you."

They made a big show of putting handcuffs on me, very gently, the cameras rolling. It probably looked harsh on television—see China dealing with this master criminal and spy—but in person it was very gentle, as if they were saying, "Come on, Harry, let's get this over with." As soon as the photographs were taken, the police took off the handcuffs. Three minutes from start to finish for the handcuffs. That's all it took.

"Now, we will formally inform your embassy," one of them said. What did they mean "formally"? Until that moment, they'd never searched my bags in my presence, although they must have made sure I was not armed when I was caught at the border. Now they made a big show of taking away almost everything I had with me—money, wallet, camera, lens, razor and toiletries, everything except my clothing, my watch, and my wedding ring—and asking me to sign a receipt.

We were now in a new stage. I had entertained the hope they'd get tired of jousting with me and simply kick me out, but there obviously was going to be more interrogation, maybe for months. Then there would be a trial. And then they could do what they wanted with me.

I had run out of the medicine I took for the disk pressing against a nerve, a condition dating back to my accident in the mine. I told the guards I'd pay to have Ching-Lee send my prescription to China, and I reminded them to send my letters to my wife. They'd work on it, they said.

Meanwhile the top officers kept trying to break me down. "Harry," they said, "nobody agrees with you. In China, everybody criticizes you."

I said, "Yes, but is the majority always right? Remember in 1957, when people like me were called rightists and sent off to the *laogai*, but later they released me and said, 'This was a mistake.' When was the majority right? Then or now?"

I tried to fight back, but I was slumping into the darkest mood I'd had since they nabbed me on the border, twenty-one days earlier. It was starting to get to me. Maybe I needed to use my life for one last grand gesture: a hunger strike.

On July 10, I did not eat lunch. I thought this was very dramatic, but nobody cared. They just looked at the full tray and took the food away. Hey, the troublemaker doesn't feel like eating today. I realized a hunger strike would work only if people on the outside knew what I was doing. The Chinese would expect me to change my mind, and they would not inform my family or my embassy until I was near death. This meant I would have to go to the end. I had to be prepared to die.

23

IN MY ABSENCE

"I want to tell you about my feelings," Ching-Lee said not long ago. She was remembering the terrifying days when nobody knew where I was. The Chinese had told me nobody cared, but I knew that my wife and my friends and the American people cared about me. I was confident that my adopted country would fight for me.

My story is not just about Room 104 in the villa in Wuhan. It is also about the woman who was home in California, starting out as a frightened wife, becoming an effective advocate for me, for our cause. I have learned all this since I came home, and I am continually impressed by, and grateful for, all she and our friends did.

"I got his last fax on June 17, and he told me he was going to Xinjiang on June 19," Ching-Lee recalled recently when describing her experiences. "He asked me to call him right away after I received his fax, and I did, but nobody answered my call, and I found it a little strange. Afterward he told me he had left early.

"Usually Harry calls me every day, but this time was different. On the eighteenth and nineteenth of June, he didn't call, and I had a feeling something happened, but I still thought he would call. By the twentieth and twenty-first, I was sure something had happened. Maybe he'd had a car accident. Maybe Kazakhstan was not safe. Maybe he'd been robbed. Maybe he'd been killed by the Communists. I didn't know. These were the worst days. The only person I could call was Jeff Fiedler, and I couldn't eat or sleep, and even Jeff cried sometimes. Before Harry left, he told me, 'If there's no news for one week, try to take action to rescue me.' "

On June 21, Jeff cautioned her, "I think we should wait a full week because if he did enter China and it's inconvenient to make a phone call and we tell somebody, that could cause trouble."

Nobody had raised the issue of my disappearance in public, and Ching-Lee and Jeff felt it was better to leave it that way. Ching-Lee felt the burden of keeping the painful secret, however, particularly because her parents were living in the house and Ching-Lee is very close to them. They began asking questions when she appeared troubled, but she did not want to spread any anxiety, at least not yet.

"I forced myself not to cry," she recalled. "I decided not to tell my parents, but on the twentieth, I was crying, and my mother said, 'Maybe I can help.' I said it was nothing, just a bad mood, just missing Harry. But the pressure was too much for me.

"On the twenty-second, I told my mother, and of course I discovered I should have told her earlier. She really supported me. She gave me spiritual support. You know, mothers are funny. No matter how old a mother is, if something happens to her children, she becomes stronger."

Mrs. Chen told Ching-Lee that everything would be all right, that I was a big boy who had been in tough spots before. She reminded Ching-Lee that many people in China would help me, and she said that it would be politically counterproductive for the Chinese to just knock me off. She took some of the burden from Ching-Lee's shoulders.

"This was the worst time in my life," Ching-Lee has said. "At five in the morning on the twenty-third, I couldn't sleep, so I called Jeff and started talking, analyzing everything. I said, 'If I were the Communists, I would kill Harry outside China.' "

Jeff then broke the news: "Ching-Lee, Harry was arrested in China." He told her the State Department had told him overnight that it had information that I was being held near the border. Ching-Lee's most overwhelming feeling was relief. I was still alive, and she could take considerable comfort in that single fact. She said she immediately went back to sleep, to gain strength for the fight ahead.

I had no way of knowing all this until much later, of course, but my friends and supporters in Washington had been working on my behalf, and so had the government of my new country.

On June 23 at ten in the morning, the American consulate in Beijing was officially notified that Sue Howell and I had been detained at the border and that the investigation of Sue had been "concluded." The news was then relayed to Washington, and at five-thirty in the afternoon, on Thursday, June 22, Donald Keyser, the director of the China desk at the State Department, sent telegrams to Beijing and Almaty, inquiring after us. The next day in Washington, he had lunch with China's acting deputy chief of mission, Lu Shumin, to raise his concern.

Meanwhile the State Department traced Sue and me back to Almaty on June 19, when we had traveled by bus to the border. By this time, Sue was surfacing in Almaty. Over the phone, Jeff helped debrief her, to get an idea of the Chinese authorities' mood and the charges against me. Washington did not know whether I had a legal entry visa, so Ching-Lee faxed them copies of all my papers, which allowed the State Department to protest to the Chinese embassy.

I had left instructions that if anything happened to me, everybody should "make noise," to alert the world to support me. Ching-Lee wasted no time raising the volume. I knew, of course, that Ching-Lee is a capable person but I never imagined how strong and resourceful she could be in an emergency. She had dealt with reporters in her old job in Taiwan, but she had always followed her boss's orders. Now she had to make decisions and speak out on her own, despite having studied English only once a week back in Taiwan.

After the news of my capture broke, David Welker, our new employee at the foundation, told her that the press wanted to talk to her, so she began giving interviews in her second language, in a country in which she had been living for not even four years. "My first interview was on the radio, over the phone," she told me later. "I prepared something, and I spoke slowly, and afterward some of my friends called and said, 'You did a good job,' but I don't know if that was true. I wanted to understand the question, and I wanted to speak very clearly.

"The next time, I had to do a live television interview, and what was worse, the interviewer wasn't there. They put a little plug in my ear, and I could hear the interviewer asking me the questions, and I had to look into a camera when my inclination was to look at other people in the room. I asked them for the questions in advance, but they did not follow the questions they had given me. I was not sure if I answered the wrong questions." Of course if you ask most people on the Sunday-morning Beltway talk shows a question, they will make a statement about whatever they want, so Ching-Lee wasn't doing anything unusual.

"One morning I had to get up at four o'clock, California time, to give interviews to *Good Morning America* and the CBS morning show—one in our family room, the other in our living room. It was very hard. I was afraid that I might not answer the questions in perfect English but I did my best. Afterward I said to myself, 'I can handle it.' Generally reporters from newspapers and magazines could somehow understand my broken English, but on television I had to learn to make fewer mistakes."

She was being modest. Later, when I saw the articles and the tapes from those months, I was extremely impressed. My wife was a media star. She made me and our cause come alive. "Harry is a man, but he is passionate," she told Seth Mydans of *The New York Times*. "He left the camps already fifteen or sixteen years ago, but he still sometimes cries over his friends who died there." She told about my dream to create a *laogai* museum just like the Holocaust museum and said that I often met with former camp members so we could share our memories. "When they get together, they are different," Ching-Lee told Mydans. "Their talking is different from our talking. They are laughing, they are crying, they have their own world." The reporters always asked why nobody could talk me out of going back. "Harry is really different," she would always say. "If he insists on doing something, then he will do it. Nobody can change his mind."

On June 28, Ching-Lee flew to Washington to visit Congress and urge our representatives to help get me out. "Harry is an American," she declared. "The Chinese government has already robbed my husband of nineteen years of his life. They have no right to keep him for a single day against his will."

These remarks were repeated on the evening news and appeared in the next day's headlines. The world is all connected now. You can sit in a hotel room anywhere in the world and watch CNN and find out what is happening. Saddam Hussein knew about the U.S. action in the Persian Gulf War by watching CNN. When Ching-Lee spoke to Congress, the leaders of Beijing had to know. Nobody could forget about me. She would not let them.

The Clinton administration, to tell the truth, was not happy with my trips because they complicated relations between Washington and Beijing, something Clinton needed like a hole in the head. But since I was a citizen, the administration fought for me. I have since seen State Department transcripts that showed just how much my adopted homeland did for one naturalized troublemaker.

On June 27, Deputy Assistant Secretary Kent M. Wiedemann met with the Chinese chargé d'affaires, Zhou Wenzhong, and asked that an American official be allowed to meet with me and that I be released from China promptly. On June 28 in Beijing, the American embassy's consul general, Arturo Macias, called on the Chinese to confirm my whereabouts. In Washington, Assistant Secretary of State Winston Lord, a former ambassador to China, summoned Zhou to insist on more information.

The unsung hero was Charles Parish, an official in the American embassy in Beijing. Because Parish speaks Mandarin, he was sent out to Xinjiang to try to find me. He left on June 29 and arrived in Ürümqi on June 30, only to be told I might still be in Horgas. Because there were no flights between Ürümqi and Horgas, Parish hired a taxi to take him the 375 miles. Twelve hours later he got to Horgas, where the Chinese officials insisted I had never been, which of course they had to know was a lie. Parish also contacted Chinese officials in Yining, and even though I had passed through their town a week earlier, they said they didn't know anything about me. On July 3, Parish located the Karamai Guesthouse, but nobody there knew anything either. He ran out of money on July 4 and had to go back to Ürümqi, where money could be wired to him.

Meanwhile in Washington, Jeff Fiedler had daily contact with John J. Foarde III, a duty officer on the China desk, who coordinated the information and was always helpful and sympathetic.

Jeff needed money for the extraordinary expenses that defending me would entail. Brian Freeman—an investment banker from New Jersey and a friend of Jeff's—gave us fifty thousand dollars when Jeff explained the problem, and through the help of Phyllis Jenkins, a friend of mine in Los Angeles, the family foundation of Kirk Douglas, the actor, later sent Jeff a check for three thousand dollars.

Two groups did not respond when Jeff tried to get them to help: Chinese-American businesspeople held back because they thought I was cutting into their profits, and American lawyers with expertise in China did not want to be identified with me because they did not want their access to China cut off. But some of my friends in Congress beat the drums for me, especially Representatives Nancy Pelosi, Frank Wolf, and Christopher Smith, and Senator Jesse Helms.

Jeff continued to give suggestions to the State Department. He told Anthony Lake, Clinton's national security adviser, that I was trying to get into Xinjiang to investigate the World Bank's presence there, and he suggested that maybe he would tell the press this. He also told Winston Lord that he had a perfect solution for continued violations of the Hawley-Smoot Act: Just inspect all Chinese imports for possible *laogai* products. "They could do it in one port, maybe Seattle," Jeff mused. "Send just two inspectors out there, and you'd have ships backed up all the way to Hawaii. That will get the attention of the Chinese government and also the American business community."

Hearing that former secretary of state Henry Kissinger was going to Beijing on a business trip, Jeff enlisted Lane Kirkland, the longtime president of the AFL-CIO, to ask Kissinger to speak up for me in his talks with the Chinese leaders. Kissinger apparently rather forcefully reminded the Chinese that holding American citizens is bad for relations between China and the United States. Jeff also got help from Archbishop Desmond M. Tutu, who spoke up for me with the Chinese trade officials in South Africa. Many other people around the world spoke up for me in their countries and in Beijing.

Meanwhile Under Secretary of State Peter Tarnoff in Washington called on Zhou to express "grave concern" about my situation. Zhou claimed I was under investigation, not in detention. On July 5 in Beijing, the American chargé d'affaires, Scott Hallford, met with Assistant Foreign Minister Yang Jiechi—same story. On July 7, Arturo Macias met with Peng Keyu of the Foreign Ministry, who gave him assurances that I soon would be able to see visitors.

The next day Fan Zhengshui, a chief in the Foreign Ministry, announced that I was being charged with "past crimes" and was being held in Wuhan. Fan also said I was charged with "sneaking" into China under a false name, stealing state secrets, and passing them outside China.

On the morning of July 9, Ching-Lee was awakened at home by a reporter who told her I had been arrested. "This sounded terrible," Ching-Lee told a friend. "I knew that if Harry was charged with spying, he could be sentenced to death. I knew we had to work harder to get people's attention."

24

I GET SOME COMPANY

On July 10, I was one meal into starving myself to death when the guards announced a surprise. "Hurry up, your friend is coming to see you," Liu said. I did not know I had any friends in this part of the world, and try as I might to persuade them, the guards were not about to tell me who it was.

I was ushered into a Crown, a Japanese-made car, with a curtain drawn around the windows so nobody could peer inside, and we headed downtown, with a lieutenant on either side of me in the back seat.

Through the curtains, I caught glimpses of the city—the riverside, the parks where I had courted the college girl I would marry. All the painful memories came flooding back: my years after prison, teaching at the university, seeking my visa, the hopes I had of starting my life over again in California, the rejection by Diana. Now I was a prisoner again. Had I gone through all those changes just to be brought back here in captivity? I did my best to keep dark thoughts out of my mind.

They took me to Wuhan Prison Number 1 and put me in a room with General Wang, who looked at me and grimaced, noticing I had not shaved since they'd confiscated my razor, two days earlier. Couldn't have me looking unkempt for company—whoever the company was. He produced a razor and told me to shave, under his surveillance.

When I was clean shaven, I was deposited in a room with a thick glass barrier for separating prisoners from their visitors. Both sides had a telephone and a police monitor, who kept his hand on the phone's disconnect button. Prisoners are allowed to talk about the weather, their family, their health, but if they veer into the details of their case, the monitor cuts off the conversation by pushing the button.

A door opened, and a man entered—not very tall, with glasses and a nice suit. "My name is Arturo Macias," he said over the telephone. "I'm the American consul general based in Beijing. I came here right away, as soon as I received notice from the Chinese government. As you probably know, there is currently no ambassador to China, so I am the top-ranking officer in the embassy."

He said he had only thirty minutes to talk, so he asked some basic questions about my name, my passport, and where I lived, to verify my identity. "I have a letter from your wife," he said, displaying it through the glass. "They won't allow me to give it to you, but I can read it to you." The note from Ching-Lee said she was fine and thinking about me. I tried not to show any emotion in front of the police. After he read the letter, he told me, "Harry, I want you to know we are all subject to Chinese law. This doesn't mean just you. It includes me, too."

I took that as a message that legal procedures were now being followed, and I also heard a subtle warning that I would have to cooperate a little, give up some information, allow my captors some face.

"Also, I want you to know your wife is thinking about you, and you have many friends in Congress."

The monitor didn't push the button in response to that, and it was quite clear that my captors had lied when they said nobody cared back home. My friends in Congress had heard about my predicament and would do what they could. Macias asked whether there was anything I needed, and I said I wanted an attorney to write a will for me. Also, I said, my back was worse, and I asked him to get Ching-Lee to send me the medicine I needed. I also wanted reading materials: Chinese lawbooks plus *Moby-Dick* and *The Old Man and the Sea*. Listing these two favorite books was my way of signaling that I was ready for a fight—just like Melville's Ahab, just like Hemingway's Old Man.

I told Macias I was not being tortured, and when he asked about the food, I said I didn't want to talk about it. In truth, it wasn't bad, but I did not want to praise them. Macias said, "I have brought some writing paper and magazines and newspapers for you." Later I would discover that he had brought a book of articles by Hemingway, two personal-computer magazines, *House and Garden*, *Architectural Digest*, three Chinese newspapers, and the March 1995 issue of *National Geographic*, whose feature topic was the Endangered Species Act and whose front cover was a photograph of a red fox trapped in a net with a headline that said DEAD OR ALIVE. Why not the February or April issue? For days, I wondered whether Macias was trying to send me a message or whether they just happened to have that issue lying around the office. Macias said that Chinese law allowed only one visit every thirty days. I asked the guards to give him a letter to Ching-Lee, but they would not let him take it.

After Macias left, I felt honored that my adopted country had made such efforts to send a professional like him all the way from Beijing to Wuhan to make sure I was all right. The United States is a country that cares for its individuals. Here I was, a naturalized citizen causing every-body trouble, and the United States did not just say, "Forget about him." I felt so good about the visit that I ended my hunger strike after one meal. I'm not even sure my captors noticed.

On July 13, a security agent gave me pain-relief pills and a small prescription-type bottle with a dark-brown liquid inside and no writing on the outside. I asked what it was, and they told me it was herbal med-icine for my back. "I can't take it," I said because I had no idea what it was.

"We did our job; don't blame us," one of the officers said.

I had no choice. A female nurse put a spoonful in my mouth, then gave me a cup of water, and she returned later with another dose.

Within two days, my nose started bleeding profusely. I lay down and held a small towel to my nose, but the bleeding would not stop. The young guard was afraid the star prisoner, the master spy, was going to die on his watch, so he put a larger cold towel on my head until the bleeding finally stopped.

The damage was already done. Within two days, blood vessels popped in both eyes, causing the whites of my eyes to turn black. When Ching-Lee saw pictures of me on television a few weeks later, she could see that my right eye was still black, and she feared I was being tortured. In a way, I was. I still wonder what the purpose of their medicine was. My eyes are constantly red from the vessels having popped: a little souvenir from my homeland.

Now that I was officially under arrest, the authorities had the right to interrogate me, but the visit from Macias renewed my will to fight. I was curious to see the mental state of China in 1995, what the authorities had on me, what they considered important, the charges that would decide whether or not I spent the next segment of my life back in their system. I was relieved when I knew that my detainment was no longer secret. Their game was now in a new phase. At least they could not secretly abolish me. Would they go back to the madness of the Mao years, when a person was guilty of being a counterrevolutionary if he was even related to a landlord? Or would they confine their charges to the specific acts they had questioned me about?

They would not supply me with a Chinese lawbook although I had given them twenty dollars to buy one, but I knew a bit about Chinese law. They could charge me with a violation of Article 32, spying, which could carry serious penalties, including death. But if they charged me with Article 166, stealing state secrets, the punishment could be anything from five to fifteen years' imprisonment or maybe even death. I had the feeling there was a major conflict between the security and legal bureaucracies and the Foreign Ministry. The prosecutors probably wanted to charge me with spying while the Foreign Ministry probably had larger political considerations and did not want to jail an American for a long time. My fate seemed caught up in the intrigues of Beijing.

One of the first questions asked of me was about the two documents Ching-Lee and I had stolen in Shanghai, which linked the factories and the camps with the government. "You held up this document to the American Congress," one of my interrogators said. I couldn't very well deny doing so, but I tried telling them that a college student had given it to me. They did not go for that and asked why I had displayed the document in Congress.

I said it was simple. "I wanted to show them that the Shanghai steel pipes are made with *laogai* labor."

They then produced testimony from the factory manager in Shanghai, who said he had left the report on his desk and that the only people in the room were Ching-Lee and me. "Come on, we know you did it," Wang said. "There's no other way that document could have gone from Shanghai to the United States."

I did what any married man would do under those circumstances. "I didn't steal them," I said. "My wife did it."

"But you knew about it," they said.

"I only knew when I got back to the United States."

I tried telling them that under American law, they could not charge me if somebody else in the office had taken the document. I told them Ching-Lee was the criminal, not me. (When I got home, I told Ching-Lee I had blamed her. She said, "That's all right, I'm not planning to go back to China soon anyway." My wife is a very understanding person.)

I kept reminding them that I needed exercise and fresh air, and now that I was actually arrested, they finally let me into the inner courtyard for thirty minutes every day. One sunny day I stripped down to my briefs, hardly caring who saw me. I just wanted to get some sun on my body after having been cooped up indoors for nearly a month. At first, I walked around the courtyard, just to get my legs moving, and the next day I did about thirty push-ups even though my back was hurting.

After a few days, I lay down on the ground and pretended to be sleeping, covering my eyes with my hands, but really I was checking out the area. Because I never saw or heard anybody else, I had assumed the second story of the villa was empty, but as I lay on the ground pretending to be asleep, I noticed several people looking out over the balcony, talking to themselves as if to say, "So that's the guy."

I wondered what they were doing up there, and then it hit me: They probably had a whole operations staff upstairs, operating telephone lines to Beijing, collecting electronic information, reading printouts. Just from what I could observe, there seemed to be between fifty and sixty people in the villa, watching me. Maybe they were even watching me on hidden monitors. I looked harder for a hidden camera in my room and in Room 104, but I never found one. It was not until I went back to the States and saw some television footage the Chinese released that I realized they did indeed have a monitor in both my room and Room 104.

~

On July 18, my interrogators showed me the 60 *Minutes* tape from my first and second trips. There I was in the hotel room, and Ed Bradley was saying I had to visit the factory or he could not sign the contract, and the general manager was scurrying around trying to arrange my visit. It brought back happy memories of our sting, but I could not afford to gloat. It would be hard for me to deny my participation since the tape had been shown all over the world, so I described the entire hotel-room episode. They were very pleased and they said, "Okay, everything you told us matched our investigation." These guys were sticklers for detail. They had gone back to the exact room, measured the distances and the angles, told me where the cameras were.

We did have a difference of opinion about whether I had committed a crime against the Chinese government. I asked them whether they had heard about freedom of the press. I was working for CBS and the BBC on my trips, which hardly made me a spy.

They were fascinated by Ed Bradley and kept asking me how much money he made. "He makes millions of dollars," I said. "Go after him." It was quite clear to me they were stunned that a black man in America could make that much money. I also nominated David Gelber, the CBS producer, as a culprit. "If I'm a criminal, they're all criminals," I said. "They paid for my trip."

The interrogation rolled on as if we were speaking different languages. "The chicken talks to the duck," as the old Chinese saying goes. When I was sitting in Room 104, I told myself, "These things don't relate to you. You are a third person." If I had related emotionally to these things, I could not have gone on.

The police also brought up my relationship with Mr. Feng, the old photographer whose pictures for the foundation were useless and who may have given evidence against me. I told them his pictures were for information, not for spying, that I had not made him visit any forbidden areas or steal state secrets.

Another charge was posing as a policeman, but I said I had bought the uniform at a street market and never wore a badge or claimed I was an officer. Of course I lied to them. I actually borrowed the uniform from a real police officer, through my friend Liu.

All these interrogations took time because the secretary had to write down all the questions and answers, and then I had to approve the transcript, often fifteen or twenty pages long, before they could continue. Most of their questions were so obvious, things in the public record, that I got the feeling they were killing time, waiting for Beijing to decide what to do with me. The interrogators never seemed to go after my network of supporters. It began to dawn on me that they could keep me indefinitely, not just weeks but for months or years.

I spent a great deal of time in my room, standing in front of the window, not dreaming but reviewing. Did I endure all that suffering just to come back here? What was the purpose of my life? On July 22, all the parts of my whole life seemed to join together. I stood with my back to the three lieutenants, my hands clasped behind me, and I saw everything, everything, in perfect order, in perfect clarity. It was a moment of truth—half meditation, as with the Buddhists; half revelation, as with the Christians—the two forces of my life blending together.

I saw myself as a teenager, inquisitive, energetic, hopeful. I saw my stepmother hugging all eight children, and I saw my father, proud of his family. Good times, bad times. I closed my eyes, and I could see my classmates and my teachers, my baseball team, the first time I went out to play shortstop, the solid feeling of the ball smacking into my glove, the burst of energy as I threw the runner out at first base. I saw the smile on Meihua's face as we parked our bicycles and kissed innocently behind a tree.

I could feel the anger, the terror, when they arrested me at college, the first time I was tortured, the faces of Chen Ming and the others who died. I reviewed the years after my release, discovering that all of China was a giant prison camp. I recalled the early years in California so vividly that I could smell the grease in the doughnut shop. Good times, bad times. Cars, speeding tickets, minor accidents, meeting people from Berkeley and Stanford, the possibilities for me in America.

I thought about my three trips back to China. Were these random experiences, or had they been heading toward something important to help the Chinese people? Was I a forgotten man, an obscure prisoner, or could I become a worldwide symbol of defiance? I did not know. My personal review ended abruptly in 1990, the year I met Ching-Lee. My mind would not allow me to review my new life.

"Hey," one of the young lieutenants said softly. "Why don't you lie down? Go to sleep. Go to bed." He was afraid I was asleep on my feet, hypnotized or something, but lost in my reveries, I just shrugged him off. I decided my life was important. I was supposed to be here. I could get through it.

General Wang was almost always calm, a big-timer used to important cases, but one day I made him really angry.

A British television company in Yorkshire had done a very nice fifty-minute documentary using some of my crude tapes from the first trip. The Yorkshire people had come to California, filmed me and Ching-Lee in our office, then riding our bicycles as we had on our visits to the camps.

Afterward the CTV network in Taiwan had edited the Yorkshire film, making a corny twenty-minute documentary about a "master spy" at work, giving it a new title, *Inside Mainland China*, and putting my name on it. It was like one of those docudramas that American television networks fob off as real news on the new generation of viewers who cannot read newspapers. The Chinese now showed me the Taiwanese version as if it were evidence.

"I was educated by your government," I told Wang. "I was taught, 'Don't trust the Kuomintang. Don't believe a word they say. It's all just reactionary propaganda.' Now you are using a Kuomintang film to prosecute me. Now you trust them?"

Wang jumped to his feet and started banging the table. "If it's true, we use it," he shouted.

"Look at it carefully," I told him. "Why do they put Chinese characters on the script, have outside people making comments? Don't you listen? The original was in English. There's no sound in this one. No dialogue. How can it be used as evidence? The Taiwanese translation is different from the British original. You'd better get the original Yorkshire film. You want to use Taiwan rumors?"

Wang blustered and grumbled, but I never heard about that Kuomintang fiction again.

They started to zero in on the alleged Silk Road trip that Sue Lloyd-Roberts and I had taken. At first, I thought they were going to take the low road of speculating about what had gone on in the single hotel room Sue and I shared—nothing went on—but they never evinced the slightest curiosity. They were more obsessed with our "spying" techniques, asking about our contacts and what we had done at different camps.

But if I lived by any rule, it was this: Never tell them anything they don't already know. What driver? What car? I had been to so many places so many times with so many drivers, I said, I couldn't remember.

"Let me give you a clue," somebody would say. "It was a fancy car."

"Oh, yeah, I remember. It was a Korean car. Good one, air-conditioning. The driver had a small mustache." That driver had taken us lots of places, places he didn't want to go, places we told him were safe. I did not want him and his family to suffer because of me, but they already knew about him. "If the driver took me to a prison camp, he didn't know what I was doing."

They assured me nobody would get into trouble. I asked whether the two officials from the Qinghai Hide and Garment Works had been fired because of the publicity from 60 Minutes, and Wang assured me they were still on the job. My interrogators tried to make a big fuss about a poignant BBC segment shot at a lonely graveyard outside the Tanan Laogai Farm, in which Sue Lloyd-Roberts talks about the thousands of prisoners who had been brought out to Xinjiang only to die there. I had guessed that the stone tombstones probably marked the graves of former prisoners who had been "released" to work or maybe marked the graves of their families while the actual prisoners had been buried in another field, with wooden tombstones. The filmmakers had stopped the film at the shot of the stone tombstone and asked, 'Is that a prisoner's grave?" I readily conceded that the BBC film had missed the distinction. "It is not true," I said, little realizing my captors would use my taped words in an attempt to discredit the entire film.

I outsmarted myself when General Wang said that the BBC documentary claimed fifteen million people were living in Xinjiang and maybe ten million of them were political prisoners. *Xinhua* had already made this charge in October of 1994, and I was prepared for Wang's statement. "This is a terrible lie," he said.

"You should check out the original English tape," I advised.

A translator was called in, and after watching the original BBC film, he said that the narrator had said, "ten million in the country."

I was sorry I had opened my mouth. It would have been better to catch them in court in such an error, but they never repeated this error.

Sometimes they surprised me with the things they did know. Once, when I was giving them a hard time, one of them said, "Don't underestimate our ability. I can just pick up the phone and dial the United States and prove you are lying. We have many friends in the United States who don't like you." Then the interrogator held out a piece of paper, folded, with only the top showing. "Recognize this?" he asked with a snarl. It was stationery from the Laogai Research Foundation. He then showed me the red seal at the bottom, which I recognized as mine.

"Let me look more closely," I said, catching a glimpse of the date, May 24, 1995. I seemed to recall sending a note to a foundation in Taiwan. Damn, how did they get that? Did China have a mole in Taiwan? Did they go through my garbage? Were they somehow able to read my mail? I had never seen any sign of tampering with my house or my security measures, but my interrogator had made his point. "Maybe that's my seal," I said with a shrug, but I could not let it end there. "Hey," I said. "You're accusing me of stealing your documents. How come you can steal mine?"

They didn't think that was funny.

Wang also surprised me one day by asking who Shannon Ramsby is. I kept a straight face and said the name did not sound familiar, but Wang tried to refresh my memory. He said, "Shannon Ramsby spent the night in the same hotel with you and your wife in Shashi."

Oh, I said, that guy. I told Wang we had met an American on a steamer going down the Yangtze and invited him to stay with us when the hotel in Shashi was short of rooms. They clearly had Shannon's name, and I could only wonder whether they knew he had flown in and out with Ching-Lee, but they never asked about him again.

~

Sometimes I was surprised by the things they did not know. They kept asking me about the foundation, my books, and my friends in Congress as if they were all intertwined. Because the Chinese government dominates all aspects of life, they assume the same is true about the United States. I told them that my friends are Democrats and Republicans, that they are affiliated with the AFL-CIO, which is liberal, and the Hoover Institution, which is conservative. They wanted to know how much money I made from Hoover, and I said eighty thousand dollars a year, which got their attention. It would also get the attention of my friends at the Hoover Institution, which does not pay me a penny.

"Who are your colleagues? How do you work together? Do you need approval for what you do? What is the purpose of the organization?"

The questions seemed prepared, probably shipped in from Beijing. The supervisor just read them, and my answers were recorded.

"How come you travel for a project like this, and Hoover doesn't know about it?"

"Hey, this is America," I said. "It doesn't work that way."

The interrogator seemed smug, as if I were hiding something, but I was just tired of their fishing expedition with the Hoover Institution.

"I'll be frank about it," he said. "We know the chairman of the Hoover Institute is also the head of the FBI."

Good grief. He was confusing J. Edgar Hoover, the former director of the Federal Bureau of Investigation, who has been dead since 1972, with Herbert Hoover, the president of the United States from 1929 through 1932, who has been dead since 1964. I didn't correct his error. I didn't want to demolish his pet conspiracy theory.

They were really testy about the BBC segment on organ transplants, their cash crop. The concept of independent reporting seemed foreign to them. "Did you actually see overseas patients over there?"

"We only spent a few hours in that hospital; how could we do that? But it was your own doctors who told us that patients come from America, Hong Kong, Macao—all over."

"You said on the BBC that it was a kidney transplant, but you showed doctors operating on a heart. Why did you say it was kidneys?"

"Look at it carefully," I told them. "The film says 'organs.' It never says 'kidneys.'"

That was their major complaint about the BBC documentary. I told them the BBC was just trying to show an operation in a modern Chinese hospital, not trying to mislead anybody. The BBC never claimed it was a kidney-transplant operation.

My interrogators tried to capitalize on a few other details in the BBC film. They said Dr. Yang in Chengdu denied making an agreement in two or three hours for a thirty-thousand-dollar kidney transplant, but Sue and I were there, and we know he did. They said we claimed there were overseas patients at Chengdu, but we merely reported that two different doctors had told us they did receive patients from all over the world. They said we were wrong in claiming that one third of the products in Xinjiang were made in prison camps and accounted for half the province's exports. I told them it was only an estimate and that they were welcome to give more complete figures, which they never did.

They also complained about the BBC segment showing Sue in front of a gravestone, claiming that it was in a burying field for prisoners when actually it was the gravestone of a local woman. I had noticed this discrepancy and had called Sue to alert her, but the film had already been shown once on the afternoon news. She rushed to have it corrected for the evening news, but it had already been sent out to the international news outlets, which is how the Chinese authorities noticed it. It is true that many prisoners are buried in unmarked fields or with makeshift wooden markers. As far as I was concerned, this was the only factual error in the entire program, but they were using every nuance against me in an attempt to blur the truth Sue and I had uncovered.

Toward the end of July, the Chinese authorities released a fifteen-minute documentary entitled *See How Harry Wu Lied*. They tried to peddle it to Hong Kong television stations for fifty thousand dollars, but nobody would touch it until the price was dropped to three thousand dollars, and then the outside world was able to view it. The first shot showed me in Room 104, obviously tired and wearing the same clothes I had worn since my capture. I could be seen answering their questions with smirks and sarcasm, arms folded and head cocked.

"Who edited the commentary?" one interrogator asks me on the film.

"The BBC," I say rather wearily.

Does the report have "any foundation"?

"I've said it's wrong," I say sarcastically.

I repeatedly agree there are a few minor errors in the BBC film, but I keep asserting it was not my intention, or Sue Lloyd-Roberts's intention, to get anything wrong. No wonder their asking price for their obvious propaganda plummeted from fifty thousand to three thousand dollars. They didn't have much on me.

In China, there was one repercussion from the film. Some big shot saw it and noticed I was still wearing my wedding ring and wristwatch, apparently a breach of their rules. A day or two after the film was seen, Wang told me he had to confiscate the ring and watch, too.

Without even meaning to, my tormentors punched a hole in my armor on July 30, when they showed the Yorkshire tape, with a close-up of Ching-Lee. I had struggled to keep her in a separate compartment of my mind, but now her soft voice, her sweet face, her intelligent words on the screen were like a knife in my heart. They had not laid a hand on me, but this was pure torture. "Stop!" I shouted. "Stop the machine!"

They were so surprised by my outburst that they changed their tone. All they wanted was for me to identify the footage; I had no compunction about dismissing it as public-record stuff. I just shut down, and they allowed me some face. The session was over.

I went back to my room and lay down on the bed, yanking my T-shirt up to cover my eyes. Now that I had seen Ching-Lee's face, I wanted to keep her there, in my mind, all night.

"Are you okay?" the young guard asked.

I was crying. I did not want him to see my tears. I willed myself to sleep with my dear wife's face before my mind's eye.

On the night of August 3, forty-five days after my capture, General Wang arrived dressed in plain clothes, accompanied by his secretary. Normally Wang and his secretary would sit behind the table, but this time they sat near me on chairs, just chatting. "Our job is almost done," the general said. "Very soon we will hand everything over to the prosecutor, but I just want to clean up your file. There's some stuff in there about your relations with a woman."

"What are you talking about?" I asked. Frankly I was curious.

"When you left camp, you became a lecturer in school, and you had some personal problems. Do you want to talk about it?"

Ah, so that was it. He was not specific, but I knew he was talking about my divorce from my first wife and the young student I had married in 1984. When someone becomes an enemy of the government, even the old wounds of his private life will be used as ammunition against him.

"Leave that file alone," I said. "It doesn't matter."

Wang could see I would not talk, and he let the subject drop. He was my age, and perhaps he could sense my old pain from being rejected.

Three days later one of the interrogators, Colonel Duan, gave me a piece of paper to sign three times, so they could check my signature on the contract for the charges of my giving money to old Feng, the photographer in Hong Kong. I briefly wondered whether they could concoct some kind of confession above my signatures, but I wrote my name in the middle of the page and knew they could not squeeze anything above or below it. Duan told me the indictment would be handed up any day now and added, "Good luck. Maybe I'll see you in the United States." Was he trying to send me a message? I asked how he expected to be in the States, and he said he had already traveled twice to Hong Kong, a fact that betrayed his standing within China's bureaucracy. "I have a nephew in the U.S.," Duan said. "Won't you welcome me if I come over there?"

"I won't be there," I replied. "I'll be in prison over here. You people are charging me with all sorts of crimes."

He just smiled as if he knew something I didn't.

The next morning I was visited by two prosecutors, who asked me a few basic questions, just for identification, and then left. In the afternoon, they returned and handed me the indictment and made me sign a receipt for it. They said they liked my cooperative attitude. I hadn't realized I was being cooperative.

Back in my room, I read the indictment carefully. I wanted to see whether they were going after me for treason or just for stealing state secrets. The former would mean execution; the latter would mean fifteen years in prison and maybe execution. The first paragraph said I had gone through "three years of reeducation through labor in Beijing for theft"—the old fifty-yuan business. How many times did I have to tell these people those charges had been dropped when I was released from camp? They never mentioned my years as a counterrevolutionary rightist. They were trying to portray me as a common criminal. I glanced at the other charges:

- Using false names to enter China
- Visiting without authorization my old prison coal mine in Shanxi to take pictures
- Videotaping without authorization the other prison mine in Shanxi twice in 1991
- Giving money to a few former prisoners
- Stealing documents from Shanghai *laogai* factories
- Giving four thousand dollars to Feng to "spy" on prison facilities
- Videotaping without permission prisons in Xinjiang in 1994
- Going without permission with Zhang to the Baimaolin *laogai* farm in 1994
- Giving false information to two foreign broadcasting companies
- Posing as a police official by wearing a police uniform in Qinghai in 1991

The indictment went on to say that the accused had committed "grave offenses by spying on, stealing, and providing China's state secrets on judicial administration to institutions and organizations outside the country or bribing others to do the same on his behalf, which seriously undermined China's national interests." I worried that the phrases "grave offenses" and "seriously undermined" might be a code for a long sentence. On the next-to-last page, I found what I was seeking: "His acts have violated . . . the provisions of Article 166 of the Criminal Law of the People's Republic of China." It was the lesser charge. They were dredging up the old fifty-yuan business from years earlier. Most of the other stuff was a matter of public record. It meant they had no proof linking me with another government. Nor did the indictment mention 60 *Minutes*. I knew why. To include the CBS show would only publicize what they were doing in the camps. They did not want to put themselves on trial. They had tried to smoke out my support system in China, and they had mostly failed.

The more I studied the indictment, the more I realized it was a classic document composed by a Communist mind. By accusing me of being a fifty-yuan thief, they avoided mentioning that I had once been accused of being a counterrevolutionary rightist. They were trying to evade this untidy episode of China's recent history. On the whole, the charges were small potatoes indeed. On the one hand, I was relieved that the Communists were not going to shoot me. But on the other hand, I was furious. These people had held me for nearly two months. This was the best they could do?

25

CERTAINLY NOT

Two very strong and intelligent women were caught up in my case. One of them was Ching-Lee Wu from Milpitas, California. The other was Hillary Rodham Clinton from Little Rock, Arkansas. The two women had something in common. Both wanted me out of China as soon as possible—though for different reasons.

I had missed the occasional rumors in the spring of 1995 that Mrs. Clinton was hoping to address the Fourth World Conference on Women, sponsored by the United Nations, which was to open in Beijing on September 4. Now that I was caught, on July 8 articles in American newspapers reported that "political differences" might prevent her attendance. I was the political difference.

This was hardly a case of our sitting down and planning to take advantage of Mrs. Clinton's trip, but once it came up, my people had to be aware of it. Although I sometimes criticized President Clinton's lack of a strong stand on trade and human rights regarding China, I never intended to put pressure on him in this way. Both Ching-Lee and I have great respect for Mr. and Mrs. Clinton. When he became a candidate in 1992, we were impressed with the Clintons' intelligence and youth and with their support for health reform and women's rights.

Unfortunately I got in the way of a trip Mrs. Clinton felt was very important. While she never said she was definitely going, she also never said she would not go if the Chinese did not release me. She watched it happen day by day while Ching-Lee stood up for me in public. "I think why the Chinese Government is doing this to Harry is because they think the Americans are weak; the American Government does not act very strong, so the Chinese act strong," Ching-Lee told *The New York Times* on July 9.

"They think maybe the American people are just concerned about money," she said. "So we have to let the Chinese Government know that we care about individual people, that the whole country is just like a big family."

Many groups and people did treat me like family. Human Rights Watch urged the United States to ask the World Bank to postpone two large loans, totaling $660 million, for highway and hydroelectric projects in China. It also suggested the White House pressure large American companies to seek my release through their contacts in China.

Right after I met with Arturo Macias, he called Ching-Lee to reassure her I was all right. At the same time, Secretary of State Warren Christopher made a public speech in which he said, "The thing that would be most conducive to good relations between the U.S. and China . . . would be the early and prompt release of Mr. Harry Wu."

Many people in Washington wanted to meet Ching-Lee, but Jeff Fiedler felt that they should start at the top. He held off everybody until he could get appointments with Senator Bob Dole and Representative Newt Gingrich. Representative Gingrich was still riding high from the stunning Republican victory in the midterm elections of 1994, and he tossed off a thunderbolt on July 9. Speaking with Bob Schieffer of CBS, Gingrich said the Clinton administration should resume diplomatic ties with Taiwan immediately, regardless of what happened to me. When the administration suggested that this was not a good time to taunt China, he backed off a bit, but he had certainly gotten everybody's attention.

When they went to meet the Speaker of the House for what they thought was a private chat, David Welker and Ching-Lee were a little surprised to find a large herd of reporters outside his office. The Speaker told them he was very concerned about me, particularly when he heard I had run out of medicine. He told Ching-Lee his wife suffered from a herniated disk, and thus he was enormously sympathetic. Ching-Lee had never been around American politicians, and she was getting an education about how they operate. She offered the Speaker a little yellow ribbon, the symbol of support for hostages that all our friends were wearing, and she was taken aback when he said, "Could we just hold up on that for a while?"

She did not understand that this gathering in the Speaker's office was a photo opportunity. The press secretary then allowed all the photographers into the room, and Gingrich said to Ching-Lee, "Now you can pin it on," and he told the reporters, "We are very concerned about Mr. Wu." As soon as the photographers were gone, Gingrich said to Ching-Lee, "Could you take this off me, please?" To Ching-Lee, the request sounded a little odd coming from a man who had just spoken fervently of his support for my plight. Gingrich must have seen the look on her face because he quickly said, "I know this is a little contrived, but Ronald Reagan taught me this."

In came another herd of press people, this time the television crews, and once again Representative Gingrich motioned for Ching-Lee to pin the ribbon on him. Spontaneous moment, take 2. In talking to the press, Gingrich said he was hoping Ching-Lee would meet either the president or Mrs. Clinton. David was sitting next to Ching-Lee, and he was in a position to notice the Speaker's aide handing him a note that read, "Prez will not see her." (At first glance, that sounded as if the White House did not want to give us public support, but much later I was assured that the official White House strategy was to reserve President Clinton for a last-resort gesture, in case things really went badly for me in captivity.) The old Ronald Reagan trick paid off. The double exposure of Ching-Lee pinning the yellow ribbon on Newt Gingrich was in newspapers and on television all over the world.

The day after she met with Gingrich, Ching-Lee was invited to the White House to meet several people, including Anthony Lake, the national security adviser. "Mr. Lake said he gave a briefing about you to the president every day," Ching-Lee told me later. "He said President Clinton was very concerned about you."

They talked for thirty-five minutes, and when the meeting was over, Jeff and Ching-Lee were asked to avoid making any strong statements to the press. Nevertheless, while Jeff and Ching-Lee were leaving the White House, a group of reporters chased them down. "They were calling out, 'Mrs. Wu, Mrs. Wu,' " Ching-Lee told me later. "I had asked Jeff how to talk to reporters, and he said, 'Be honest with them. Just tell them there is nothing to discuss.' " Ching-Lee stopped on the White House lawn as the swarm of reporters shouted questions at her. They asked her whether she was satisfied with what the government was doing, and Ching-Lee answered, "So far." They also wanted to know what Ching-Lee thought about Mrs. Clinton's upcoming trip.

"Would you urge her not to go?" a female reporter asked.

"Certainly," Ching-Lee replied spontaneously.

"Why?"

"Until my husband comes back."

It was perfect television. "That answer went around the world in ten minutes," Jeff recalled. The headlines essentially said, MRS. WU ASKS MRS. CLINTON NOT TO GO TO BEIJING.

Ching-Lee had given an honest answer, and Jeff was not unhappy with the response. As of that moment, Mrs. Clinton could not go to Beijing without appearing to be insensitive to Harry Wu and his loyal wife. "I wonder if that reporter had not asked me, would I have connected those things," Ching-Lee said later. "She reminded me I wanted to help my husband."

On July 13, Representatives Newt Gingrich and Benjamin Gilman and Senators Bob Dole, Jesse Helms, and Alfonse D'Amato collectively urged President Clinton "to announce that the U.S. will not participate at any level or in any fashion in the upcoming U.N. Conference on Women as long as Harry Wu is detained in China. Anything less would send a tragic signal of disregard for the human rights of any American citizen." The heat was on the Clintons. I was later given to understand that someone in the State Department advised Mrs. Clinton that the president would incur fierce criticism if she announced she was going to Beijing. Afterward Mrs. Clinton apparently became a major advocate inside the White House for getting me out of China as soon as possible.

My wife was invited to appear on all the television shows. She debated one woman who said women's issues should not be held hostage by one Harry Wu. Ching-Lee countered that human rights were as important as women's rights. Ching-Lee's position was that Mrs. Clinton does not represent just women; she is the first lady of the United States and represents all Americans, including me. Ching-Lee said that if Mrs. Clinton went to China while I was being held, it would send the wrong message.

From helping to run an office in Taiwan, Ching-Lee had now gone to making public statements about the foreign policy of the United States. She kept telling Americans that the Chinese regime is far more impressed by strength than by weakness or even good manners or good intentions, but this seems to be a lesson every administration needs to be reminded of every four years or every eight years.

Most countries have a policy about not making deals with terrorists, and I support that. Was I being held hostage? In a way, I was. Did Washington privately assure China that Mrs. Clinton would go to Beijing if the Chinese released me? I have no idea. But if I had been making that deal, I would have made sure Wei Jingsheng's freedom was included in the bargain. Mrs. Clinton for me was a bargain for China.

After delivering her manifesto on the White House lawn, Ching-Lee continued her campaign in London. She had been hoping to meet a few members of Parliament and government officials, but she did even better. As it happened, Cathy Saypol, the publicist for *Bitter Winds*, my book about my years in the camps, had also done the publicity for Margaret Thatcher's memoir and had given Mrs. Thatcher a copy of my book. The former prime minister of the United Kingdom had just finished reading it when my story broke, and she invited David Welker and Ching-Lee to her office.

"This was our first stop in London," Ching-Lee told a writer later. "We arrived at her office and Mrs. Thatcher came out and shook my hand and asked how I was, and then she held my hand and led me into her office. She had obviously read Harry's book, and she wanted to know very specific details about what was happening. She was curious about the significance of their holding Harry in Wuhan. She kept telling me incidents she had read in *Bitter Winds*. We must have been there forty-five minutes."

David Welker said, "She wanted to know all the details of the trip, so we went over a big map of China, and she wanted to know about the discrepancy of names on the passports, and we assured her it was a legal change of name. She also wanted to know about Harry's physical condition, because her husband also suffers from a herniated disk, and she knows how painful it can be." David said that Mrs. Thatcher has "a funny way of tilting her head when she asks a question, and after a while all of us were tilting our heads."

Mrs. Thatcher urged Ching-Lee to make sure I never tried to get into China again because I was valuable working in the free world. With her usual assurance, she told Ching-Lee the political reality was that I would be released without going to jail.

When she learned that David and my wife had a lower-level appointment in the British Foreign Ministry, she said, "Not high enough! Not high enough!" and made a phone call to arrange for them to see Jeremy Hanley, the chairman of the Conservative Party, who had just been appointed minister for Asian affairs.

David and Ching-Lee also went to Parliament, where they met with seventy or eighty people, including several members of both houses. Later they staged a protest outside the Chinese embassy. David, Ching-Lee, and one student dissident were allowed to march up to the door and make a statement, with some camera crews behind them. When nobody answered, they slipped their letter of protest under the door. Then they made a tour of the BBC building, giving interviews to some of the major television and radio programs in the United Kingdom. Tony Blair, the leader of the Labour Party, happened to be there and shook Ching-Lee's hand and wished her well.

After four days, they took the new Channel Tunnel to Paris, where they gave a press conference at the office of France Liberté, Danielle Mitterrand's organization devoted to human rights. They also spoke to members of the French National Assembly, but the reaction there was not as strong as in England.

Many other governments put pressure on China, particularly Australia, whose foreign minister, Gareth Evans, publicly urged Beijing to "look leniently" on whatever I might have done.

I had spent a lot of time in world capitals, speaking up for millions of prisoners, and many of my friends did not hesitate to speak up in my hour of need.

Some, though, were not so helpful. James Lilley, for example, a former ambassador to China, seemed to dismiss my work to expose China's cruelty as the act of a man who had what he described as a Chinese "martyr complex." Did Lilley really mean that any Chinese person who criticizes the government deserves the trouble he gets? It was, to say the least, a callous view.

For all its help, the State Department also tried to portray me as a bit of a loose cannon. On July 14, *The New York Times* reported that the State Department had urged me not to travel to China in 1994. J. Stapleton Roy, a recent American ambassador to Beijing, said that my changing my name to Peter H. Wu could be construed by the Chinese as trying to deceive them. He also said that the United States did not want to be portrayed as helping to plan my missions inside China. "We laid out our concerns at length, did our best to make the dangers explicit and to help him understand that should something go awry, our ability to assist would be limited," one official told *The New York Times*.

Seven days later the House of Representatives discussed China, not just my arrest but also the labor camps, China's sharing of missile secrets with other countries, and China's use of forced birth control. But after much debate and administration lobbying, the House voted, 321 to 107, not to cancel China's MFN trade status. It was the wrong message to send to Beijing.

My government was sticking up for me in many other ways, however. On July 28, Secretary of State Christopher once again urged China to release me, and he repeated the demand on July 31 from Andersen Air Force Base in Guam, as he traveled to Brunei for a meeting of Asian foreign ministers. "It would be very difficult for me to envisage any circumstances in which President Jiang Zemin would be able to come to Washington to meet the President if Harry Wu is not released," Christopher said.

Christopher met with his counterpart, the Chinese foreign minister, Qian Qichen, for ninety minutes on August 1 and did not make any further public demands for my release. Beijing continued to assert that I had slipped into China using false documents and that my actions could be construed as spying. Qian, however, said my fate was up to the domestic judicial system and that the Foreign Ministry could not intervene, which may have been partly true, if there was an internal power struggle between the Foreign Ministry and the Public Security Bureau. All the stories from Brunei, however, made it clear that Mrs. Clinton's trip still depended on my release.

Mrs. Clinton's proposed trip was drawing closer. On August 9, Ching-Lee sent her the following letter, written with the help of Jeff Fiedler:

Dear Mrs. Clinton:

As your decision regarding the U.N. Women's Conference comes nearer, I thought I would take this opportunity to present my personal views to you.

The issues to be raised at the conference are important to women around the world. While holding it in Beijing has always been a questionable decision, it is the reality.

Your decision, though, it seems to me, is much less concerned with venue than it must be with China's arrest and continued detention of my husband, Harry Wu. No matter the arguments made about the conference being a non-Chinese gathering, it seems to me that if you attend you will not be signaling the importance of women's issues, but rather that Harry's fate is unimportant to you. I am speaking about the public perception, not your personal feelings, for I have every reason to believe that you and the President care very much what happens to my husband.

Your public activities carry great symbolic importance, and your traveling to Beijing would confer great prestige upon the Chinese government. But, this would be sending a confused signal to the leaders in Beijing about the resolve of the United States to press for Harry's release.

People might say that my views are narrow, and I am only thinking about my husband, and not larger issues. Perhaps, this is so. But as a wife who stands up and admirably defends her husband from attacks, I think if anybody can understand my position and feelings, it is you. Recently, the Chinese produced a propaganda film which included bits and pieces of Harry's interrogation. It contained vicious, and scurrilous charges about him as well as the bogus claim that he "confessed" to "fabricating" information. The

entire Chinese government propaganda machine has been working to create a distorted picture of my husband, a U.S. citizen.

Mrs. Clinton, my husband is a tireless human rights activist.
Last year, for instance, he traveled alone in northeast China
where he visited and photographed a women's forced labor camp.
In a recent congressional hearing on the *laogai,* he persuaded an
extraordinary woman, who survived nearly twenty years in the
camps, to come forward and talk about the special problems of
women prisoners. Now he is being held prisoner because of these
and other revelations about China.

I urge you not to go to Beijing unless my husband has been
released. I am certain that you can find many other ways to under-
score your commitment to women's issues.

Thank you very much for your consideration. I look forward to
some day meeting you personally.

Sincerely,
Ching-Lee Wu

That same week the White House began floating rumors that Mrs.
Clinton was planning to go to Beijing no matter what. Jeff Fiedler faxed
a copy of Ching-Lee's letter to Tony Lake, and the rumors seemed to
quiet down. "We would have released the letter to the press, and I think
they understood that, too," Jeff later said. It never came to that.

26

I DECIDE TO COOPERATE

The same day in August that Ching-Lee sent Mrs. Clinton her letter, I was hustled back downtown to the prison, where I met Daniel W. Piccuta, the first secretary and consul in the American embassy in Beijing, a dark, handsome guy dressed in a business suit, who could speak Mandarin fluently. I was elated at seeing another American stride in, bringing his air of freedom and self-respect.

Piccuta asked how things were going.

I told him I had been indicted, and he asked me what the authorities had said about my attitude. "They said it seems cooperative," I replied.

"Excuse me, Harry, but what did you say?" Piccuta asked. "I missed it."

"I said they think I'm cooperative."

Piccuta smiled. "Harry, I think this is very important. I'm happy to hear about 'cooperative.'" He said it so pointedly in English that I knew he was urging me to continue, that this would help me. Then he said, "Harry, you look healthy. Are you okay?"

I said I was all right, not being mistreated, my food was okay, but the guard decided that this was a sensitive subject, and he said, "Hey, you shouldn't ask about that." With my tone, I tried to indicate that I was still suffering, my back was still hurting, which caused pain down to my legs.

Piccuta was clever about giving me some news, saying, "Harry, I saw you on CNN. You looked bad, but to my eyes you seem okay." The message was not about my health. The message was CNN. "Harry, you are very, very famous," Piccuta went on, well aware the guards could not be expected to understand the massive, worldwide impact of CNN, that Piccuta's use of the word *famous* told me the world was watching. (Later I learned that Ching-Lee had proposed the word *famous* to send me the message.)

Piccuta said that on July 27, he had had a good meal with Ching-Lee and Jeff Fiedler, and he read me a letter from Ching-Lee, emphasizing two sentences. The first was "I went to the big house, next door to Jeff's office." My Washington office is across Lafayette Park from the White House. This meant the government was involved in my case. The second sentence was "I saw Philip's Aunt Margaret in London," a reference to our friend Philip Baker, a human-rights activist. I didn't know whether Philip had an aunt named Margaret in London, but then I almost laughed out loud when I realized Ching-Lee was telling me she had met with Margaret Thatcher. I was overjoyed, and my spirits soared. People knew. People cared. Leaders cared. I could not thank Piccuta for this, but he had given me hope.

His implicitly conveyed message was "We are putting pressure on the Chinese. Give the Chinese a way to save face. Cooperate. You can get out." He told me he had brought some books and magazines and even a copy of the *International Herald Tribune*, which the Chinese would have to censor first. He assured me Ching-Lee was all right.

When I got back to my room, I felt greatly relieved. They wanted cooperation? I'd give them cooperation. I told them to get their senior people in to see me, that I was ready to go along with the game.

Around midnight, General Wang appeared, again in plain clothes, along with a secretary. He was surprised that I wanted to see him, having taken his leave four days earlier. "This is very unique because my job is finished," he said. "I'm coming here because you want to talk to me."

I asked him about the meaning of the indictment. Why had they not mentioned many of the things we discussed? What was the sense of my confessing all this stuff if they were not going to put it in there?

He liked my new attitude, and he worked up a "confession," which began, "After thinking carefully and making a self-examination, I have sincerely drawn the conclusion that the following facts show that I have damaged the interests of the Chinese government directly or indirectly and that I have violated Chinese laws." I admitted entering forbidden labor camps, videotaping other camps, posing as a researcher, and I said I was sorry I had damaged the interests of the Chinese government, and I thanked them for their hospitality. I just admitted the obvious, fudged a few secrets, promised to retire from my foundation and get out of politics. It wasn't the first time I had made a confession that was only partly true. I had done it lots of times in camp; whatever I had to do to survive I would do. Piccuta's veiled advice had told me the time was right for a confession.

"I keenly regret and feel remorse for the consequences of what I have done," the confession continued. And it said that in the future "I will not be used by international anti-Chinese and anti-Communist forces." And finally it said, "At present, it is evident that I have violated the laws of China, and I am responsible for my mistakes and crimes."

I was lying. They knew I was lying. I knew they knew. But they had no problem making a deal with somebody they knew was lying to them. That is how their system works. Everybody understands. I signed the paper, said good night to General Wang, and everybody — including me — went off to get a good night's sleep.

On August 13, I was given the reading material from Piccuta. When I opened the *International Herald Tribune*, I saw that the censors had clipped out several articles, but they had left in two articles about China. One story was from Beijing, saying Henry Kissinger had told Chinese leaders that solving the Harry Wu issue would improve relations with the United States. I'm sure Kissinger's words helped protect me, because the Chinese respect him for all the great favors he has done them, including arranging President Richard Nixon's pathbreaking trip in 1972.

The other item raised my spirits even more. This was an article from *The New York Times* by A. M. Rosenthal, its former editor, now a columnist, who has been one of the leading advocates for human rights around the world. I could not believe my good fortune that my keepers had not censored Rosenthal's column, but the headline, VICTORY OVER THE STU-PIDS, never mentioned the Chinese. Rosenthal wrote that "the com-mandants of the gulags of the world and their security-ministry masters have two things in common, in whatever country they operate. They have a taste for torture, and they are very stupid." He went on like that for a while before giving examples: "Lord, Lord, how dull these people are. But for impenetrable stupidity I have rarely known anything like the film the Chinese made and sold to Western news organizations. This film is supposed to show that Harry Wu confessed that his reports are false. . . .

"Of course, Harry Wu was heard confessing to nothing except maybe some editing errors by a BBC editor of his own organ documentary. The gulag film really shows how hard Mr. Wu resisted, not that they had broken him."

Then Rosenthal did something Chinese journalists can never do. He criticized the government of his own country: "American diplomats are doing their personal best to help Mr. Wu. But if he is released it will not be because of irresistible U.S. Government pressure.

"There has been none applied that Beijing would recognize. . . .

"The only realistic hope is that some Chinese foreign-service officers who are not brain-dead will be able to overrule the security police, who gave Mr. Wu and his fully documented reports world recognition by arresting him instead of stopping him at the border and sending him back."

Rosenthal added, "Harry Wu has won his victory. The only way China can now cut its losses and save face is to set him free. May God bless Harry Wu."

As I read his words, it was like having a friend in the room with me. Somehow, whether through carelessness or intention, Rosenthal's words had slipped past the stupids. Once again I was persuaded: I could beat these people.

~

Right after my "confession," the mood changed. At first, all my guards had treated me as if I were a dangerous enemy, as if I might suddenly sprout a hundred arms and strike them dead with swords, but the longer I stayed, the less of a devil I became. I was curious to watch the evolution of the young lieutenants because they were the new generation, they had been children when I left China, and I wanted to see whether they had any more spunk, any more independence, any more honesty than the older generations. They had heard me talk back to their superiors, and they could see that their superiors respected me. Some of the eighteen lieutenants who were rotated around the clock remained distant, loyal to the party, but most of them struck me as naturally good human beings.

One example: I developed a terrible itch from athlete's foot because Wuhan is very humid and hot, and one of the guards said, "Tomorrow, I'll get some medicine for you."

"Don't do it," I said. "You will break the rules. You will get into trouble." He didn't insist, but I was convinced he would have gotten the medicine for me if I had let him.

During the last three or four weeks, I would tell them, "Look, I know you're not allowed to talk to me. That's okay. Just listen. If you understand, nod your head. If you don't understand, shake your head sideways. I'm a human being. I want to talk." I sang songs. I told them stories. I told them about things in America. They broke their silence to comment on the red-and-black Chicago Bulls cap I had carried as a prearranged signal to one of my contacts inside China. One of the lieutenants even had a Chicago Bulls T-shirt of his own.

The world is getting smaller. Even though almost all of China is cut off from *60 Minutes* and CNN, the guards wanted to know about Magic Johnson's being diagnosed as HIV positive, and they wanted to know why Michael Jordan had come back to basketball after his year of playing baseball. They knew these famous athletes from the 1992 dream team at the Barcelona Olympics. They wanted to know about the famous chase of O. J. Simpson in the Ford Bronco and about his murder trial, and they listened to me tell them about how American lawyers are supposed to protect defendants—a difficult concept for Chinese. I told them about Susan Smith, the young mother who was convicted of drowning her two kids in her automobile in a lake in

South Carolina. And I told them about Rodney King's accusing Los Angeles cops of mercilessly beating him and how some people had rioted when the cops were acquitted. I tried to explain how Rodney King had his rights, just like everybody else.

They would look at the magazines I had received from Piccuta; in *House and Garden*, the pictures of houses and cars and shrubbery must have looked so opulent to them. I told how I had two cars, one for me and one for my wife, and about the automatic shift with cruise control—because Chinese cars usually have a clutch and a stick shift. I told them what kinds of cars I have, how I applied for a driver's license, how many speeding tickets I'd gotten.

Some of the young lieutenants seemed to understand what I was doing in my crusade against the camps. Many Chinese people have suffered in the *laogai* or have family members or friends who were sent off to the countryside during the Cultural Revolution. Now they saw this stubborn man refusing to give in, willing to come back from America for this cause. Did they know that my cause was also their cause? Not one of them ever said a word that could have compromised him, but I could look into their eyes and see it. They all knew what their country had done.

On the night of August 12, I had two visitors. One of them, a short, older man, maybe around five feet two inches tall, introduced himself as Judge Zhang Tianshe and informed me that he would preside at my trial and his colleague Cao Yongping would also take part. Judge Zhang was polite, friendly, professional. The bullying was over. "You have received the indictment, and in eight to ten days you will go to court," he said.

"That's too soon," I said. "I don't have time to prepare. I need a lawyer." The judge said that was no problem, and he handed me a list of lawyers qualified to handle a case of this magnitude. China does not have a vast supply of lawyers, the way America does. For most of Mao's regime, lawyers were hardly allowed at all, and their principal job was—and still is—helping the judiciary resolve cases. In Shanghai and

Beijing, there is a growing number of international lawyers, but the judge's list contained exactly one lawyer in all of Wuhan qualified in that field. I told the judge to get me whomever he could.

A day or two later two court-appointed "defenders," Xu Deyuan and Zheng Zhifa, showed up, saying they would charge the standard fee of $750. "We are concerned about justice. We will protect your interests," one of them said.

Just to see whether they had my interests at heart, I wrote a letter that said, "I received an indictment, they said I would go to trial in eight to ten days, here is my lawyer's name, and I need the money to pay for it." I handed them Daniel Piccuta's business card and said, "Fax this to my embassy."

Two days later they returned, claiming they had gone to court to look at my file.

I told them, "You have to know this is a political case. I don't think you'll be able to defend me."

They said, "No problem, we'll be able to help you."

I told them that if they wanted to help me, they could question my indictment's reliance on the use of Article 166, which prohibits stealing government information. The lawyers seemed a bit dubious about what they could do. "Come on," I said, "I'm not a government official. I'll admit what I actually did, but I didn't leak secrets."

I wrote four pages to the American embassy and asked the officials there to fax my wife so she could look up affidavits from CBS and the BBC that declared that I was under contract to them, that I was a journalist, not a spy. "Will you send it to my embassy?" I asked. "It's my right under the law." Of course I wasn't clear about the law since nobody had furnished me with a lawbook. I was also never informed of the evidence and witnesses that would be used at my trial even though the information was probably available.

A few days later the lawyers admitted they hadn't faxed my request. "I can't do that," one of them said. "If I did, Public Security would take care of me."

He was not wrong.

27

TRIAL AND VERDICT

I woke up the morning of August 23 and solemnly said good-bye to all the young guards. "They know what they're going to do," I told them. "They're going to throw my tired old body back into the camps." I don't know whether I really believed that, but it was a possibility.

A couple of the guards began to snicker. They liked my style, but my main caretaker, Officer Liu, played it straight. "Come on, what are you talking about?" he said loudly. "You'll be back here tonight. Everything will be all right."

The police almost apologized when one of them said, "According to the procedures, we have to put handcuffs on you."

"Can I refuse?" I asked with a smile.

Everybody was laughing as I got into the waiting car, with court police taking videotapes for the record. The courtroom was unpretentious, maybe seventy-five feet by sixty feet, with most of the sixty seats empty, except for a few television crew members and news correspondents. The officers told me that because my trial involved "state secrets," the public was not allowed to attend. I glanced around the room and was cheered by the sight of Daniel Piccuta from Beijing, along with a Chinese official from the Foreign Ministry.

My back was hurting, and I did not look forward to standing for hours or days, so I asked for crutches, but the guard said no. "You might use them as a weapon," he said, adding that I could sit down whenever I wanted and that I could have pain pills if I needed them. I started off standing in the dock, my two hands gripping the railing. I'm afraid I presented rather a sorry picture. I was weak and disheveled, with my white shirt rumpled and my sleeves rolled up. I was running out of clothes—and energy.

I looked at the tribunal and saw three judges—Zhang Tianshe, the presiding judge, who had come to the villa; Cao Yongping, who had accompanied him; and Li Liqing, the first female judge I had ever seen. She was a very modern judge—permed hair, makeup, lipstick, onc-inch heels. In some things, at least, China has made a lot of progress. To a man who had spent two months in captivity, with only an occasional secretary or nurse in his field of vision, the middle-aged judge was a welcome sight.

The prosecutors opened the case by showing the BBC documentary on organ transplants, saying I had claimed the film depicted a kidney transplant instead of the heart surgery it really was. Under questioning, I admitted that the footage was not a kidney transplant, but I told the court the film claimed only that it was an "operation" in China. They showed a few other videos from CBS and the BBC, saying that the images gave away state secrets. They showed my picture of the watch-tower in Shanghai, taken from a public building, and they called on a police officer from Shanghai, who testified that the document I showed to the U.S. Congress was classified and that Ching-Lee and I had been present when he put it on the factory official's desk. I corrected them when they showed film from one coal mine and said it was the other. The prosecutors and the judge could not tell one coal mine from another, but they kept the mislabeled film in my file. Then they brought three witnesses who had actually seen me on my trips in China.

The first was my pal Hang, who had taken me into the Number 13 Laogai Detachment, the Guozhuang Coal Mine, on my second trip. He looked miserable and guilty about being there, but we both knew he had no choice. Our eyes met, and as one ex-prisoner looking at another, I could see that he was just playing his part, that he would not give up anything to hurt me. They asked whether he recognized me, and he said, "Yes, that is Wu Hongda," and under questioning he admitted I had visited him at the coal mine and given him three hundred dollars. I was proud of him. He gave the Chinese something they could use, but he never volunteered anything about what I was doing at the mine.

The second witness was my old campmate Zhang, who had taken Ching-Lee and me around the work camps in 1994 and with whom I had stayed. The prosecutor asked him to identify me, and Zhang said, "Yes, I recognize him. I helped him travel through the camps, and he took some pictures." They showed photos from the Shanghai Number 2 Brigade, located in Anhui Province, and Zhang said, yes, we were there. You bet we were. It had been on worldwide television. Zhang wasn't telling them anything they didn't know.

The third witness was the Communist official from the Shanghai Laodong Steel-Pipe Factory, who, when asked to identify me, began a loud harangue about my character. "He is a bad guy, a liar," he started shrieking.

The judge stopped him and said, "Please, don't get emotional; just answer my questions."

The man calmed down and said he had seen the document in the office the day Ching-Lee and I were the only visitors.

"I was there," I said. "That doesn't mean I did it. You don't have a direct witness." I was just giving them a hard time. In my earlier interrogation, I had blamed Ching-Lee for stealing it, and they also knew I had displayed the document in the United States Congress. The man still had my Meftech card, too. My giving it to him was hard to refute.

Then they showed more evidence against me, including testimony from three different taxi drivers who had taken me around Sichuan, Xinjiang, and Anhui provinces.

Next they accused me of posing as a police officer, but I said I didn't have a badge or shoes or a belt, that I just bought a police uniform because it was cheap and available. I said if the police had stopped me, I would have said I was not an officer. They showed a blurred picture made from a surveillance video, and the prosecutor said, "This is Harry Wu in a police uniform."

"Look again," I said. "There is another officer in the photo. Neither is me."

They presented a photo of me in a police uniform. "That's from the Yorkshire video," I said. "It was taken in California. You can't use that as evidence."

They also presented a report from my friend Liu, who had "admitted" buying the uniform for me. In 1991, we had actually arranged what he would say if his role was discovered. They interrogated him in 1992 and tried to get him to lure me back to China, but I saw through that. All he "confessed" to now was what they already knew, that he had gotten me a uniform. He was very loyal and brave to hold back information on my network of supporters inside China.

Finally the prosecutor said that Feng, the old photographer, had confessed to having been hired by me to get "illegal information." They even showed the contract signed by Feng and me that set the payment at four thousand dollars, and they showed samples of my signature.

The prosecutors went over my alleged offenses. They noted I had claimed that giving money was not bribing people and I had said that the "stealing and spying" in several places had been conducted by "a man named Chen," totally obscuring the fact that I had been accompanied by my wife on the trips. They noted that I took only "part of the responsibility" for the police officer's uniform and that I had denied bribing Feng to take pictures.

"After being brought to justice, Peter Wu, the defendant, confessed his crimes with honesty, and the attitude of admitting his crimes is good. Therefore we request the court mete out punishment lightly," the prosecutor said.

I heard the word *lightly*, and I tried to interpret it. I still figured they could give me a long sentence, but at the very least they were not going to execute me.

I was disappointed in my homeland. Despite the court's pretensions, it could not make a case in its own chosen show trial. The only thing the Chinese had going for them was their need for conformity, the fear of the individual. I had rocked their boat. I was not a spy. China's system, with all its abuses, is so obvious that the government could not hide them from a wandering misfit with a handheld video camera. The Chinese officials could throw me in jail for the rest of my life, but they couldn't make me out to be anything more than a pest, an annoyance, a troublemaker. I had won.

When the prosecutors finished presenting their evidence, it was time for my lawyer to make his closing statement. He had never discussed any of this with me, and he had presented me with no court documents, so I expected nothing from him, but he actually made two good points.

Regarding my wearing a police uniform, he came up with the regulation saying that a police officer on duty must be wearing a full uniform: shoes, hat, badge, and belt. "Wu Hongda was wearing only the pants and the shirt," the lawyer said. "This means he was not legally posing as a police officer."

The judge rejected the argument, but I appreciated my lawyer's logic.

And to the charge that I had given bribes to people, the lawyer said I had given small gifts to friends of mine because I could afford it and because I sympathized with them.

I was rather impressed with the lawyer's performance. Then the judge asked whether I had anything to say.

"First of all," I told them, "everything I said, I said. Everything I wrote, I wrote.

"My second point is about so-called state secrets. Everything today came from films shown by CBS or BBC or Yorkshire Television. If it's a photograph in downtown, it was taken on busy streets. There's a watchtower in the middle of a busy city. I took these pictures, and you charge me with stealing state secrets? Does this mean everybody should cover his eyes? If people look at the tower, they observe state secrets. What is the definition of *state secrets*? If I'm staying at a fancy four-star hotel, in a room on an upper floor, there's no problem taking pictures. But if I observe the hotel's security system, banking system, maybe that's getting into state secrets.

"Finally, the Chinese government has tried to tell the world I'm a thief. The fact is in 1960, I was sentenced to three years as a penal criminal for stealing fifty yuan, but when I was released in 1979, the authorities said I wasn't a thief. They said, 'You tried to escape to betray our country.' During my interrogation at the villa, the officers had the facts—that I was not a thief—but now the indictment still lists the fifty yuan. I don't understand your purpose. But I am happy to be called a thief," I continued. "If your document today says I was sentenced to three years for being a thief, why did I undergo reeducation through labor for another six years? Later I'm going to sue Beijing for compensation for my other six years."

After four hours, my trial was over, and the judges said they would deliver the verdict the next day. As I walked out of the courtroom, I came face-to-face with Daniel Piccuta, who gave me a smile and a wink, as if to say, "I'm with you; hang in there."

~

"See, you lost; you came back," said Officer Liu back at the villa, reminding me of my prediction that I was heading for the *laogai*.

"Tomorrow they get me for sure," I said.

Later that afternoon I was called back into Room 104. I was a little surprised to see Judge Zhang and Judge Cao. "Are you okay?" one of them asked. They said they were worried about my health and my attitude.

Oh, so that was it. If I refused to go to court the next day, the show would be ruined.

"What do you expect from the verdict?" Zhang asked.

"I just want to get out of here. There's no reason to keep me here. If there were a helicopter, I would grab the ladder and pull myself up. I don't care about tomorrow's verdict. The whole thing is unacceptable."

"Of course I don't know the verdict yet," Judge Zhang said calmly, "but I'm pretty sure, because the Public Security officials tell us your attitude is good, that things will go well for you."

We were back to saving face again. We Chinese want everything to look good so that nobody is embarrassed in public.

"If I don't go, what happens?"

"According to Chinese law, whether you appear or not, we will still announce the verdict. Will you come?"

"I'll think about it. I haven't decided yet."

"I know your health is bad, but I promise you I will announce the verdict in twenty minutes, so please be patient. I know it's painful, but you will see. We have prepared some pain-relief medicine for you. It will be good for you."

"I don't know," I said. "You are charging me with serious things. It is clear by now that I could get at least fifteen years, maybe death." I painted a gloomy picture, just to remind them of the camps, in case they had forgotten.

Zhang just laughed. "I don't think it will be so serious," he said. "The Chinese government is concerned with humanity." Then he emphasized that I had to appear in court the next morning.

We left it at that and said good night. I thought it best to leave them unsure of whether I would actually show up. They wanted to play with my mind? Very well. I would play with theirs.

⌐

The next morning I started bustling around my room, putting everything in order: my books, my magazines, my clothes. The guards asked me what I was doing. "I'll never come back to this room," I said. "They're going to send me to the *laogai* again."

"Aw, come on, don't make jokes," one of them said.

"I'm serious. I looked at your regulations. The sentence is death. Maybe they will kill me."

Officer Liu looked at me and said, "I guarantee you will come back to Room 101. Do you want to make a bet?"

"I trust you, but I trust your government more," I said. "I have great faith in the legal system's living up to its rules."

I looked at the younger guards, kids from the Tiananmen Square generation, kids who knew there was something else out there. I needed to keep up my bravado, pretend I was the tough guy, but I knew anything was possible. They could move me to a jail for a few days just to scare me, or hold me for a few months just as the Iraqis or the Iranians do to the occasional American businessman they catch. Or maybe they would send me away for years, play hardball, try to use me to extract some contract or concession from the Americans for the MFN status or a presidential visit to Beijing or a new Boeing contract. You never know. I was just a chip in the game.

It was time to go. At eight-fifteen in the morning, we got into the car and headed for the courthouse. The day before, they had made me wear handcuffs right into the building, but this time, when the car arrived in the courtyard, with television crews waiting, the officers took off the handcuffs.

I was ushered into a small waiting room with about four or five chairs against the wall. About thirty minutes later, at nine o'clock, I was called to the courtroom, which was still half-empty except for some so-called journalists and people with cameras and Daniel Piccuta, faithfully sitting there.

Judge Zhang promptly rejected the defenses I had made the day before, went over the details of the charges again, and announced the verdict: "Peter Wu, the defendant, is convicted of stealing, spying on, and buying China's state secrets and providing them to institutions and agencies outside China. Therefore, he is sentenced to thirteen years in prison and a supplementary penalty of expulsion from China.

"Peter Wu, the defendant, is also convicted of practicing fraud by disguising himself as a state functionary. Therefore, he is sentenced to three years in prison and a supplementary penalty of expulsion from China.

"In consideration of the compound penalty for two offenses, he is sentenced to fifteen years in prison and a supplementary penalty of expulsion from China.

"If the defendant disagrees with this verdict, he can appeal directly or through this court to the Hubei Provincial High People's Court of the People's Republic of China within ten days of the next day upon the receipt of this court decision."

The words *fifteen years* and *expulsion* leaped out at me, but I could not logically connect the two phrases. I also heard *right to appeal*. My spirits plummeted. The verdict made me sound like a common criminal. I thought of my father, years ago, back in Shanghai, telling me, "Never cry. And never give up." I thought of Ahab chasing the great white whale. I thought of Jean Valjean, persecuted for stealing a loaf of bread. To hell with their verdict. I made up my mind to appeal.

Usually when a guilty verdict and a sentence are announced, the defendant is immediately bound over, handcuffs clapped on wrists, and taken directly to jail. But the police officer standing next to me very kindly put his hand lightly on my shoulder and said, "Mr. Wu, please come with me," and ushered me out of the courtroom. As I was leaving, I passed Daniel Piccuta, who tried to smile reassuringly, as if to say, "It could have been worse." I wondered whether he had heard the fifteen-year sentence the same way I had.

I was brought into the waiting room again, but it had been rearranged, with a table set up in the middle, a white cloth over it, leather chairs arranged on all sides. Police officials stood around, relaxed, informal, smoking and chatting. After about twenty minutes, the three judges came into the room.

"How is your health?" Judge Zhang asked.

"Okay," I replied.

"Have you paid attention to your verdict? We respect your opinion. Did you notice we never mentioned anything about the petty-theft charge?"

I didn't say anything.

"You have the right to appeal your sentence within ten days," he went on. "If you appeal, the hearing will take place in a month and a half, and then there's a final judgment. What do you think?"

"I want to appeal. I was not allowed to place any evidence before the court. I had no witnesses on my side. My lawyers prepared nothing. Nothing. I want to appeal."

"Are you sure you want that? Didn't you pay attention to your sentence? We considered your health, your family waiting for you."

"You just said I have the right to appeal. You're saying I must serve fifteen years and then you expel me."

"You don't understand," the judge said. "According to our law, we can apply an additional sentence first."

I thought about my father's words to me when I was a boy: "Never cry. And never give up."

"I want a fair trial."

"Wu Hongda, you are very stubborn. Now I'm beginning to learn about you. As a judge, I've finished my job. You are foolish. To be honest, they've already decided to deport you first, but if you want to appeal, we will apply the immediate sentence."

Expulsion first? Why didn't they say so in the first place? "All right," I said. "I won't appeal."

Everyone in the room seemed to heave a collective sigh of relief. At least, I was not a total lunatic.

"Sign the paper; you can leave. Two or three days—you'll be on your way home."

I was given a document that contained several key provisions. "I accept the court decision" was one phrase. "I give up the right to appeal" was another. But the judge had said "deport you first." That was all that mattered. I signed.

Back at the villa, it was lunchtime. "You lose the bet," Officer Liu said. All my stuff was back in my room: my camera, my money, my credit cards—everything. Only then was I sure it was real. They would not have given me my belongings unless I was truly leaving. About an hour later I was handed all the legal documents confirming my expulsion.

The funny thing was weeks later I happened to look more closely at my airline tickets for the return flight, and I noticed that they had been purchased at eight in the morning on the day the verdict was handed down. The judge did not announce the verdict until nine. So much for the separation of the executive and the judicial branches of government.

But I look at it this way: The last time China's rulers had me, there was not even the pretense of a trial, and it took me nineteen years to get out. This time I had lawyers and judges and a four-hour trial, and I was being released after sixty-six days. As far as I was concerned, that is progress.

28

OUTTA HERE

For my last ride out of China, there were no curtains on the windows. Outside the black Toyota van taking me to Wuhan Airport was timeless, endless China: workers in the fields, people carrying baskets alongside the highway, bicycles, cars, the rivers and the lakes, the sky, the land. But the modern buildings and the industrial clutter made me realize this was the Deng Economic Dynasty rather than feudal China. I wish I could say I was sentimental, tears dripping down my cheeks, knowing this was it, that I'd never see my native land again. But I kept using sarcastic humor to keep other emotions from overwhelming me. I counted sixteen people with me, guards and officials, all piled into a lengthy motorcade. I said, "Come on, it's not necessary. I'm a free man now. I can get out to the airport by myself." No one cracked a smile. They were tired of my smart-aleck attitude.

As soon as we got to the airport, it was announced that the flight to Shanghai would be delayed for two hours. I was taken into a security office so the other passengers would not be contaminated by me, and I was offered tea and snacks. My guards' job was finished, and now they could talk to me. This was my last chance, at least for a while, to gauge the mind of totalitarian China.

"What do you think will happen to you when you go home?" one of my senior escorts asked me.

"I don't know," I said. "I don't know what's happened outside."

"Well, try to imagine what your life will be like," he said. "We're just chatting."

"Maybe my book will sell better than before," I said.

"What do you mean?"

I said, "If yesterday only ten people knew about the *laogai*, today a thousand people, a million people know about it."

He did not pursue the Western notion that any publicity is good publicity. Instead, he asked, "What is the first thing you want to do when you get home?"

"I want to hire some young people to stay with me for a while."

"What do you mean?"

"I'm used to my attendants twenty-four hours a day, being with me, peeping through the peephole at me while I take a bath. In the beginning, I was uncomfortable, but now I'm getting to like these guys."

He looked at me and muttered something. I think the best translation would be "wise guy."

He continued in friendly fashion. "I just want to let you know: Don't come back. They will put you back in jail. They will make you serve your fifteen years."

I found it significant that he used the word *they*. It reminded me that this was a high-level case, that this senior official was only doing his job, and that by using *they*, he was trying to put some distance between himself and his masters.

"Look, let's have a chat," he continued. "Do you think we handled your case properly?"

"No, it was handled all wrong."

"Why?"

"If I were the Chinese government and I stopped Harry Wu at the border, I would not arrest him, but I would escort him to Beijing. I would have a dinner with him, arrange for Communist scholars to talk about the *laogai*, maybe have a debate. I would offer Harry Wu, 'Which camp do you want to see? Whatever—your choice—I'll let you go. I'll let you take pictures, whatever you want. And then, okay, you are free; you can travel in China. You can leave. I give you all the conveniences.' "

He looked stunned. Maybe I was being facetious, but it's true: The Chinese don't know how to put their best face before the world. They could say, "You saw bad things; okay, show the film on Western television. But China is changing; the people respect the modern government." There is an old Chinese saying, "Release the bell," which means that if you tie a bell on somebody or maybe on an animal, you then have the dangerous task of removing the bell. The Chinese cannot remove the bell inside their minds; they are stuck in their old ways, in a culture of intolerance that is thousands of years old. I wanted to stand up and shout at him, "You have turned millions of your own people into the enemy. You suppressed them, damaged them, prosecuted them, and you continue to do this." But what was the point? I just wanted to go home, home to California.

Another two-hour delay was announced. My friend Officer Liu came up to me and said, "Wu Hongda, we need money."

"For what?"

"You missed your flight from Shanghai to San Francisco, so we have to put you on a foreign airline. We have to pay cash."

"I have to pay my own deportation fee?" I asked.

Officer Liu looked downcast, the way bureaucrats do when they are thwarted. "Come on, Wu Hongda, you want to go home; we're concerned about your family. You don't want to stay here. It's only a thousand dollars, that's nothing for you."

I was beginning to regret lying to them about my eighty-thousand-dollar salary. "No, you're responsible for that," I told Liu. "You're the ones who took me. I didn't want to stay here. You want to expel me, expel me."

He looked even more forlorn. "Come on, don't be stubborn. Solve the problem."

That's how it went. I was supposed to save their face. I said I didn't have any cash, but I'd be glad to pay by credit card. Liu looked stricken, and he said, "No, you cannot go to the counter. Come on, you want to go home. We have a good result. You need medical care. Why not solve the problem? I was in charge. I'm responsible. Don't give me a hard time."

I told him I'd pay with a traveler's check. I still had three thousand dollars in checks already signed by me and another two thousand dollars worth of unsigned checks, just in case I needed to give somebody untraceable money. I peeled off ten one-hundred-dollar traveler's checks. "The only thing is," I explained, "you'll have to sign them once here and once in front of the clerk."

Liu stared at me blankly. It was apparent he had never seen traveler's checks. "Look, it's easy," I said, pointing to the blank line. "You just sign your name: Liu Ah Go."

In the Mandarin language, there is an expression for Everyman, Ah Go, which translated literally means "puppy" or "young dog." Everybody knows it means John Doe; it's not an insult. I meant, "Just put your John Hancock on it." Liu, however, took it personally.

"You call me a dog?" he snapped. "You are the dog! You are the running dog of the imperialists, and you try to insult me."

Now I got mad. I was a thousand dollars away from going home, but I had had it up to here with these people. "You don't want it? Give it back! Don't give me any shit. I'm just telling you how to use it."

He finally figured out what I was trying to tell him, and he cashed my check and bought me a ticket.

When it was time to board the flight to Shanghai, the police turned on a video camera with a bright flash blinding my eyes, which were already shot from the wonderful herb medicine. I held up my hands to shield my eyes from the glare, and Officer Liu started yelling at me. "What are you doing?" he squawked.

"I cannot see my way," I said.

They turned out the lights, and I could walk again. And that's how I left Wuhan—still squabbling with them.

All sixteen officers accompanied me on the flight from Wuhan to Shanghai. We arrived in Shanghai around eleven-thirty in the evening, and they walked me straight across the tarmac to a giant Air China 747. My escorts were all chattering and waving documents, and suddenly I thought to myself, "Hey, wait a minute, this is an Air China flight! What about that foreign carrier?"

I stood in the doorway as the Americans and the Chinese in first class stared at me, wondering who this bedraggled man was who had caused their flight to be delayed. "You are our special guest," the flight attendant told me. "We had a special order to wait for you. Orders direct from Beijing."

I was handed my passport, then my ticket, then the medicine Ching-Lee had sent over, which I could have used for the past two months, and finally the Chinese lawbook I had paid for two months earlier, which Dan Piccuta had delivered but they never turned over to me. The attendants started to close the door.

"Hey, Officer Liu, where's my thousand dollars?" I shouted.

He slapped his forehead in a universal gesture of chagrin, as if to say, "Oh, my goodness, I totally forgot." The door slammed shut, and that was my last vision of my homeland—somebody stiffing me out of a thousand bucks.

29

HOMECOMING

Ching-Lee and my friends did not have much advance notice of my homecoming. After meeting me on August 9, Daniel Piccuta had sent word that he hoped for a speedy trial, but with no date set, Ching-Lee and David Welker went to Switzerland on August 17 for the annual meeting of the United Nations Commission on Human Rights.

The Chinese delegation tried, but failed, to pressure the commission to cancel a press conference Ching-Lee had scheduled. Ching-Lee responded by passing out copies of the *Congressional Record* with the testimony on the *laogai* that I and others had given in March. During a working session of the conference, Ching-Lee quietly handed a copy to a young man from the Chinese delegation, who politely said, "You know, things were bad in my country in the past, but now they are better."

She replied, "I don't think you know all the details. Things are still very bad there."

Suddenly an old fox from the delegation spotted the young man talking with Ching-Lee and rushed over, as if to rescue the younger man.

"The Kuomintang was very bad," the official said.

"I am not talking about 1949," she said. "I am talking about today," and they continued raising their voices until the moderator on the dais rapped his gavel and asked for silence.

On August 18, while she was in Geneva, Ching-Lee learned that my trial was set to start on August 23 and that Beijing threatened to postpone it indefinitely if word leaked out. She and Jeff agreed not to talk about the trial, and they rushed home four days later to be ready just in case I was released.

Our neighbors had not forgotten us. They had been supportive of Ching-Lee throughout the ordeal, and many of them hung yellow ribbons on the house, and one of them sent over some home-cooked meals, and one of the children on the block drew a picture that said, I LOVE YOU, HARRY.

Because California is more than half a day behind China, Ching-Lee was getting reports at bizarre hours. Early in the morning on August 23, she heard I had been convicted, and then she had to wait twenty-four hours to learn the sentence. Our house became a kind of mission control as reporters crowded outside and David Welker, upstairs in the office, monitored the phone. He had grown tired of answering calls from reporters from all over the world, so he taped a message, urging them to wait until there was news. Ching-Lee was downstairs with her parents and her brother and sister-in-law and two nieces from Taiwan.

Late in the morning of August 24, David looked out the window and noticed the press corps becoming even more agitated. Then somebody left a cheering message on the phone machine: "Mrs. Wu, you must be very excited. Your husband has been put on a plane." As soon as that reporter hung up, another reporter left the same message.

"Ching-Lee, come upstairs," David yelled. "I'm not sure, but something has happened. Reuters is reporting that Harry is on a plane."

David called John Foarde, the conscientious official at the State Department in Washington, who echoed the reports: "We're hearing the same thing. I'm just waiting for the call from Beijing." Suddenly Foarde said, "Beijing is on the other line. I'll call you back." A few minutes later, Foarde called back to say Beijing had confirmed I was on the Air China flight.

Ching-Lee broke the good news to everybody in the house, touching off cheers and hugs, while David went outside to organize the press.

Ching-Lee asked David to draft a short statement she could read to the press, so he wrote a few notes on a three-by-five card. Then she and her mother and one of her nieces went out to the lawn. Ching-Lee said she appreciated everybody's help and was very happy and was looking forward to our being reunited as a family. The reporters asked whether this was part of a deal by the White House and whether Mrs. Clinton was now going to Beijing, but she just thanked them and went inside without stirring up anything.

Jeff Fiedler had been en route from Chicago to Washington, but now he rerouted himself to San Francisco while David handled the details. The office of Representative Pete Stark in Fremont, California, arranged a reception at the airport, including medical care in case I needed it, and Mayor Peter McHugh of Milpitas lent a minibus from the city's Senior Citizen Department to carry the entire Wu party to the airport. A second car followed in case I wanted privacy. Ching-Lee and the others piled into the minibus, carrying a big bouquet of yellow roses, and drove forty minutes, straight to the airport and right onto the tarmac.

Meanwhile Jeff had landed, and he and David arranged for Ching-Lee to give a brief statement to the nearly one hundred milling journalists. She said she was delighted I was coming back, and added, "Harry is so dedicated; he insists on doing this job. Because of his personal experience, he wants to expose the horrors of the *laogai* system."

I was oblivious to all this. I tried to sleep in the coach section on the nonstop flight but was still fuming about Liu ripping off my thousand dollars, still furious about the medicine and lawbook they had not given me when I needed them. But mostly I wondered how I would get home to Milpitas. I had no idea whether anybody in the United States knew I was en route, and the Air China pilots and crew were not helpful. Usually when I catch a flight at the last moment, I call from the airplane to arrange a ride home, but the Air China plane did not have a telephone. Perhaps I would simply rent a car to drive to Milpitas; maybe I would surprise everybody in the evening—"Hey, what's for supper?" I had no idea what was in store for me.

We were heading east, out of the sunlight, into the darkness, and after nearly thirteen hours in the air I saw the lights of the Bay area, the bridges and the freeways, the offices and homes where people pursue their lives in freedom in this crazy land—a situation that was once described, in the musical *Flower Drum Song,* as "living in America like chop suey," meaning all different ingredients mixed together. The Bay area, my new hometown—I saw it glistening below, and I allowed myself a dash of emotion, a touch of sentiment. I could walk off this plane and flash a piece of plastic and rent a car, make a phone call, do whatever I wanted to do—a free man in a free country, my country.

⌐

At dusk, the big Air China plane swooped down into the airport alongside San Francisco Bay. When the plane stopped taxiing, I figured it would take at least fifteen minutes for the passengers ahead of me to get off, but the attendants came back down the aisle and said I could leave first. I reached up and grabbed all the books and the medicine and my travel bag and walked toward the open door. At the last moment before exiting, I pulled on the Chicago Bulls cap that was to have been our signal of recognition if the trip had worked out.

Just outside the open door, I spotted Jeff and Ching-Lee, who was carrying yellow roses. She looked so good to me, the face I dared not envision, that I just put down my luggage and wrapped my arms around her, and we hugged in the doorway.

"It's okay," she whispered in my ear. "Everything is fine." (Months later Ching-Lee admitted to friends, "He didn't look so good to me. His hair hadn't been trimmed in sixty-six days. He had the same clothes he'd been wearing. He looked very tired.") Then I saw Jeff's bearded face, and he looked good, too, so I hugged him. He and Ching-Lee grabbed my bags, and we started walking down the corridor. Everything seemed so strange. I was in a daze.

Ching-Lee noticed I was limping and wanted to know whether I had been tortured. No, I said, my legs hurt because I did not have any medicine for my back.

"But I sent it to you in Wuhan," Ching-Lee said.

"They just gave it to me today, when I got on the plane in Shanghai." She muttered something not very nice in Chinese.

They took me into a private room, where a doctor checked my blood pressure and my heart rate and finally pronounced me healthy enough to go home on my own. They had brought a wheelchair, but I was determined to walk out of that airport on my own.

"Harry, there are reporters here," Jeff told me. "Do you want to talk to them?" My first reaction was no, I was too tired to speak, so they informed the reporters I would not be speaking, which must have annoyed them considerably. Later, when I realized how much "noise" the press had made about my capture, I was sorry I had not seen the reporters right away. Also, hundreds of people had shown up at the airport, wanting to cheer for me, but I just wanted to see my family and get home, so I never got the chance to wave to them. Until days later I did not understand how many people had been concerned about my plight.

As we walked through the corridors, Ching-Lee kept telling me things that had happened, and I kept nodding, but later she realized, "Harry didn't remember anything I told him."

We turned a corner, and I saw Ching-Lee's parents, and I fell down on my knees, so grateful to have parents who would come to the airport for me. I saw Ching-Lee's brother and his wife and their daughters, and then David Welker gave me a hug and said, "I'm glad to see you, my friend."

"I'm glad to be here," I said.

They all said I looked skinny and gaunt, but they said I was surprisingly coherent, considering what I had been through. They asked whether I had been interrogated day and night, and I had to say, no, it wasn't all that bad.

As we left the terminal, I saw the Milpitas minibus with a big yellow ribbon wrapped around it; I would not have to rent a car to get to Milpitas after all. I got into the car with David, Jeff, Ching-Lee, and the driver, with the rest of the family and friends following in the bus.

As our little motorcade headed south, I started talking. First I told them about the sixteen guards all the way to Shanghai, and then I worked my way backward to the astonished look on the judges' faces when I said I wanted to appeal.

"Sounds like you," Jeff said.

When we pulled onto our block, I was amazed to see all the lights from the television crews that had assembled in front of our house. Our neighbors were out on the sidewalk, waving and clapping, and there were yellow ribbons on all the houses, including ours, where a Milpitas police officer was standing guard. Dozens of reporters and television people clamored for me to speak. For months, I had wanted to tell my story to the world, but now I had very little energy left. "I'm very proud to be an American," I told them. "If I were not an American, I don't think I would have been let out."

I thanked them for coming, and then I went inside, to my beautiful California home. I insisted on walking around, inspecting everything, putting away my bags, then sitting on the white leather sofa in the living room, surrounded by family. Ching-Lee's two little nieces were running around. A couple of Chinese friends came over, and I told stories: about the spider eating a cricket, about the judges, about the young lieutenants who knew all about Magic Johnson and O. J. Simpson, about my train ride across China, about the terrible nosebleed, about Wang and the stupid questions straight from Beijing. Occasionally I banged my two fists together for emphasis—Wang and me, butting heads, lying, telling the truth, playing cat and mouse.

After a while, people started to fade—the nieces, Ching-Lee's parents. Jeff used the tiny guest room. Then Ching-Lee said she was going upstairs. I looked at David and realized that every bed, every couch, was taken. "I'll sleep on the floor in your office," David said.

The whole house was finally quiet. I crawled into bed next to my wife and took her in my arms and told her I loved her.

"I thought about you all the time," she said. "Did you think of me?"

"I have to tell you the truth," I said. "I could not think about you. It would hurt too much. I could not have gone on." It was dark, and I could not see Ching-Lee's face, but she whispered softly, "I understand." Soon I could hear her drifting away to sleep. I closed my eyes and gave thanks for being home, but I could not sleep. I could not.

sleep because I was mad. Liu had taken my thousand dollars. I sat up in bed and put my feet on the floor.

"Harry, where are you going?" Ching-Lee murmured.

I told her I was going to write a letter about Liu.

("I wasn't that surprised," Ching-Lee said weeks later. "That's Harry. He has to fight for what is his.")

I slipped out of our bedroom and tiptoed to my office. I stepped over the sleeping figure of David Welker and sat down at my word processor.

"To: Government of the People's Republic of China, Beijing.

"As I was escorted by five uniformed policemen and about eleven plainclothes officials at the Wuhan Airport, waiting for expulsion, there was a plainclothes policeman named Mr. Liu, aged forty-two . . ."

I got stuck on a phrase. I needed some help with the English. David will never forget what happened next. The poor kid had been on duty for two months, worrying about me, helping Ching-Lee, living in many different time zones. His mind finally eased, he had fallen into a deep sleep. At four o'clock in the morning, I poked him, saying, "David, wake up."

He opened his eyes and stared at me, incredulously. "Harry, what in the world are you doing?" he asked.

I told him I was writing a letter to the Communists. He fixed the sentence for me, the two of us sitting around in our underwear on a warm California night.

"Okay, you're finished; go back to sleep," I told him.

"Now I know you're home," David said.

30

SETTLING DOWN

Ching-Lee was no longer the same woman I had met almost six years earlier. She had a new level of confidence and initiative. I was embarrassed to even think it, but perhaps I had underestimated her. She did not go out of her way to tell stories about her adventures while I was away, but only a fool could miss them. She had chatted with Margaret Thatcher and Tony Lake and Newt Gingrich. She had mastered the fifteen-second sound bite for television. She had learned to joust with the Chinese.

I heard the story about the big eight-day celebration in San Francisco to honor Shanghai, its sister city. Ching-Lee had tried to pressure government officials to call it off, but the affair was too late in the planning stage. So they decided to protest in person. Imagine the organizers' shock on July 16, when Ching-Lee and Representative Nancy Pelosi and Milpitas's mayor, Peter McHugh, all showed up at an outdoor party and with the mayor of Shanghai standing there, began chanting, "Free Harry Wu!" The Shanghai mayor had to notice a plane overhead, pulling a large banner that also said FREE HARRY WU. To this day, we do not know who paid for that plane. There was another rally for me in Los Angeles, organized by our friend Ann Lau.

People recounted the stories of Ching-Lee's courage, and the more I looked at the tapes made during my absence, the more I realized that

Ching-Lee had taken a terrible situation and turned it in our favor. She had persuaded people to care about me. She had forced people to care about the *laogai*.

I was embarrassed about telling all the interviewers that I had not dared think about her for fear I would crack up. How could I not think about this beautiful and brave woman who had backed me up at home? The second night, when things were quiet, I said to her, "You don't tell me all the things you did while I was gone. But I hear from other people how much you did. I see the articles. I see the tapes. I did not know these things."

"I did them for you," she said, "because I love you. I am your wife."

I knew she was smart, a working woman, but also sweet and kind, beyond the stereotype of the Asian wife who would do whatever her husband wanted. I never imagined she would become a public figure, but now I found myself saying, "Wow, this is another Ching-Lee." I became so overwhelmed by my feelings that I whispered, "I look in your eyes, and I have to ask you, Will you marry me again?"

"Don't be ridiculous," she told me. "We are already married. No need to get married again."

Since those first days and nights when we were reunited, Ching-Lee has spoken about the changes in her. "Of course I am different," she has told people. "Even before Harry was captured, I knew I was changing, but I didn't dare talk because I didn't feel I understood the *laogai*. I always could talk to people," Ching-Lee has said. "It was part of my job back in Taiwan. When Harry was busy with an appointment, or when he was tired, I felt sad, and I wanted to help, to share the burden. Not just paperwork. Not just typing. Then, when Harry was arrested, many people asked to talk to me. At first, I didn't tell very much, but afterward I learned a little bit. I was still very careful not to make mistakes, but I realized I could talk about this. When Harry came back, he said, 'I underestimated her.' I understood what he meant. At first, people just wanted to talk to him, but now it's okay. I'm still different. I realize people want to talk to me, too. I can talk to television people. Recently I gave a talk to a high school. My speech is different. I can do this."

Ching-Lee is still my loyal wife, and sometimes she urges me to slow down, to stay home, to stop running around the world every day so we can have a normal life together. Recently we have even been talking about starting a family. In the meantime I have trouble saying no to a speaking engagement across the country, jumping on airplanes every day. I know I've got to slow down and spend more time with Ching-Lee. I remember those brutal days when I thought I might not see her again.

It was difficult settling in that first full day. I finally did sleep a little, but at ten o'clock the next morning I invited all the reporters inside the house, into our little den. Naturally the first question was about the announcement that day that Mrs. Clinton would indeed go to China. Her announcement was not specifically linked to my release, but there was no doubt in my mind about the cause and effect.

"She had to judge by herself to go or not to go," I told the reporters. "But if my release is part of a deal, if this is a condition for Mrs. Clinton to go to China, I will be angry about it. The release of Harry Wu does not mean the Chinese human-rights record has improved. The police told me, 'You are lucky you are an American citizen.' This made me very sad."

The reporters wanted to know how I had survived my captivity. Was I tortured? Did they interrogate me around the clock? I had to be honest and tell them it was not so terrible, that I almost always felt in control of what I was telling them. "I lied to them," I told the reporters. "And so what?"

I could see them shifting uneasily in their chairs. Americans like to think everybody is bound by the same rules: to tell the truth at all times, to mean what you say and say what you mean. But I was dealing with people who could not be trusted, so I had to match them. "I said if they released me, I would stay away from politics and have a good life with my wife," I continued. "Why should I be honest with them? I deal with men as men deal with me, and they lied to me from the very beginning." This was a battle I had to continue.

I was asked whether I would ever try to get into China again.

"I don't know," I replied. "I just got back. I'll have to think about it."

~~

One of the first phone calls I received was from Daniel Piccuta in Beijing, who was overjoyed to hear I was all right. Immediately after my verdict, he had seen a Chinese official and volunteered to escort me to the airport if I was expelled. The official told him that I would have to serve my sentence first. Piccuta then went to his hotel room in Wuhan, where he could have been reached, but it was not until half past midnight that anybody called and then only to say, "Harry Wu's plane just left Shanghai."

Another call was from Don Hewitt of 60 *Minutes*, who asked whether his crew could come out and do a segment about my trip, and I said of course. They sent out my old friend, that famous American importer of steel-pipe, Ed Bradley. I got a big kick out of telling him, "You know the number-one question they asked of me in China? 'How much money does Ed Bradley make?' "

Bradley interviewed Ching-Lee and me together. Asked whether Mrs. Clinton had done enough about China, Ching-Lee said, "I think she really should do something for those who are still inside Chinese prisons, who are wrongly accused, . . . those faceless, nameless people."

"She should condemn the Chinese gulag system," I added, "condemn human-rights abuses in China clearly, frankly, publicly."

Bradley asked whether it would be fair for an American president's wife to criticize the Chinese during a conference in their own country.

"And you want to save the Chinese Communists' faces?" I sputtered on camera. "And you don't care for these dissidents suffering in the gulag system? What do you care?"

Well, yes, the look on Ed Bradley's face said he cared.

~~

The Chinese did not waste any time before trying to discredit me. As soon as I was on the plane, they released a barrage of statements meant as character assassination. "A man who was morally corrupt and did many evil deeds," the *People's Daily* called me. The newspaper said I began as a thief when I was a college student, bringing up the old fifty-yuan charge, trying to make me sound like a petty thief all over again.

The article conveniently skipped over my nineteen years in the *laogai* and went on to say that while a college instructor in Wuhan, I had stolen public property, faked documents to get radios and electric fans, and forged my superior's signature on travel-expense forms. I had also tried to seduce a student at the university, which was absolutely true, although I did not have to try that hard. She and I had been equal partners in the short time of happiness we had together. I was characterized as "morally degenerate" and accused of a lack of patriotism. "His heart was full of hatred. He felt China owed him, and he wanted to settle an old score with China."

That is true. China owes me nineteen years. And I am just one of millions.

~

The following day Anthony Lake, Clinton's national security adviser, called and welcomed me home, and I thanked him for the government's efforts in my behalf. *The Washington Post* carried a headline, MR. CLINTON TO MEET MR. WU. Lake was asked, "Do you have a plan to meet Harry Wu?" and he said, yes, very soon, but it never happened.

We stayed home and watched on television as Hillary Clinton went to Beijing, right on schedule. I would have been delighted if Mrs. Clinton had stayed home to protest the Chinese policies on human rights, and I would have been delighted if she had torn into their treatment of prisoners during her main speech before the conference. What she did was deliver an impassioned speech praised by many people around the world.

"It is time for us to say here in Beijing, and the world to hear, that it is no longer acceptable to discuss women's rights as separate from human rights," Mrs. Clinton told the delegates.

I would have loved her to have been more specific about the Chinese policy of forced sterilization or forced abortions or the frequent charges of female infanticide committed by parents who want a son. She did not do that, but the force of her words in that setting had to be obvious to Beijing, which had not allowed Tibetan exiles or delegates from Taiwan to enter the country.

"Freedom means the right of people to assemble, organize, and debate openly," Mrs. Clinton said. "It means respecting the views of those who may disagree with the views of their governments. It means not taking citizens away from their loved ones and jailing them, mistreating them, or denying them their freedom or dignity because of peaceful expression of their ideas and opinions."

She also told the delegates: "If there is one message that echoes forth from this conference, let it be that human rights are women's rights and women's rights are human rights, once and for all."

The next day we watched clips of the security officers showing the hard face of communism to all those women, all those troublemakers from all over the world. The Chinese government had arranged the most inconvenient site for one important session on September 5, the town of Huairou, forty miles from Beijing. Thousands of delegates were forced to stand outside in a downpour because the auditorium was too small to accommodate all of them, and there were some unpleasant moments when officers pushed and shoved the unhappy delegates.

Almost nobody in China was able to hear Mrs. Clinton's talk, but the Chinese leaders were undoubtedly proud to have the first lady of the United States in their country. The leaders of the country heard her, and so did most of the free world. She was under a lot of pressure, some of it from Republicans and human-rights activists in the United States, to publicly repudiate Beijing. I had been afraid she would just be a polite guest at the conference, just save China's face, but instead she delivered a powerful message that human rights are universal.

After I told the story about hanging my calligraphy on the villa wall, the saying about the rain falling in the ocean, I noticed my father-in-law spending even more time in his room, working on his own calligraphy. One day he brought out his newest work, a beautiful rendering of the Buddhist saying with his own seal on it, and he gave it to me as a gift. I was so touched that I had it framed and placed on the wall facing my desk. Even at the busiest times, I stare at his calligraphy and remember,

"The rain falls in the ocean, neither increasing nor decreasing." It reminds me, "Stay calm."

~~~

As the days went on, I collected stories about things that had happened while I was in captivity. I found out that Senator Dianne Feinstein of California had happened to be in China while I was being held. As the former mayor of San Francisco, she had visited President Jiang Zemin, who used to be the mayor of Shanghai, San Francisco's sister city. Senator Feinstein asked Jiang to release me, but Jiang insisted he could not interfere with the wonderful separation between the executive and the judicial branches of government.

On August 24, Senator Feinstein was at the Shanghai Airport, waiting to fly out. Jiang sent a special officer to the airport to reassure her, "Harry Wu will depart from China today." Everything was prearranged. At about the same time, I had been sweating out my verdict. I'm glad to know the authorities had already bought my ticket and told my senator not to worry. I just wish Jiang had told me as well.

~~~

Not long after I got home, I talked on the phone with Meihua, who had seen me on television in Shanghai and now understood the mystery of what I had been doing on my trips to China.

"Are you all right?" she asked, and I said I was okay.

"Don't try again," Meihua said, "Take care of yourself. You are almost sixty years old now. We don't have that much time. You should enjoy yourself and your family. I am always thinking about you. If you care about my feelings, don't take any risk."

I thanked her for the advice but made no promises. Nowadays we exchange a letter or two, occasionally speak on the phone. She always sends her regards to Ching-Lee, and recently her family discovered some old pictures of us, and she also told me she has a second granddaughter.

I give the Chinese leaders some credit: They have never hurt Meihua because of our association, because they know I never discussed my missions with her. Things have improved at least this much. A well-known troublemaker in California can pick up the telephone and call his childhood girlfriend in Shanghai without fear—so far—that Big Brother will interfere.

One unexpected reaction to my trip came from the BBC. Some people there were upset because I'd conceded a few points to enable my captors to save a little face. To be sure, I had conceded only aspects of the documentary that were obviously misleading: The operation shown was indeed a heart operation, although the BBC never claimed it wasn't. I had told the BBC that the grave markers were not necessarily those of prisoners. But these small points did not, in my judgment, discredit the entire documentary or the BBC, which is the greatest news-gathering network in the world.

Still, some of the BBC regulars in China had their visa status threatened, and that put a lot of pressure on my friend Sue Lloyd-Roberts. Some BBC reporters in Beijing had heard rumors that I had been drugged, and that this had so impaired me mentally that I was somehow capable of uttering the most grotesque absurdities during my interrogation and trial. Now that I was free in the United States, the BBC asked to interview me by satellite to clear up the matter. I was glad to do it because I respect the BBC, so I went to a studio in New York to be interviewed long-distance by one Peter Snow, who kept calling me Mr. Wu, with aggressive British politeness. I tried to describe my isolation in the villa, but Snow kept coming back to how depressed I looked in that Chinese propaganda film. He asked me a question that I remember as "Mr. Wu, we heard they were forcing you to use medicine. Did that influence your brain to cause you to say this? Why did you say the BBC film was untrue?"

I suddenly realized I did not want any part of his questions. I liked neither his tone nor his base insinuation. I pulled off my headset and abruptly said, "The interview is over." As I walked out of the studio, I told some people, "Those guys in China did not interrogate me as hard as this guy from the BBC."

Remembering the letter my captors had shown me, a letter I had written in my own house, I improved my security as soon as I got home. Yes, I have a pistol in the house. Yes, I put a security camera on my property. And yes, I went out and bought a paper shredder.

Note to the Communists: Please feel free to go through my garbage. All you're going to find is three-day-old beef and broccoli.

We all had our fifteen minutes of fame. David Welker had his photograph on the front page of *The Washington Post*—the two of us hugging at the airport. The Chinese would notice it, of course, and I'm sure David thinks this association will keep him from ever getting a visa to visit China, but someday he will have a great career in the diplomatic corps or private industry. He loves the Chinese language, he loves the Chinese people, he loves China. He'll get back there again.

On September 8, I was invited to Washington by the House Subcommittee on International Operations and Human Rights of the Committee on Human Relations, where a dozen representatives compared me to Natan Sharansky, Lech Walesa, Raoul Wallenberg, Aung San Suu Kyi, and others who have stood up for human rights. I was enormously flattered to be included in such distinguished company. But as an old shortstop from Shanghai, I was especially delighted when Representative Nancy Pelosi, now from California but originally from Baltimore, compared me to the great shortstop of the Baltimore Orioles, Cal Ripken, Jr., who had just broken the baseball record for consecutive games played. "I think we have our own iron man with us here today," Representative Pelosi said. Then she praised Ching-Lee: "Sometimes you just wanted to think things might be hopeless, but Ching-Lee's leadership and her strength were an inspiration to all of us. She would never show any weakness; therefore we could not."

Ching-Lee thanked the subcommittee for its support. "People who attack the federal government should go through the experience. It was eye-opening. I have no complaints at all. I was kept closely informed day and night about what was going on. I know that the officials involved in the effort to secure Harry's freedom in Washington, in Horgas, in Beijing, and in Wuhan worked very hard."

For my part, I began by telling the members, "Before I say another word, let me say thank you from the bottom of my heart."

We had other people to thank. I went to the Netherlands to receive the annual Beggar's Medal, one of the major peace prizes in the world. Several members of Congress spoke of nominating me for the Nobel Prize, but I urged everyone to support Wei Jingsheng, who has been brave and outspoken while living in China and continues to suffer. He is far more deserving.

Another victory had been scored while I was being held in Wuhan. My old friend Bob Windrem at NBC had produced one more investigation into a company suspected of buying forced-labor products. His film had been shown on *The NBC Nightly News* on June 26, following a visit by correspondent Fred Francis to the Asbury Graphite Mills of Asbury, New Jersey. H. Marvin Riddle, the president of the company, told NBC he did not know where his company's graphite comes from, but his son, Stephen, the executive vice president of the company, told Francis that the graphite comes from the Qingdao Mines in Shandong Province.

"Do you know as a company that most of the labor on expandable graphite from Qingdao is forced labor?" Francis asked.

"We know that, yes," Stephen Riddle said.

"How do you know that as a business?"

"From, from, from see . . . from visiting that—and from talking to people in the graphite industry or other industries that have been over to that area of China . . . I mean, everybody tends to look the other way," Stephen Riddle said.

"Including you?"

"Including us, yeah."

"Have you ever worried that your company, Asbury Graphite, is in violation of United States law?"

"Yes."

NBC also interviewed Representative Frank Wolf of Virginia, who called on the Customs Service to investigate companies buying goods produced by forced labor in China. I was glad that public officials like Wolf and journalists like Windrem were keeping up the pressure. Now that I had been caught in China, I had to prove I could still be effective monitoring the *laogai* system.

The last fallout from 1995 was my investigation of the World Bank's projects in Xinjiang. Because I was nabbed at the border, I never got to look at the projects, but we eventually stirred up more information than I could have imagined. With the help of Jeff and David and Ching-Lee, we issued a report on October 23, 1995, entitled *The World Bank and Forced Labor in China: Mistake or Moral Bankruptcy?*

We noted that the World Bank's own staff appraisal report of July 31, 1991, had failed to mention the existence in the Tarim Basin area of seven large *laogai* camps and fourteen forced-labor camps run by the XPCC, which also runs at least thirty farms in that area.

We emphasized the military aspect of the Corps, and then we reprinted an article in April of 1995 by the Chinese news agency, Xinhua, that reported, "Since the early 1990's, Xinjiang has been carrying out a large irrigation program funded by the World Bank, which is aimed at helping 540,000 people who live in the western part of the Taklimakan Desert. . . . So far, about 53,000 hectares of desert land [almost 205 square miles] has been reclaimed with 70 per cent planted with crops."

Beijing was giving the World Bank credit for water projects in the Tarim Basin, but the World Bank was still being coy about its relationship with the Corps. We counted up 263,732 prisoners in XPCC farms along the river, the great majority of them Han Chinese, but the World Bank's reports stress the help to the indigenous Uighur people.

The report by the Laogai Research Foundation called on James Wolfensohn, the new president of the World Bank, to investigate the extent of forced-labor camps in the Tarim Basin. We also asked for an independent study of the World Bank's projects in Xinjiang and elsewhere in China, and we urged the World Bank to formulate an official policy barring the use of forced labor in all its projects, with appropriate sanctions against countries that violate the policy.

The World Bank sent a team over to Xinjiang. On December 20, 1995, it issued a report entitled *Findings of an Investigative Mission to Xinjiang, Executed November 5–18, 1995*. The fifteen-page report noted that it had been stimulated by our October report. It said that its Tarim Basin project was actually concentrated in two river valleys, the Weigan and the Yerqiang, populated mostly by Uighurs, and it claimed that most of the camps I had visited in 1994 were outside the drainage area served by the World Bank projects. The report also said that only one penal institution was even remotely near its projects, the "Pailou Prison and its associated farm." But the report added that investigators had visited Pailou Farm and found that "even with respect to indirect water benefits, Pailou Farm has not in any way benefitted from the project." The investigators said that records and interviews indicated that the farm had not grown or changed in twenty years.

The World Bank listed its other projects in Xinjiang. At the Xinjiang Agricultural Development Project, which closed on December 31, 1994, the World Bank claimed, "none of these teams has witnessed any indications of penal activities or facilities." At a Rural Water Supply and Sanitation Project in the Aksu region of Xinjiang, the World Bank team did note penal facilities, but by and large, "even on State Farm No. 7 of Aksu Branch, the Bank project served its intended beneficiaries, who are certainly neither prisoners nor soldiers, but poor transplanted peasants from eastern provinces."

The report eventually got around to "links of implementing agencies to penal institutions." It conceded that the Xinjiang State Farms Organization "has historically referred to itself most frequently" as the XPCC, and it listed all the facets of the XPCC without ever mentioning the military. It did note that the Corps "also maintains a Prison Bureau," which "reports directly to the Prison Administration Department" in Beijing.

Toward the end, the World Bank report summed up by saying,

The Tarim Basin Project and the other projects implemented by agencies of the Xinjiang Regional Government are unconnected to any military organization. As for the two projects where the Xinjiang state farms had implementation responsibilities, the mission was assured that the functions of this organization had no relation to the People's Liberation Army. The continued use of military terms to describe levels in the organization structure (commander, regiment, etc.) was attributed to the origins and heritage of the Corps and its members, many of whom are second and third generations of the first military personnel decommissioned in Xinjiang in the early 1950s. The mission found no evidence to confirm or contradict this strong assurance.

The report also said, "The mission uncovered no evidence that any forced (prisoner) labor has been used in the implementation (construction) of any Bank project in Xinjiang."

In an accompanying press release, the World Bank claimed it had looked at all 159 of its current projects in China and that the inquiries were "conducted independently of the Chinese government, which cooperated fully with the Bank." The press release did note that the XPCC "is responsible for administering some prisons and adjacent farms on behalf of the central Ministry of Justice," that "some of the farms benefitting under the Water Supply and Sanitation Project—including one visited by mission members—are in close proximity to prisons and prison farm areas."

It was not hard to refute the claims that the XPCC had no contemporary military function. Week by week, we kept coming up with more evidence—from the Chinese government itself—that the XPCC was still an instrument of force. Perhaps the most blatant example was an uprising in the Corps's own backyard, on April 4–6, 1990, twelve miles from Kashir, in the southwest corner of Xinjiang, near the border with Kyrgyzstan. In rural Baren, several thousand Uighurs protested the closing of mosques, and troops fired on the demonstrators. The Chinese government claimed twenty-two people were killed, whereas others said the toll was as high as fifty. According to Amnesty International, in its report *Secret Violence in Xinjiang*, published on October 10, 1992, "Armed groups from the nominally civilian XPCC brigades participated in quelling the demonstrations."

In the Corps's own *Xinjiang Military Reclamation*, my foundation found references to the same uprising: "In the struggle over two days and two nights, the militia of the XPCC caught fourteen rioters," who had been shouting out slogans like "We don't trust socialism."

Shortly before the World Bank sent its team to Xinjiang, it might have discovered a report by the BBC Monitoring Service, on October 10, 1995, which described a visit to Xinjiang on October 1 by Vice Premier Jiang Chunyun. Jiang was quoted by Xinhua as saying, "Practice shows that the officers and men of the PLA [People's Liberation Army] units and the armed police forces, the cadres and policemen of the Public Security front, and the staff and workers of the Corps are worthy of heroic rank that the party and people can completely trust."

Or the World Bank might have noted the visit to Xinjiang on September 8–13, 1995, by Zhu Rongji, China's economic guru. Xinhua wrote that Zhu "also affirmed the irreplaceable role of the Corps in consolidating border defence, stabilizing the border, fostering ethnic unity and developing regional economy."

On April 4, 1996, we issued our reply to the World Bank, a twenty-four-page report with a twenty-four-page appendix. The report is entitled *The World Bank and the Chinese Military: Ignorance—Incompetence—or Cover-up?* We gave thirteen pages to documenting the military functions of the XPCC and then noted how "The World Bank Avoids Using the XPCC's Real Name." In the appendix, we ran the photograph of the home office with the two names, XPCC and XAITC. We wrote, "We believe that the World Bank has accepted Chinese lies and repeated them to the world in 'Findings,' and probably knew that the organization they had agreed would implement the Xinjiang Agricultural Project was the quasi-military Xinjiang Production and Construction Corps."

We also found fault with the World Bank's findings, which say, "As explained by the Regional Justice Bureau, the prisons and laogai farms under the Corps are among a limited number of prisons within the country specially designated by the Ministry of Justice to handle prisoners performing reform-through-labor." In fact, we have identified over 1,000 *laogai* camps in China, and the government itself has claimed 685 prisons and reform-through-labor facilities, a figure that does not include those run by the Corps. So we took exception to the World Bank's use of the word *limited*.

We also had a problem with the bank's description of a "farm" adjoining the Pailou camp and with its saying it served "poor transplanted peasants from eastern provinces." Most likely these are people who are not quite "reformed," who are detained to work in Xinjiang for the rest of their lives.

It should have been clear to the World Bank that the Corps works with prisoners. We obtained a copy of the *Northwestern Militia*, a Xinjiang publication, that states:

> In the autumn of 1983, the State Council decided that 100,000 prisoners from Beijing, Tianjin, Shanghai and Guangzhou were to be sent to the XPCC for detention and labor. The Corps had a shortage of prisons and lacked preventative measures. . . . The Corps' policymakers and representatives of the 2.2 million land reclamation warriors voluntarily offered to complete the task for the Central Party leadership. They organized 86 militia squadrons of over 4,000 militia members; and, in one year's time of detention, not one prisoner escaped.

This was not during some mass-hysteria purge ordered by Chairman Mao. This was at the peak of Deng's economic reforms. The Chinese government calculatingly committed one of the largest prison transfers in history, and the XPCC was the agent for this movement.

Finally, we chided the World Bank for listing four projects in Xinjiang but not listing the forty-million-dollar Seeds Project it had mentioned in its March 13, 1984, staff appraisal report. This project had been lauded by the XPCC itself in several of its yearly reports. Having visited several *laogai* cotton farms in 1994, I find it hard to believe that the XPCC was not using cotton seeds from the World Bank project. As we wrote in our report, "This is why the World Bank failed to include the 'Seeds Project' in 'Findings.' For if they had included it, the World Bank would not have been able to state as it did that: 'No evidence was found of any benefit, direct or indirect, to forced labor camps or military "special farms." ' "

In our conclusion, we called for an independent international commission to study how the World Bank funds are being used in Xinjiang. The failure to mention the Seeds Project suggested to me that the World Bank might have other connections to hide. The bank clearly serves the undeveloped regions of the world, but I hate to think American money is being used to strengthen the *laogai* system.

Our report on the World Bank was a milestone for me. The Laogai Research Foundation had come up with rich evidence that the XPCC has military and penal wings that the World Bank tries to minimize. The importance of my work was obvious. No longer could anybody dismiss me as just a freelancer with a penchant for dangerously roaming around China.

31

THE FUTURE

Wherever I go, people say, "Harry, you're not going back to China, are you?" They get this look on their face, half terror, half bafflement, which says, "Grow up, Harry. Be a good boy. Give it a rest." But this is not some children's game of hide-and-seek played behind the Great Wall. This is a compulsion on my part, a matter truly of life and death. I go to China to get the Chinese authorities to stop — to stop the camps. The real question is not, When will Harry Wu stop being such a bad boy? The real questions are, When will China stop locking up dissidents? and Why doesn't the rest of the world do anything about this?

I have nothing against the nation of China, and I surely have nothing against the people of China. I don't want to stop China's economic gains. I am happy if the Chinese people eat better. No more famines because Mao had a bright idea. I'd wager that if Marx got a day pass back from wherever he is, he would visit China and say, "This is not what I had in mind."

Every day Deng and his people have danced on the grave of communism, but they still practice totalitarianism. I don't want to sit in California and persuade people in China to riot before the guns of the army. Beijing knows how to stop riots with guns and tanks, but if revolution means change, then the revolution has already started. The yuppies of China are getting richer by the day, and the crooks make money on drugs and prostitution, but the peasants have been dispossessed of the land they worked for ages. What will China do with its prosperity? What steps will it take to join the other economic powers?

My strongest message is to the United States, my adopted country. I don't believe the American people support the behavior of the Chinese government. In the United States, people are constantly waving the flag and talking about freedom. What about prisoners making artificial flowers at night after breaking rocks all day in a quarry? I believe the American people would boycott goods made in China if they realized they were made by the forced labor of prisoners, political or other.

The United States must be a leader to make the world understand what is happening in China, but as we went into the 1996 presidential campaign, the only thing clear about President Clinton's policy toward China was that it was not working. We need real teeth in U.S. policy. If we're going to share goods and secrets with the Chinese, let's make sure they don't use them against their own people. Stop exchanging high-tech goods with them. I'm still angry about being detained at the border and then escorted by guards who were using Motorola cellular phones.

I'm so angry that I keep going around talking about my native country to anybody who will listen. I have no politics. My liberal American friends get this sour look, and they say, "Why do you talk to Jesse Helms?" Let me tell you something. Politics aside, Jesse Helms was the warmest of all the public figures Ching-Lee met with while I was in prison. He cares about prisoners. You think Jesse Helms likes it when I go to Seattle to speak up for the Boeing union or when I lobby against fifteen thousand booing Wal-Mart stockholders? Right, left—I don't care.

I have friends in Germany who belong to the Green Party, who talk openly about the history of the concentration camps, who condemn any slave system in the world. I have right-wing supporters in France who ask, "Harry, should I go to China?" and I say, "Don't go, because they just arrested Wei Jingsheng again." So it isn't just the left, and it isn't just the right.

Lately I have discovered I am a troublemaker to many overseas Chinese who criticize Deng and his regime. The new theme is "I was at Tiananmen Square; we criticized our government, but everything you do hurts our country." Let's face it: Tiananmen Square was in 1989. That's a long time ago. Many of the bravest people of that week eventually made their peace with the system. What will they do to change things? One woman, named Mo Li Hua, from Hunan, around forty years old, was not at Tiananmen Square, but she was jailed in that movement and later escaped to Sweden. She has told me, "I admire you, but you are trying to stop business with the Chinese." Mo's argument is that the money goes to our motherland. She distinguishes between foreigners and Chinese. Many Chinese dissidents, honest people, brave people, still have their prime loyalty to the system. What's good for China must be followed. I cannot accept this.

I love going to American colleges, to bring my message to the younger generation. My speeches take me to some of the most interesting corners of the country, places that give me hope, remind me what a great country this is. For example, I was invited to Haverford College, a wonderful little Quaker school outside Philadelphia, in the fall of 1995, crisp cold air outside, the electricity of ideas and emotions inside the packed auditorium. It was dark in the audience, but I could see that many of the faces were Chinese and Japanese and Korean and Vietnamese—the new generation of Americans. I always try to tell from the accents, the attitudes, the looks, the behavior, where people come from. Are they from Taiwan or Hong Kong or mainland China or the United States? What point of view are they likely to hold?

At Haverford, somebody in the balcony asked, "Are you a traitor?"

I could not judge the intent. Friend or critic? I didn't know. It was a fair question. I said, "Yes, I am a traitor to communism. But I am not a traitor to the Chinese people." I love my old country. I violated its law, yes; I slipped in to embarrass the tyrants who rule China, but it was their Communist law I violated. I was honored to break it.

Most of the audience at Haverford applauded this response, but lately more hecklers have been showing up. I suspect that the Chinese government is mobilizing all its students who are in the States. I don't mind. Let's have an open debate, no holds barred. At the University of Toledo, in Ohio, one student said, "I lived in China twenty-seven years, and I never heard of the *laogai*. You sold your soul to foreigners. That BBC tape was totally a fabrication."

"Did you see the tape?" I asked.

"No," she said, "but I heard about it."

"You've got to see it," I said.

I just want to start a dialogue. That's what college is for.

Sometimes it gets sticky. I was at the University of Oklahoma in March of 1996, and a group of Chinese people interrupted my speech, calling me anti-Chinese. One guy even turned out the lights in the auditorium, but I happened to spot him, and I pointed him out, and the security guards started to eject him from the building.

"You are a troublemaker!" he shouted at me.

"Thank you," I said. "Every time you call me that, I am happy. You are publicizing my new book."

I guess I am really a troublemaker. Deep down I do not think of myself as a hard guy. I love the Chinese people. I love humanity. I have seen so many people in the camps die, flicked away like so many cigarette butts. I learned at an early age that life belongs to you only once. We are all born with the same end, whether it comes thirty years or eighty years later, and that is death, but the question is how much we enjoy our lives, how much we are allowed to enjoy our lives.

When people accuse me of hating China, of trying to overthrow China, I say, "Don't tell me about politics. Enjoy your life. If people want to sing a song, let them sing. If I want to read a book, I read a book. If I want to say something, I say it. In China, everything has a political label. The Chinese say, 'That's a capitalist song.' "

Let it go. Politics is not natural. The place for the human being is with the family. Love. Sex. Food. Music. Literature. Do something good for other people. We are all entitled to this. All right, we have to vote for politicians to handle things, but never forget that we pay the politicians; they are not our masters. If anything, they are our servants, our workers. China goes to the opposite extreme. If someone disagrees, the politicians silence him or her. If someone refuses to shut up, they will not hesitate to kill him or her.

I try to help my friends get out. In 1996, Liu Jingqin, who had accompanied me on my journey to Qinghai in 1991, got permission for himself, his wife, and their middle daughter to join two other daughters in New York City. I flew to New York to meet them on perhaps the most appropriate day of the year — July Fourth, Independence Day. We embraced at John F. Kennedy Airport, and they joined the millions of immigrants trying to make a life for themselves in the free world.

If China is so wonderful, why are so many people running to get away from Hong Kong before 1997, when the city falls under Beijing's sway? Why are they flooding into Vancouver, Seattle, Los Angeles, other parts of Asia, and Europe? Hong Kong is dead. I tell you this right now. All those multinational companies that want to maintain Hong Kong as a financial center, the way it was as a British colony, are kidding themselves. Colonies need two things: political support and economic support. Colonies must be special. Beijing won't allow Hong Kong to be special because then it would have 1.2 billion people moving to Hong Kong, this little dot at the edge of China.

China will try to get Taiwan, too. It's inevitable. They are locked against each other like two plates of earth, rocking and grinding, preparing for the earthquake. The Chinese cannot tolerate a thriving democracy run by Chinese people directly across the water from them. Otherwise the mainland people will say, "Hey, how come they vote? How come they speak their minds? How come they are so prosperous?"

Should the world be afraid of China? Of course it should. I'm not saying China will start the next big war or take over the world. The Chinese have great resources — people and land — and one could say China has a bright future a hundred years from now. I am worried about the next five or ten years.

I don't think China knows what it wants. What is China? The yuppie with the cellular phone? The peasant digging with his hands? The bureaucrat with the list of suspects? China needs to know where it stands in the world.

It is not hard to see that communism as an ideology died many years ago. The Chinese people were the first to know this, but even the party leadership has caught on. Deng Xiaoping has said he does not care whether the cat is white or black so long as it catches mice. That's fine. But the United States and the rest of the world seem intent on providing the cheese to help the Communists catch the mice on their terms.

American policymakers and analysts are constantly reminding us that China will soon have the largest economy in the world. What seems to be lacking in this discussion is the implication of an economic giant's turning into a military and political giant. This is already happening in China, where nobody talks seriously anymore about building the socialist paradise. Chinese nationalism grows more fervent every day. In my sixty-six-day captivity in 1995, I was no longer a "counterrevolutionary rightist" but, rather, a "criminal" who "steals state secrets" and "passes them on to hostile foreign organizations." Any leader who ignores the deep-rooted Chinese nationalism does so at his or her own peril and at his or her nation's peril.

The Chinese are operating on several assumptions: that people are more interested in their own economic development than in freedom and democracy, that the party can remain in power even though communism has failed, that the United States and the rest of the industrialized world will pursue economic gain at the expense of human rights in China, and that China can expand its military without significant resistance from the United States.

In my view, the United States is still hoping that China's hybrid form of capitalism will lead to democracy. More likely it will lead to the creation of a new form of a totalitarian, supernationalistic military state.

What policy should the United States pursue? Some people argue for a policy of containment in the old cold-war sense, but I find that outmoded and unthinkable. Recent U.S. administrations seem to favor an ad hoc policy of engagement, which strikes me as little more than mercantilism. I believe the United States and other developed nations should articulate a policy of restraint: restraint of their own support of China and pressure for restraint within China. The United States and other nations can begin a policy of restraint in the following ways:

1.   Condemn the continued existence of the *laogai* in China. Don't let the Chinese confuse the issue by using the new term, *jianyu*, making believe the *laogai* is a simple prison system. They are using prisoners, political and otherwise, for forced labor. The *laogai* continues.

2.   Make clear to the Chinese that their repression of dissidents will have real costs. Other nations should enforce existing laws against importing slave-labor products, make new laws about it, and enforce them. These countries should demand verification of every product they import from China. If Washington can do this with diesel engines, it can do it with grapes and wine and tools and boots and flowers. Should all Chinese goods be boycotted? No, but I do endorse specific, short-term boycotts of companies that clearly traffic in forced-labor products. If I were an unscrupulous businessman, I would want to do business with China, which has a huge labor pool but no unions. The United States should insist the Chinese not make profits on the backs of prisoners.

3.   The United States could try revoking the most-favored-nation status. Just for a year. Archbishop Desmond Tutu has said that the Western boycott of South Africa may have hurt more black people than white people at first, but in the long run the white leaders gave up apartheid not out of a sense of morality but out of pragmatism. If the U.S. president withdrew China's MFN status, that might hurt Chinese workers in the short term, but it would hurt business leaders in Hong Kong, Taiwan, America, and China even more. Canceling the MFN privilege would get their attention.

4.   There is no reason why China should be the largest customer of the World Bank when there are other needy and much more democratic developing countries. At the very least, there should be pressure on the World Bank to look more carefully at its projects in the same region as the Xinjiang Production and Construction Corps.

5.   Once and for all, the Chinese argument that human rights are not universal should be condemned in meaningful ways, like pressuring the UN Commission on Human Rights to hold more hearings on the camps. If it's interested, I've got a list of witnesses.

6.   Keep China out of the World Trade Organization. Each administration says China does not qualify for the WTO because of its lack of overall economic development, but Western countries should list forced labor as a specific reason for keeping China out. The United States began

bristling about economic sanctions only when the Chinese persisted in pirating U.S. pop music. That's not right, but maintaining a system of virtual slavery is worse. Let's condemn both.

7.   All Chinese acts that violate international norms—such as the sale of missiles and nuclear technology to troublemakers like Syria, Iran, and Pakistan—should be immediately condemned, not swept under the rug. A consistent response is necessary if the United States is to have any credibility with the Chinese and end this danger to world peace.

8.   The legitimate demands of the people of Taiwan, Tibet, and Hong Kong to determine their own future should be respected, supported, and linked to other aspects of U.S. policy. Particularly in the case of Taiwan, the United States must make very clear that the cost of any use of force by the mainland Chinese will be extremely high. I know the United States sent ships to the Taiwan coast during the tensions before the Taiwanese elections in March of 1996; exercises like this must be powerful and consistent.

9.   Other nations should stop selling China the technology and the equipment used by the military and the police against dissidents.

10.   More information is flowing into China through computers, but the Chinese people need even more honest and accurate information in order to evaluate their system and make decisions. International broadcasts to China should be greatly expanded.

I truly believe that the Chinese people can develop their own form of democracy, but not as long as the aspirations of the people are repressed. The irony is that U.S. policy aimed at a stable China only results in a tense and unstable leadership. History is replete with examples of the United States trying to prop up dictators who have lost legitimacy with their own people. The United States and other powers must not be lured by their economic gain from trade with China. They must practice restraint themselves and urge restraint within China.

~

As I approach sixty, the traditional age of wisdom, I know I have not been very wise. I know only one thing: When China's rulers decide to be good boys, I, too, will be a good boy. I don't want to fight this battle forever. They took away my youth, and I cannot forget. It is too late for the years already lost to Wei Jingsheng. It may be too late for me to have children, too late for grandchildren, too late for the Wu family in Shanghai, broken and dispersed by the Communists. No Number One Son. No Number One Daughter. My story ends with me. But maybe it will not be too late for the next guy.

Will I ever go back to China? I am Chinese. My soul is Chinese. My homeland is beautiful. Next time, I want to go back on a pilgrimage. Next time, I want to go with Ching-Lee, carrying presents for what is left of my family. We will present our passports at the international airport. The customs officials will look up at her and say, "Wu Ching-Lee, your visa is in order." They will look up at me and say, "Wu Hongda, Peter H. Wu, Harry Wu—whatever your name is—your visa is in order. Have a nice day."

We will visit the mountains, the temples, the rivers, the cemeteries. I will bring Ching-Lee to the graves of my father and my two mothers. We will bring flowers and arrange them on the ground.

I will bring corn buns to the earth where Big Mouth Xing is resting. "Here, you ornery foul-mouthed lug, here are your corn buns."

I will meet Wei Jingsheng for the first time. He will be home in Beijing, writing a book, running for office, working as an electrician again—whatever he wants to do.

People tell me never to think about going back to China again. Nobody tells Harry Wu what to do. I will go back.

Front door next time.

ACKNOWLEDGMENTS

I wish to thank all the people who helped with this book:

My wife, Ching-Lee, who worked so hard and put up with my long trips. I promise soon I will stay home more.

Her parents, Chen Hsien-Cheh and Chen Yen You-Mei, for also being parents to me.

Jeff Fiedler, for being my friend and caring so much about the cause.

David Welker, for bringing a new burst of youth and skill to the foundation.

Robert L. Bernstein of Wiley Publishers, who encouraged me to write the book.

Peter Osnos and Steve Wasserman of Times Books, whose vision and careful editing made the book better as we went along.

Esther Newberg of International Creative Management.

My friends who have shared parts of my trips to China: Sue Lloyd-Roberts, Shannon Ramsby, and Sue Howell. And some who cannot be named because they are still in China.

The many journalists and writers who have made their own contributions to the story of China: Americans like Ed Bradley, David Gelber, Norman Lloyd, Ned Hall, Bob Windrem, George Lewis, and Orville Schell, and Britons like Roger Finnegan and Tim Tate.

Others who helped were: Jean Pasqualini, Lodi Gyari, Linda Pfeifer, John Creger, Charles Lau, Yuan-Li Wu, Andrew Nathan, Peter Huvos, Maranda Shieh, Philip and Bing Baker, Ignatius Ding, Barry Chang, Grace Chiu Chen, Ann Lau, George Mo, Nancy Li, Yu-Sheng Chang, Bob Sensor, Phyllis A. Jenkins, A. M. Rosenthal, Madeline Joyce, Alexandra Leroux, Joseph Brodecki, Isabelle Woog, Jill Lin and Douglas J. Krajnovich, Michelle Cheng, Beth Thomas of Times Books, Andrea Miles of the U.S. Census Bureau, Kevin Tedesco of 60 *Minutes*, Jack Horner of International Creative Management, Nancy Alderman of Wiley Publishers, Katherine and Dr. Joseph Ho, Amnesty International, Human Rights Watch, AFL-CIO, Support Democracy in China, Silicon Valley Democracy for China, many Chinese and Tibetans in the United States, and many other people around the world.

The Vecsey family of writers, teachers, and lawyers: George, for helping me write the book. Marianne, for getting so involved in the project. Laura, for listening. Corinna, for her legal expertise. David, for his help with transcribing, writing, and editing.

And finally, all the good people who invited me to their homes, their schools, their towns, their countries in the past year. Through your friendly smiles and handshakes, your good meals and comfortable rooms, your kind words and prayers and helpful deeds, I have been able to keep going. Through thousands of friends, I have come to realize just how many people care about the *laogai* prisoners in China.

INDEX